"THE PINK BOOK"

Handbook of the

D1503192

Government & Federal Agency Securities

& Related Money Market Instruments

34th Edition

The First Boston Corporation

PROBUS PUBLISHING COMPANY
Chicago, Illinois

Library of Congress Cataloging-in-Publication Data Available

ISBN 1-55738-168-2

Printed in the United States of America

1 2 3 4 5 6 7 8 9 0

FOREWORD

This 1990 edition of the *Handbook of U.S. Government & Federal Agency Securities* – or, as it is more commonly referred to, the "Pink Book" – marks the continuation of a tradition that began in 1922, when First Boston began publishing the book to provide factual information on the activities, instruments, and institutions of the U.S. government securities and money markets. That information is of use to a wide range of people: investors and other market participants as well as students and teachers of economics and finance.

The last several years have been extraordinary ones for the financial markets, and the world's financial system as a whole continues to undergo rapid change. This book, the product of our position as a major broker-dealer in government and money market securities, is designed to aid in understanding some of those changes and their implications for the future.

The *Handbook* is prepared by First Boston's Economist Department, which provides comprehensive economic research of interest to issuers of securities and to investors. The department's economists, under the direction of Chief Economist Dr. Neal M. Soss, analyze worldwide monetary and fiscal policies to assess their impact on interest rates and help put economic events into useful perspective for our clients.

Thanks are owed to the many First Boston colleagues and U.S. government agency employees, too numerous to mention here by name, who contributed their expertise to this book. Able production assistance was provided by Jackie Freeman and research assistance by Norman Louie.

Zwen A. Goy
Editor, *Handbook of U.S. Government & Federal Agency Securities*
Assistant Vice President, Economist Department
July 1990

Table of Contents

Exchange Rate of the Dollar Against the Japanese Yen and the German Mark

(September 1985 = 100)

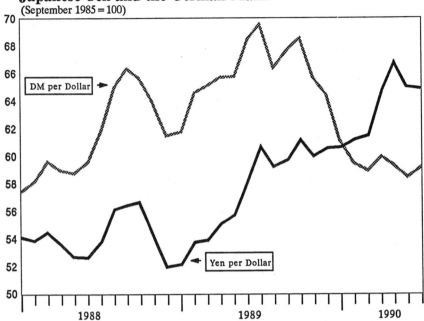

Merchandise Trade

(In billions of dollars, SA)

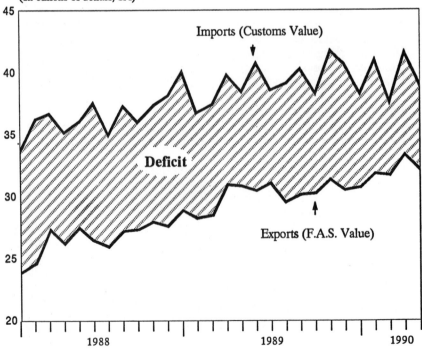

Source: U.S. Bureau of the Census.

6

The Economic Environment

The two years covered by this 34th biennial edition of the *Handbook*, from Spring 1988 to Spring 1990, witnessed a remarkable economic achievement. From the start, the American economy attained full employment — and preserved it throughout. Previous episodes of full employment often led to serious inflation and related problems, with recession soon to follow. This time, in heartening contrast, inflation accelerated only moderately and economic growth persisted, albeit at a slower pace. Although interest rates rose at first, they later fell back. Stock prices continued their recovery from the "Crash of 1987" to accomplish new all-time highs, and the dollar's international financial standing improved.

While for America the two years were unusually orderly, for most of the world they were exceptionally turbulent and exciting times. Most gripping, and most unexpected, were the revolutionary outbursts against Communist political and economic domination. In early 1989 the world rejoiced as mainland China surged toward freedom, only to shudder soon after at the brutal suppression on Tiananmen Square. At that juncture, who would have believed that within the next few months all of Eastern Europe would cast off the Soviet as well as the Communist yoke? Or that in a year Germany would be poised at the threshold of economic reunification, while the Soviet Union's survival as a unified nation was in question?

These were by no means the only startling upheavals. Apartheid was ending in South Africa. Japan was rapidly transforming itself into a consumption rather than an export-driven economy, amidst governmental scandals and ultimately a stock market plunge. Western Europe surged toward economic integration scheduled for 1992. Virtually all of Latin America was wracked by profound political and economic crises. Even Canada to our north became embroiled in a constitutional confrontation that threatened to break up the country.

Life in the United States was more tranquil. To be sure, we suffered an unusual spate of natural disasters. These included a San Francisco earthquake at the instant a full baseball stadium awaited the start of the 1989 World Series, as well as a run of serious droughts, storms, and floods. The economic repercussions were substantial, but largely transitory.

Rather, it was a manmade disaster—the tide of bankruptcies in our financial services industry—that was more ominous and longer lasting in its consequences. For years many savings and loan associations had been overextending themselves in response to deregulation and inflation; only now were the spectacular dimensions of the problem revealed. The cost of making good on the federal insurance of savings accounts was estimated in the hundreds of billions of dollars, and in 1989 the Administration and Congress had to create the machinery for meeting this huge obligation. In the course of closing hundreds of insolvent institutions, the government was destined to become the reluctant owner of an enormous quantity of real estate and other assets of dubious value. While selling off these assets might eventually recapture large sums, it was also sure to depress prices and construction in the affected regions.

Another dangerous sequence developed in the threatened or actual default of the excessive debts that some companies had incurred in paying for the merger and acquisition wave of the latter 1980s. The instruments (including "junk bonds") used to fund these highly leveraged transactions had been widely distributed among financial institutions and the public. Now the soundness of some of these credits—and of the lenders— was called into question. Several prominent business and financial entities went under but, due perhaps to a combination of good fortune and close official attention, no cascading of bankruptcies developed.

The experience reinforced an emerging trend for more sober credit appraisal, both by lenders and by supervisory authorities. As regards commercial banks, a stricter approach was internationally codified by a formal 1988 agreement in which the world's principal banking authorities undertook to enforce uniform and stiffer capital requirements. For the United States, this meant a less permissive credit climate for years to come.

Inevitably these financial troubles hampered business, particularly in real estate and retailing, most notably in the Northeast. They did not impede, however, the mainspring of the economic uptrend, which was the growth of exports in response to the cheapening of the dollar in 1985–1987 and the subsequent surge of demand from the booming economies around the world. In the opening quarter of 1990, the physical volume of exports was some 24% greater than that of two years earlier. In dollar terms, the trade deficit was still running at the high annual rate of $95 billion, but this was down substantially from the record annual shortfall of $170 billion in 1987.

In view of the export strength, it was probably just as well that domestic demand was lackluster. With the country's labor supply already stretched—the unemployment rate hovered consistently around a fifteen-year low of 5.3%—robust domestic buying might well have triggered serious inflation. Even so, the rise in nonfarm private labor costs (net of productivity gain) doubled from about 2½% per year in 1987 to 5% or more in late 1989 and early 1990. The speed-up in consumer price inflation was less, but this, too, reached a 5% pace, the fastest since 1981. Corporate profits were squeezed between the rising input costs and less-rapidly rising output prices.

At those times when businesses were trying to boost inventory, presumably expecting that rising costs were going to be reflected in higher prices, the economy seemed stronger. The Federal Reserve and financial markets worried about inflation and pushed up interest rates. Having dealt with the recession fears engendered by the "Black Monday" stock market crash of October 1987, the Federal Reserve began to raise short-term rates smartly in the Spring of 1988, lifting the federal funds rate more than three percentage points over the next year, almost to 10%. By Spring 1989, however, businesses had overshot their inventory targets and the pricing climate was softening. Now the economy seemed more vulnerable and the Federal Reserve relented, gradually bringing the funds rate down to 8¼% by year end. Long-term Treasury bond prices fluctuated in anticipation of every small shift in Federal Reserve posture, but on the whole the markets were less concerned about inflation dangers than were the authorities and more inclined to see a weakening economy. Developments abroad made the United States seem even more than usual a safe haven, reassuring financial markets about the outlook for willing capital inflows to cover the current account deficit. As a result, mid-year 1990 long-term Treasury bond yields of about 8½% were actually lower than those in early 1988, despite a clear increase in the level of short rates. The margin of long-term rates over short became the narrowest since the "inverted" yield curves of 1981, largely wiping out a major source of financial industry earnings.

With respect to the market for Treasury and agency securities, the two years under review witnessed few major innovations. Nor did the deficit's intrinsic size or pattern of financing change significantly despite annual political confrontations over the federal budget deficit and machinations to meet the legislative "Gramm–Rudman" targets. The chief new element was the heavy additional borrowing required to fund the federal insurance of thrift institution deposits. This involved the creation of two new agencies, one of which, the Resolution Funding Corporation (REFCORP), issued its own securities for the purpose of providing permanent financing for the other, the Resolution Trust Corporation (RTC). The interim working capital needs of the RTC, which in the short run are huge, are to be in effect financed by the Treasury. The extent to which such borrowings would be counted into the "official" budget deficit was a subject of negotiation. From the standpoint of the economy as a whole, these operations amount to a huge reshuffling of the public's assets and the government's liabilities without significant economic impact.

By mid-1990, the country faced a prospect dramatically different from the Cold War conflict to which we had become accustomed. Democracy and capitalism had won a great triumph. But the collapse of the Soviet bloc, however welcome, also diminished our influence over the noncommunist nations and necessitated the reordering of foreign policy priorities. There was also the promise of a sizable "peace dividend," although the reduction of military spending was bad news for some industries.

Throughout these two years, there was incessant debate as to whether the longlived economic expansion, 7½ years old in mid-1990, might soon end, and whether the "landing" would be "soft" or "hard." No recession had yet occurred, however, nor did any seem nearby. A more apt metaphor is perhaps that, on reaching full employment, we had to downshift from the fast lane. Although this may well be the best our economy can do, for many Americans it may not be good enough, setting the scene for future political battle.

Changes in Real Output and Prices

(Quarterly, at seasonally adjusted annual rates, in percent)

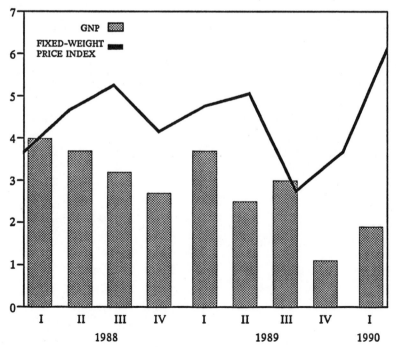

Source: Bureau of Economic Analysis.

Selected Interest Rates, Government Security Prices, and Money Supply–1988

	Federal funds rate (monthly average)	3-month Treasury bill rate (monthly auction average)	3-month commercial paper rate (monthly average)	Offering quote (end of month)[1] 8s Nov. 15, 1990 Price	Yield	8⅞s Aug. 15, 2017 Price	Yield	Money supply (seas. adj. annual rate of change in %)[2]
Jan.	6.8	5.9	6.9	101–11	7.45	104–22	8.44	9.5
Feb.	6.6	5.7	6.6	101–22	7.30	105–18	8.36	9.4
Mar.	6.6	5.7	6.6	100–29	7.61	100–26	8.80	7.6
Apr.	6.9	5.9	6.9	100–8	7.89	97–26	9.09	8.7
May	7.1	6.3	7.2	99–8	8.34	95–4	9.36	5.4
June	7.5	6.5	7.5	99–26	8.08	98–26	8.99	5.2
July	7.8	6.7	7.8	99–1	8.46	95–18	9.32	2.7
Aug.	8.0	7.0	8.3	98–16	8.75	95–1	9.38	1.8
Sept.	8.2	7.2	8.2	99–4	8.45	98–14	9.03	1.3
Oct.	8.3	7.3	8.2	99–16	8.27	101–3	8.77	3.0
Nov.	8.4	7.7	8.7	98–15	8.87	97–19	9.11	6.0
Dec.	8.8	8.1	9.1	97–31	9.19	98–14	9.03	3.3

Source: Federal Reserve Bulletin & The First Boston Corporation.

[1] Prices expressed in thirty-seconds.
[2] M2 monthly averages as revised.

Chronology

January 1988

- The October 1987 stock market crash cast a shadow over the economic outlook as 1988 began.

- Early in the month the dollar rebounded from all-time lows, boosted by central banks' intervention. The strengthening of the dollar triggered strong stock and bond market rallies.

- A Presidential Commission led by Senator Nicholas Brady concluded that the financial system had been seriously threatened in the October 1987 crash and that major regulatory changes were needed to forestall a repetition.

- The New York Stock Exchange announced limits on computerized program trading on days when the Dow Jones Industrial average moved more than 75 points.

- The trade deficit for November showed sharp improvement to $13.2 billion, sparking market rallies.

- By month end the focus turned to whether the Federal Reserve would push interest rates lower as new signs of sluggishness in the economy were perceived. Long-term bond yields fell below 8½% for the first time in six months.

February 1988

- The prime rate was cut to 8½% from 8¾% on the second.

- The federal funds rate drifted down to 6⅝% at mid-month. Administration spokesmen urged the Fed to ease monetary policy further.

- Bond prices continued to rally amid growing speculation that inflation and the economy were slowing. Employment gains were weaker in January than in previous months.

- Further narrowing of the trade deficit, to $12.2 billion for December, was seen as confirmation that trade problems were easing, especially with Japan.

- Fueled by speculation of lower interest rates, the Dow Jones Industrial Average moved sharply higher in the later part of the month to close at 2071.62, the highest level since the crash.

March 1988

- As the month progressed, the economy appeared to gain some strength. Housing starts, employment growth, and personal income improved. Exports surged.

- Consumer credit grew $5.4 billion in January. This was the largest increase since September, another indication that consumers had shaken off any post-crash gloom.

- The Tokyo stock market, which had fallen less than most other major world markets in the October crash, surged back to pre-crash levels.

- Takeover stocks gave some buoyancy to an otherwise lackluster U.S. stock market. Toward month end the stock market skidded on worries over interest rates and a weakening dollar. The DJIA closed the month at 1988, down 83.56 points.

- The bond market took its cue from the stock market. Yields rose to 8.77%, a gain of 44 basis points for the month, on generally light volume.

April 1988

- Continued signs of a surprisingly resilient post-crash economy led the Federal Reserve to reverse its mid-winter easing. Fed funds rose to 6¾% and then to 6⅞% by month end. Securities markets were, naturally, volatile.

- The DJIA reached a post crash high of 2090.19 on the eighth and continued to climb until a disappointing trade report for February on the 14th caused the market to skid 101 points to 2005.63. The dollar was also clipped, by about 2%.

- The Tokyo stock market's NIKKEI average soared to a record high of 26,769 on the seventh, surpassing its pre-October 1987 high.

- As the· pound came under upward pressure, British authorities lowered their prime rate to 8% from 8½%. This was the lowest rate since April 1978. Canada's prime rate, however, rose on the 21st to 10¼% from 9¾%.

- The U.S. Supreme Court ruled that Congress had the power to levy taxes on municipal bonds.

- The yield spread between three-month Treasury bills and long-term bonds fluctuated near 300 basis points as bond yields rose above 9% in the second half of the month.

May 1988

- The fed funds rate continued climbing as the Federal Reserve tightened in response to signs of a rebounding economy and heightened fears of inflation. By Memorial Day, the funds rate topped 7¼%.

- Commercial banks hiked their prime rate to 9% from 8½% on the 11th. Stock prices retreated as interest rates rose.

- Continued upward pressure on the pound led to another cut in the British lending rate, to 7½% from 8% on the 17th.

- The Tokyo Stock Exchange raised margin requirements to 60% from 50% on the 17th. This did not deter the NIKKEI average from achieving another record high, of 27,820, on the same day.

- The First Boston Corporation began trading on the Tokyo Stock Exchange on the 23rd, underscoring the continuing push towards globalization of financial markets.

- The American Midwest suffered the driest spring since the Dust Bowl days of 1934. Grains, oilseeds, and livestock prices trended upward in anticipation of a poor harvest.

- On the last day of May, the New York stock market shook off the gloom and rose 74.68 points. This nearly made up all the ground lost earlier in the month.

June 1988

- The month began with a rally in the financial markets. Prices of Treasury notes and bonds rose by as much as 1¾ points.

- The DJIA took off after Memorial Day, gaining a record 115 points in the first week of June. By month end, the Dow was up 70 points more, recording several post-crash highs along the way.

- Economic statistics indicated that a strong expansion in the manufacturing sector was underway. Fueled by export growth, orders received by manufacturers were up for the second month in a row and spending on factory construction surged. The trade deficit dropped in April, continuing a string of lower deficits.

- The dollar's relative stability came to an end. It began to strengthen against major currencies, gaining 6% versus the yen, and nearly as much against the pound and DM during the month. Aggressive intervention by the German central bank early in the month failed to contain the soaring dollar.

- The Fed pushed the funds rate up another notch to 7½%, but the strength of the dollar allowed long-term interest rates to fall back below 9% and stock prices to rise over 100 points.

- Volume on the NYSE hit 310 million shares on the eighth, the highest of the year thus far and the sixth highest ever, on the strength of Pacific Gas and Electric Company's 98 million traded shares. This represented the highest daily volume ever in a single issue.

- An even higher volume was reached on the 17th, when 344 million shares traded.

- In another attempt to moderate the Tokyo stock market boom, margin requirements were raised to 70% from 60%. Undeterred, the NIKKEI continued to reach new heights, closing at records on the seventh, on the ninth and then again, at 28,342, on the 17th.

- European interest rates were generally on the upswing. Britain's base lending rate was raised four times during the month in ½% increments to close the month at 9½%. German repo rates were increased twice. By month end Austria, Belgium, the Netherlands, Switzerland, and Japan had also boosted their rates. Gold lost $20.20 over the month.

- The Federal Savings and Loan Insurance Corporation announced that it expected to pay out $1.35 billion to liquidate two savings institutions in California, using up 40% of its total funds. The savings and loan industry announced it was losing money at a rate in excess of $13 billion per year.

- The U.S. current account deficit widened to $39.75 billion in the first quarter. For the first time in 30 years, net investment earnings were in deficit.

- Hot, dry weather returned to the Midwest causing grain prices to resume their climb. More than forty percent of the nation's counties were termed drought disaster areas.

- The Toronto seven-nation summit conference turned out to be a pleasant meeting. Free-market policies were given credit for the general prevailing conditions of lower inflation and lower unemployment. All agreed to try to encourage further economic growth. The controversy surrounding the issue of farm subsidies, however, was not resolved.

July 1988

- The relentless snugging of monetary policy continued, with fed funds at 7⅞% by month end. An employment increase of 346,000 during the prior month added to the perception of strength in the economy.

- The Dow Jones Industrials reached another post-crash high of 2158.61 on the day after Independence Day, then drifted downward for most of the month.

- A few days later, a post-crash high in bill yields was reached. Rates continued to climb for the rest of the month. Three-month bills ended at 7.12%, a rise of 40 basis points on the month. The long bond closed at 9.22%.

- The Democratic Party convened in Atlanta from the 17th to the 21st and nominated Michael Dukakis as its U.S. Presidential candidate and Lloyd Bentsen as the Vice Presidential running mate.

- The prime rate was raised to 9½% from 9% on the 14th.

- Rains fell in the Midwest on the 18th and the 20th. Grain prices plummeted. Drenching rains fell again on the 25th, causing the Commodity Research Bureau price index to suffer its second largest drop ever the next day. The drought was effectively over, but not before having inflicted severe damage to the harvest.

- The more the Fed tightened, the stronger the demand for the dollar became. On the 25th, the dollar had a banner day, gaining over one percent against the major currencies. Gold lost $16.30 an ounce.

- European interest rates continued to rebound, too. The British raised their base rate to 10½% from 9½% in two steps. The pound yielded virtually no more ground over the month, nor did the yen, but the German mark lost 3½%.

August 1988

- Just ahead of the Republican Presidential nominating convention, the Federal Reserve boosted the discount rate to 6½% from 6% on the ninth and hiked fed funds to 8⅛%.

18

- The prime rate followed, rising to 10% from 9½% on the 11th.

- Other interest rates also increased: three-month Treasury bills by 37 basis points and long bond yields by 22 basis points to a high of 9.44% on the 22nd. Bond yields subsequently eased back to 9.29%.

- The Treasury was unable to hold its quarterly 30-year bond auction because the $270 billion statutory limitation on the public's holdings of Treasury bonds with coupons greater than 4¼% was exhausted. A 248-day cash management bill was sold instead.

- George Bush was nominated as the Republican Party's candidate for President, with Dan Quayle as the Vice Presidential candidate, during the convention in New Orleans held August 15 to 18.

- The DJIA lost 97.08 points over the month.

- The Japanese NIKKEI stock average reached a new high of 28,366 on the second.

- In an effort to curb the dollar's rise, the Fed and the Bundesbank intervened against the dollar on the 16th. By the following week, most European central banks joined the Fed in intervening against the dollar.

- On the 25th domestic interest rates were boosted in Italy, France, Britain, Germany, Switzerland, Austria, the Netherlands and Canada. Belgium and Japan followed suit a few days later.

September 1988

- A further uptick in federal funds above 8¼% did no harm to broad financial valuations.

- The DJIA gained 81 points over the month.

- The yield curve continued to flatten. The difference between the three-month Treasury bill rate and 30-year

Treasury bond yield narrowed to 151 basis points at month end, half of what it was in the latter part of April.

- Gold prices fell below $400.00 per ounce on the 21st and continued to slide for the rest of the month, closing at $394.40. Over the month, gold lost $36.90.

- Stock index futures trading began on the Tokyo and Osaka stock exchanges.

October 1988

- U.S. monetary policy went on hold, pending the November presidential elections.

- Long-term Treasury bond yields fell about one-quarter percent to 8¾% from 9% over the month, and the VA mortgage rate was cut to 10% from 10½% on the 28th.

- Huge merger and acquisition activity boosted the stock market. Kraft accepted a $13.5 billion buyout offer from Philip Morris. The combined entity formed the world's largest consumer products company.

- The DJIA reached another post crash high of 2158.96 on the 10th. Three more highs followed, the last on the 21st when the Dow closed at 2183.50.

- The dollar began to slide from the second week on, tumbling four to six percent in value against the major currencies by month end.

November 1988

- George Bush was elected President and Dan Quayle Vice President on the eighth.

- Fed funds ticked up ever-so-slightly to 8⅜%. Signs of solid economic growth in October — especially a strong employment report, with the 5.3% unemployment rate at a 14-year low and a rising capacity utilization rate — shifted financial market sentiment towards pessimism as to the future direction of interest rates.

- The dollar's continued weakness prompted Japanese and U.S. intervention during the first few days of the month. On the 18th, heavy concerted G-10 intervention again tried to boost the dollar, but to little effect. Over the month the dollar lost 3.3% against the yen, 3.1% against the German mark, and 4.8% against the British pound.

- Long-term Treasury yields rebounded above 9%, while three-month Treasury-bill rates rose above 8%.

- Scheduling of the Treasury's midquarter refunding was again disrupted by debt legislation problems. It was not until the 10th that Congress repealed the statutory limitation on the Treasury's long-term bond authority. The 30-year bonds were auctioned a week later at 9.10%. Earlier, the 3-year notes were auctioned at 8.59% on the eighth and the 10-year notes at 8.94% on the ninth.

- The U.S. prime rate rose to 10½% from 10% on the 28th.

- British monetary policy tightened again, as the base rate was boosted to 13% from 12% on the 25th.

- German unemployment fell to 8% during October, a six-year low. Economic growth in Western Europe generally was expanding at the fastest rate in a decade.

- The NIKKEI average reached a new high of 28,490 on the 11th, was followed by succeeding highs on the 16th and 22nd, and closed the month at still another high of 29,579. The yen at one point reached 121.03 to the dollar, a 40-year high.

- The volume of stock and bond trading was generally anemic. The New York Stock Exchange experienced the lowest trading volume in nearly two years on the 28th, when 72.1 million shares were traded. Whatever strength there was in prices was based in blue chips and takeover-target stocks.

- Intense bidding for RJR Nabisco Inc. between Kohlberg, Kravis, Roberts & Company, an investment firm, and

F. Ross Johnson, chief executive of the takeover target, attracted widespread attention.

December 1988

- With the presidential election settled, Federal Reserve tightening resumed. The funds rate rose above 8½% at midmonth and to 8⅞% by Christmas.

- Strong employment growth was reported, as well as other generally buoyant economic data.

- Yield curve flattening continued. Long-term Treasury bond yields hovered within a few basis points of 9%. By month end, this represented 10 to 25 basis points less than other coupons from two years out and only 65 basis points more than three-month bill yields.

- The VA mortgage rate was increased to 10½% from 10% on the 16th.

- The French, Belgians, and Dutch hiked official rates on the 14th. Next day, the Germans followed with a ½ percentage point boost in the Lombard rate to 5.5%. On the day after that, the Swiss raised their discount rate to 3.5% from 3% and the Belgians again increased their Lombard rate, this time also to 5.5%.

- The Frankfurt stock market ignored rising interest rates and vaulted to a yearly high on the DAX index on the 19th, then again on the 20th, and again on the 27th, reaching 1340. This represented a 35% gain since the beginning of the year.

- The NIKKEI also reached several new highs during the month (on the 2nd, 7th, 27th, and 28th, when it closed at 30,159).

- Japanese Minister of Finance Miyazawa resigned on the 12th, over the Recruit Co. stock scandal, to be replaced by Tatsuo Murayama.

- Drexel Burnham Lambert settled charges of security law infractions out of court by paying a $600 million fine.

- The Canadian Parliament ratified a far-reaching free trade pact with the U.S. on the 24th.

- Soviet leader Mikhail Gorbachev made a proposal for large troop reductions in Europe on the seventh.

- Pan Am Flight 103, on its way from London to New York, was blown up over Scotland by a terrorist bomb on the 21st, marring the holiday season.

Dow Jones Industrial Average

(Monthly average of daily closing prices)

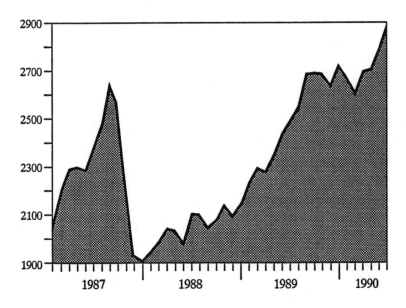

Selected Interest Rates, Government Security Prices, and Money Supply–1989

| | Federal funds rate (monthly average) | 3-month Treasury bill rate (monthly auction average) | 3-month commercial paper rate (monthly average) | Offering quote (end of month)[1] | | | | Money supply (seas. adj. annual rate of change in %)[2] |
| | | | | 8s Nov. 15, 1990 | | 8⅞ s Aug. 15, 2017 | | |
				Price	Yield	Price	Yield	
Jan.	9.1	8.3	9.0	98–4	9.15	100–5	8.86	0.5
Feb.	9.4	8.5	9.4	97–14	9.65	97–0	9.17	1.8
Mar.	9.9	8.8	9.9	97–8	9.86	97–9	9.14	3.4
Apr.	9.8	8.7	9.8	98–4	9.32	99–9	8.94	1.0
May	9.8	8.4	9.5	98–23	8.95	102–16	8.64	-1.6
June	9.5	8.2	9.1	99–22	8.23	108–16	8.10	6.3
July	9.2	7.9	8.7	100–9	7.75	110–12	7.95	9.8
Aug.	9.0	7.9	8.6	99–14	8.48	106–8	8.30	7.6
Sept.	9.0	7.7	8.7	99–13	8.55	105–27	8.33	6.3
Oct.	8.8	7.6	8.5	99–31	8.03	109–26	7.99	6.9
Nov.	8.6	7.6	8.4	100–5	7.82	110–4	7.96	7.2
Dec.	8.4	7.6	8.3	100–1	7.95	109–2	8.05	7.6

Source: Federal Reserve Bulletin & The First Boston Corporation.

[1] Prices expressed in thirty-seconds.

[2] M2 monthly averages as revised.

January 1989

- The Federal Reserve greeted the new year with another tightening, as fed funds rose above 9⅛%. Short-term bill yields followed, rising above 8½%, but long-term bond yields fell back to 8⅞%. The yield curve was nearly flat.

- Domestic interest rates were raised in Germany, Switzerland, France, the Netherlands, and Austria on the 19th.

- The dollar leaped on the news that the United States shot down two Libyan jets on the fourth day of the year. Despite several interventions by U.S. and European central banks, the dollar continued to strengthen against the major currencies all month long.

- Major stock markets around the world soared, reaching post-crash or record levels in New York, Tokyo, Frankfurt, and London. The Dow Industrials scored post-crash highs on 11 of the 21 trading sessions, gaining 174 points on the month.

- George Herbert Walker Bush was sworn in as the 41st U.S. President on the 20th.

- Japan's Emperor Hirohito died on the seventh. His son, Akihito, succeeded to the Chrysanthemum Throne.

February 1989

- The Federal Reserve picked up the pace of tightening as economic reports showed new risks of inflation. The discount rate was raised one-half point to 7% on the 24th, and the funds rate soared above 9⅜% by month end. Long bond yields rose to 9⅛%, as three-month rates grazed 9%. At times, bill rates rose above bond yields.

- A record $1.75 billion of noncompetitive tenders was submitted in the three-year Treasury note auction on the seventh, which came at 9.18%. Both the 10-year note and the new long bond were auctioned at 8.91%.

- Commercial banks hiked the prime rate to 11% from 10½% on the 10th, then to 11½% on the 23rd.

- In the first major initiative of his presidency, President Bush announced his FSLIC rescue program on the sixth.

- The New York stock market paused, but the Tokyo market continued to scale new records, reaching 32,452 on the NIKKEI average on the 23rd, the day before Emperor Hirohito's funeral.

- The Soviet Union completed its troop withdrawal from Afghanistan, nine years after the intervention began.

- For the first time in a year monetary policy remained unchanged for a month.

- The rise in market short rates continued, however. By the 20th the three-month bill yielded more than the 30-year bond. The trend grew more pronounced during the balance of the month.

- Three-month bill rates peaked the day after Easter, with average rates at the weekly auction above 9%. That auction and the two-year and four-year auctions held over the next few days attracted large amounts of noncompetitive tenders.

- Michael Milken, Drexel Burnham Lambert's highly-paid and highly-visible junk bond promoter, was indicted on 98 felony counts, including securities fraud and insider trading.

- Canadian banks raised their prime rate to 13½% from 12¾% on the 22nd.

- The oil tanker Exxon Valdez ran into rocks in Alaska's pristine Prince William Sound, spilling 11 million gallons of crude. Oil futures soared. The cleanup would cost well over a billion dollars in the first year, but remain far from satisfactory to environmentalists.

- The FDIC took over another 45 insolvent S&Ls, whose assets amounted to $13.6 billion. That brought the total under FDIC control to 118 institutions. About 800 more S&Ls were estimated to be "sick."

- The dollar continued strong on foreign exchange markets. By month end it was up over 7% on the Deutschemark and 6% on the yen from the turn of the year.

- John Tower's nomination to become Defense Secretary was rejected by the Senate, after much rancorous debate.

April 1989

- On the first day of the month, the NIKKEI average pushed above 33,000. By month end it added another 700 points.

- The G-7 finance ministers and central bank chiefs met during the first weekend. They warned that further strengthening of the dollar could undermine ongoing trade adjustments and world stability.

- U.S. interest rates declined as fear of further Fed tightening dissipated. Although fed funds continued near 9⅞%, three-month bill yields fell back to about 8¾% and bond yields moved back below 9%.

- Declines in rates, especially in the short end, and some cooler economic statistics, helped push the DJIA to several more post-crash highs. Over the month the Dow added 125 points. (Curiously, the DJIA closed at 2304.80 on three days of the first week.)

- The Bank of Japan intervened against the dollar on the third. This was its first dollar sale for yen intervention since the Plaza agreement in 1985. A week later, the Fed sold dollars.

- Europeans raised key rates again. First the Swiss, then a week later the Germans, followed by the Dutch, Danish, and Austrians.

- Japanese Prime Minister Noboru Takeshita resigned on the 25th over the widening Recruit Co. influence-peddling scandal.

- Solidarity trade union was legalized in Poland.

May 1989

- After an unusually public debate involving Federal Reserve factions, the Administration, and the press, the federal funds rate began to inch down. Although the move was small, the direction was clear.

- The new bellwether long bond was auctioned at 9.11% in mid-month, but by month end the bond market rally pushed the yield down to 8.60%.

- The stock market responded by resuming its upward momentum, gaining 61 points in the month to close at 2480 on the Dow.

- Inspired by a new spirit of liberalization, Chinese university students began to assemble in Beijing's Tiananmen Square.

- Repeated and massive interventions against the dollar failed to prevent it from gaining 7.5% against the yen, 6.9% against the pound, and 5.4% against the DM. An $8.86 billion U.S. trade deficit helped the dollar climb to a nine-month high. Gold dropped below $370 an ounce.

- Interest rates and stock prices continued their unusual parallel rise on foreign markets. Rates rose in Australia, Britain, Canada, Switzerland and even in Japan, where a discount rate hike to 3.25% was the first since March 1980. Stock prices in London rose to a post-crash high on the fifth and the NIKKEI average closed the month at a record 34,267.

- The U.S. cited Japan, Brazil, and India under the Trade Law's Section 301, alleging unfair trade practices. Sanctions were to follow if the situation had not improved after an 18-month negotiating period.

- RJR Nabisco Inc. sold $4 billion of junk bonds, a record, to help finance the company's buyout for $25 billion, also a record, by Kohlberg, Kravis, Roberts and Company.

- Lt. Col. Oliver North was convicted on three charges and acquitted on nine others in the so-called Iran-Contra trial, which resulted from the Reagan Administration's attempt to arm Nicaraguan contra rebels.

- On the final day of the month, Japan announced the selection of Foreign Minister Sosuke Uno as its new Prime Minister.

- A massacre took place in Beijing's Tiananmen Square on the fourth. Chinese government troops fired on university students who were demonstrating for democratic reforms.

- The Ayatollah Khomeini, leader of Iran's revolution, who deemed America the "Great Satan," died in Iran on the fifth.

- Solidarity outpolled the Communist Party in Polish elections on the fifth.

- With turmoil in Asia and Europe, the dollar's strength continued to build, fetching over two German marks and 148 yen at midmonth. Concerted intervention and tighter European monetary policies managed to contain the dollar later in the month. On the 30th, the Bundesbank raised its discount and Lombard rates one-half point to 5% and 7%, respectively. Swiss, French, and other European authorities also tightened.

- The employment report for May reinforced other signs pointing to a softening in the U.S. economy.

- Fed funds fell back below 9½% during the month. Short-term T-bill rates fell to 8¼% while the long-bond yield plunged over 50 basis points to only 8% at midyear.

- Commercial banks cut the prime rate, which had been on the rise for over a year, to 11% from 11½% on the fifth. The same day, the VA mortgage rate was cut one-half point to 10%.

- A growing scandal in Japan concerning the recently installed Prime Minister Uno and a geisha caused declines in the yen and the Tokyo stock market by the latter part of the month.

- Energy prices fell after an OPEC meeting ended in discord early in the month, without agreement on quotas.

- On the first, Carl Icahn sold $2 billion of Texaco stock he had acquired in a takeover attempt, making this the biggest single stock sale ever. The broad market was unaffected.

- Trading in stock index options began in Japan.

July 1989

- As fears of inflation turned to concern about possible recession, the environment generally became one of declining rates. Fed funds fell about 50 basis points to 9%. Two-year notes were auctioned at 7.75%, while long bond yields fell slightly below 8%.

- A prime rate cut on the tenth to 10½% from 11% by Chase Manhattan Bank ignited a spectacular stock market rally. The DJIA rose 221 points over the month. By month end, the 10½% prime rate had become general.

- The VA mortgage rate fell to 9½% from 10% effective on the 17th.

- On Bastille Day, on the 14th, France celebrated the bicentennial of the French Revolution.

- The G-7 Economic Summit was held in Paris from the 14th through the 16th. The group expressed confidence in the world economy but called for action to protect the environment and to impede laundering of drug money.

- London's stock market reached post-crash highs in the first half of the month, then again near the end of the month.

- The Japanese Liberal Democratic Party lost its majority in the upper house elections on the 22nd. Prime Minister Uno announced he would resign the following month as the furor over his geisha association did not subside. Toshiki Kaifu was selected to succeed him as Prime Minister. The stock market surged to new records during the remaining part of the month and closed at 34,954.

- More than half of the U.S.'s petroleum came from imports, for the first time since 1977, the result of higher usage and lower domestic production.

- Time Inc. acquired Warner Communications for $13.4 billion.

August 1989

- Interest rates dipped during the first three days of the month, then ticked up at midmonth when investor psychology suddenly turned less positive. Fed funds stabilized for the time being near 9%.

- The thrift rescue bill (The Financial Institutions Reform, Recovery, and Enforcement Act of 1989) was passed on the eighth. The legislation created two new federal agencies, The Resolution Trust Corporation (RTC) to oversee the resolution of insolvent S&Ls and The Resolution Funding Corporation (REFCORP) to provide funding for the depositor rescue. The bill called for outlays of $166 billion over the coming decade. Subsequently, this cost appeared to be vastly underestimated.

- Expectations of lower rates supported a stock market surge. On the 24th the DJIA soared to an all-time record high of 2734.64, surpassing the previous high of 2722.42 reached on August 25, 1987, before the crash.

- London and Tokyo stock markets also continued to boom.

- Demands for political autonomy sparked huge demonstrations in the Baltic States.

- Signals of sluggish economic activity came from weak construction and manufacturing sectors. But signs of rebound came from employment, output, and sales statistics. The trade deficit was smaller than expected.

- A federal jury in Chicago indicted 46 commodities brokers and traders on the Chicago Mercantile Exchange and the Chicago Board of Trade on charges of stealing and skimming investors' profits.

- Telephone company workers went on strike in 20 states and the District of Columbia primarily because the companies had proposed to shift some health care expenses to employees.

- B. Altman and Bonwit Teller department stores filed for bankruptcy protection.

- In Poland a noncommunist Prime Minister, Tadeusz Mazowiecki, was elected by a huge vote. Communists had held power for 45 years.

September 1989

- The DJIA reached a new record of 2752.09 on the first. But the market took a breather for the rest of the month.

- Revelations that Campeau Corporation's highly leveraged empire of department stores was suffering severe cash flow problems and might experience debt repayment snags roiled the junk bond market.

- Drexel Burnham Lambert Inc., the Wall Street house that raised vast amounts of money through the use of high-yield junk bonds, pleaded guilty to six counts of securities fraud in what constituted the largest such case ever on Wall Street.

- The London stock market's FTSE 100 surpassed its precrash high, reaching a peak of 2443 on the sixth. Tokyo's NIKKEI also soared to new records. For the quarter both indexes were up over 8%.

- A reassuring CPI report for August, unchanged from the month before for the first time in over three years, contributed to an easing of inflation fears.

- Taking advantage of the first major crack in the Iron Curtain, East Germans by the thousands fled to the West through Hungary during the weekend of the ninth.

- Again and again, the Fed and also the central banks of Japan and England intervened against the dollar. On the

22nd the G-7 issued a communique declaring the "rise of the dollar in recent months inconsistent with economic fundamentals." After that, the dollar declined somewhat for the rest of the month.

- Mitsubishi became the first Japanese financial institution listed to trade on the New York Stock Exchange.

- Columbia Pictures agreed to be acquired by Japan's Sony Corporation for $3.4 billion.

October 1989

- The stock market moved higher during the first part of the month, buoyed by takeover activity and some encouraging economic statistics. The DJIA set new records on five consecutive days, despite talk of lower corporate profits and troubles in the junk bond market.

- On Friday the 13th, a breakdown in the financing arrangements for a buy-out of United Airlines sparked a mini-crash in the stock market, producing the second largest daily decline in the DJIA of 190.58 points, or 6.9% of its total value.

- Foreign markets echoed the drop. The NIKKEI average fell 1.8%, Australia 8.1% and London 3.2%. Frankfurt lost 12.8% of its value in the biggest drop there ever.

- The worst fears eased on the following trading day as the DJIA recovered 88.12 points, about half the losses of the 13th. By month end the stock market regained some stability.

- Interest rates were raised a percentage point each in Germany, Britain, France, the Netherlands, Switzerland, Austria, Belgium, and Denmark at the end of the first week in a concerted effort to curb the dollar's value. Japan followed a few days later by boosting its discount rate one-half point to 3.75%, all to little avail in lowering the U.S. currency.

- Moving in the other direction, the Federal Reserve dropped the funds rate another quarter-point to 8¾%. Market interest rates fell sharply in conjunction with the Friday the 13th stock market break but subsequently rebounded to end the month with only slight net declines. REFCORP began raising funds for the thrift depositor rescue with a $4.5 billion 30-year bond, auctioned at 8.15% on the 25th.

- Hungarians dissolved their Communist Party on the seventh.

- East Germany, trying to stop the flood of people leaving for the West, changed leadership on the 18th. All told, about 400,000 people were estimated to have escaped the Communist regime.

- The UK's top financial official, Nigel Lawson, quit apparently in a dispute with Prime Minister Margaret Thatcher. John Major was appointed the new Chancellor of the Exchequer.

- Mitsubishi Estate, a major Japanese developer, bought 51% of Rockefeller Center, Radio City Music Hall and other buildings in mid-Manhattan for $846 million, antagonizing some of those who saw this deal as a symbol of the decline of U.S. economic dominance.

- A severe earthquake hit San Francisco on the 17th just as baseball's World Series was getting under way there.

- About 57,000 machinists of the Boeing Company went on strike on the fourth.

November 1989

- On the seventh anniversary of this economic expansion, the economy appeared to be on a severe downward slide. Consumer spending was down. Signs of sluggishness in the manufacturing sector became more pronounced. Weak auto sales, home construction, and corporate profits all contributed to a generally gloomy outlook. Fed funds ticked down a quarter-point to 8½% in the first half of the month.

- After much delay, Congress passed legislation raising the Treasury's permanent debt limit to $3.123 trillion, thereby allowing the Treasury to resume its regular schedule of auctions. Three-year notes came at 7.77%, 10-year notes at 7.94%, and long bonds at 7.87%.

- On the eighth, a Midwestern bank cut its prime rate ½ percentage point to 10% while some anticipated a Fed easing. Around Thanksgiving, confusing statements by the Fed chairman and a lower funds rate around the holidays gave what turned out to be false signals of an easing in Fed policy. It took a couple of days for the vain hope to dissipate and for traders to tally up their losses. By the 28th the Midwestern bank's prime rate was back up to 10½%.

- GE announced plans to buy back $10 billion of its stock.

- Strict limits on computerized stock trading were announced by the NYSE. Program trading was believed to exacerbate market instability.

- At around midmonth the Tokyo stock market resumed its upward gallop, setting several new records during the rest of the month. It closed with the NIKKEI at 37,269, another new record.

- The Boeing and the last of the telephone companies' strikes ended.

- The Berlin Wall was breached and East Germany allowed its euphoric citizens free travel through its western borders on the ninth, for the first time since the Wall was erected in 1961.

- Bulgarian Communist leader Zhikov stepped down on the tenth, amid public pressure. Next day, Communist leaders urged free elections without guarantee of Communist supremacy.

- Massive public demonstrations in Czechoslovakia led to a lifting of travel restrictions on the 14th, and two weeks later to an announcement of plans to cast off Communist domination and form a coalition government.

- W. German Chancellor Kohl announced long-range German reunification plans on the 28th. The Deutschemark continued to appreciate against the dollar as the opening of Eastern Europe was seen as potentially most beneficial to the German economy.

December 1989

- Fed funds traded at around 8½% until a few days before Christmas, when the rate inched down another quarter-point to 8¼%.

- Lingering unease about real estate loans came to the fore about the third week. The Dow declined, but only for a few days. The DJIA ended the month 47 points higher than it began.

- For the year as a whole, yields on short Treasury bills declined 56 basis points to 7.78%; yields on long bonds fell 102 basis points to 7.97%. The Dow, on the other hand, added an impressive 585 points, or 27%, to its value.

- President Bush and General Secretary Gorbachev met at the Malta Summit on storm-tossed ships over the first weekend. The Cold War appeared to be abandoned.

- Moscow admitted that the 1968 Czech invasion was "erroneous."

- The U.S. invaded Panama on the 20th in order to capture the strongman, General Noriega, and bring him back to the U.S. to face charges of drug trafficking.

- Yasushi Mieno became the new governor of the Bank of Japan on the 17th. On Christmas Day, Japan raised its discount rate for the third time in 1989, by half a point to 4.25%. Throughout everything, the Tokyo stock market bounded ever higher, establishing 13 records and rising 4.85% in the month. The NIKKEI average closed the year at a record high of 38,916, a gain of 26% on the year.

- Lithuania officially abolished the constitutional guaranty of Communist Party monopoly on power and shortly after, on the 20th, the Lithuanian Communist Party declared itself independent of the U.S.S.R. Communist Party.

- In Romania, the transition from Communism was more difficult. Riots took place on the 18th and fighting continued until President Ceausescu and his wife were executed by firing squad on Christmas Day. The new leader promised free elections in the Spring.

- The West German mark surged 5% against the dollar while the Japanese yen remained unchanged. For the year as a whole the dollar lost nearly 5% of its value against the German currency but gained 15% against the yen.

- The German stock market rapidly recovered from its October break, and closed the year at 1790.37 on the DAX index, a record high. During the year, it gained 34% in value.

- Domestic oil production during 1989 fell by a record half million barrels per day. Imports rose to provide 46% of the oil used in the U.S., a near record and the highest share in more than a decade.

January 1990

- The new year began with a 56.95 point surge in the Dow to a new record of 2810.15. For the rest of the month, however, recurrent reports of weaker corporate earnings together with a falling bond market, brought the DJIA down by 266.91 points, or 9.5%, before recovering slightly in the last trading day.

- Large banks cut the prime rate to 10% from 10½% on the eighth, the first decline in this rate since July. Nevertheless, bond yields rose 50 basis points to around 8½% by month end on signs that the economy might have bottomed, dashing hopes of a Fed easing. Rumors that the Japanese were scaling back their investments in the U.S. also fed the declining bond market.

- In the early days of the month, concerted intervention took place against the surging dollar in an effort to boost the yen. The dollar declined against the DM to a 20-month low on the eighth as rising interest rates in Germany boosted its currency.

- The Tokyo stock and bond markets took a pounding all month long. Bond yields rose 1¼ percentage points to 6¾%. The stock exchange lowered margin requirements on the 11th, but this did not stop the slide in the NIKKEI average, which totaled 4.4% for the month.

- General Noriega surrendered to the U.S. military on the fourth and was brought back to the U.S. to stand trial.

- Beijing ended martial law on the tenth.

- In another blow to the junk bond market, Campeau Corporation's Allied and Federated department stores filed for Chapter XI bankruptcy protection from their creditors on the 15th. About $7.5 billion of debt was outstanding.

- To quell fighting between Azerbaijanis and Armenians, President Gorbachev sent in the Red Army on the 15th. Azerbaijan threatened to secede from the Soviet Union if the troops were not withdrawn. A cease fire was agreed to on the 25th.

- The Bulgarian Parliament revoked the Communist Party's monopoly on power on the 15th, virtually the last Eastern European ally of the Soviet Union to strip the Communist Party of its dominant role.

- Poland dissolved its Communist Party on the 29th.

- On the 30th, markets were roiled by a CNN report that Mikhail Gorbachev was planning to resign from his post as

Communist Party General Secretary and retain solely his position of President. Mr. Gorbachev denied that he had such plans.

- President Bush proposed deeper troop cuts in Europe on the 31st.

Selected Interest Rates, Government Security Prices, and Money Supply–1990

| | Federal funds rate (monthly average) | 3-month Treasury bill rate (monthly auction average) | 3-month commercial paper rate (monthly average) | Offering quote (end of month)[1] | | | | Money supply (seas. adj. annual rate of change in %)[2] |
| | | | | 8s Nov. 15, 1990 | | 8⅞ s Aug. 15, 2017 | | |
				Price	Yield	Price	Yield	
Jan.	8.2	7.6	8.1	99–26	8.22	103–26	8.51	3.1
Feb.	8.2	7.8	8.1	99–27	8.20	102–22	8.62	8.6
Mar.	8.3	7.9	8.3	99–24	8.39	101–9	8.75	5.1

Source: Federal Reserve Bulletin & The First Boston Corporation.

[1] Prices expressed in thirty-seconds.
[2] M2 monthly averages as revised.

February 1990

- The decline in the U.S. bond market slowed. Yields in the Treasury's quarterly refunding, however, reflected the deterioration in interest rate expectations that had taken place since the November auctions. Yields on the 3-, 10-, and 30-year issues all came in over 60 basis points higher compared to the previous quarter.

- Drexel Burnham Lambert went out of business on the 13th, one day after rumors became widespread that it was in mortal trouble. The firm that dominated the high-yield, high-risk market collapsed under the combined weight of sharp declines in the value of junk bonds in its holdings and of investigations and heavy fines for securities laws violations by its employees.

- Japanese bond yields continued to climb, surpassing 7%. Stock prices maintained a turbulent downward slide, the

NIKKEI falling to 34,592 at month end, a decline of nearly 11% since the beginning of the year. The yen fell to the lowest level in eight months against the dollar.

- The stock market traded within a narrow band, and eked out a gain of 36.71 points on the Dow over the month.

- German reunification was much discussed, with only the terms of currency exchange still open to question. German bond yields rose more than 100 basis points as concern over the inflationary consequences of currency reunification came to the fore.

- Hundreds of thousands protested in Moscow in an effort to end the Communist monopoly on political power. A few days later, General Secretary Gorbachev endorsed the call for the Communist Party to relinquish its power monopoly, and the Party officially agreed to do so.

- Nelson Mandela, leader of the struggle against apartheid, was freed from his 27-year long imprisonment in South Africa on the 12th.

- Lithuanians elected to Parliament, on the 25th, mostly those candidates who backed secession from the Soviet Union.

- Nicaraguans elected Violeta Chamorro to succeed as President the Sandinista Daniel Ortega.

- The Soviets began to pull out troops that they had stationed in Czechoslovakia.

March 1990

- The Federal Reserve's monetary policy remained unchanged. Fed funds traded near 8¼% as they had ever since Christmas.

- The dollar's continued appreciation chiefly against the yen triggered heavy and concerted anti-dollar intervention during the first few days of March. Still, the yen lost

6.3% of its dollar value over the month, and 10.0% over the first quarter.

- In an effort to head off inflation and to keep the yen from weakening further, the Bank of Japan raised the discount rate by one percentage point to 5.25% on the 20th. This was the fourth hike since May.

- The bloom came definitely off the Japanese stock market as the NIKKEI average slid 13% further in March, accumulating a loss of 23% from its 1989 year-end value and in the process wiping out the gains of the preceding 14 months.

- The German stock market continued to surge. It closed the quarter at another record high, 1968.55 on the DAX index, a 10% gain over the year thus far.

- Domestic markets maintained comparative stability. A generally more optimistic outlook developed as signs of some pickup in the economic expansion appeared. Short and long rates fluctuated within narrow bands, while the stock market managed to gain 79.73 points on the Dow to close the quarter at 2706.98.

- Over the quarter as a whole, however, the DJIA lost 46.22 points, while the long bond yield rose 65 basis points to 8.62%. Three-month bill yields advanced 26 basis points to end the quarter at 8.04%.

- Lithuania, a constituent Republic of the U.S.S.R. since the Second World War, declared itself a sovereign and independent state on the 11th. The government of the U.S.S.R. rejected the declaration as invalid.

- In a stunning reversal of its history, the U.S.S.R. peaceably legislated an end to the Communist Party's monopoly on power within the Soviet Union and adopted a presidential system of government on the 13th. Mikhail Gorbachev was officially elected President of the U.S.S.R. on the 16th.

Budget Receipts, Expenditures and Debt

(In billions of dollars)

Fiscal year	Budget receipts	Budget expenditures[1]	Surplus (+) or deficit (-)	Total Federal debt at end of fiscal year[2]
Administrative Budget				
1910	0.7	0.7	--[3]	1.1
1920	6.6	6.4	+0.3	24.3
1930	4.1	3.3	+0.7	16.2
Consolidated Cash Statement				
1940	6.9	9.6	-2.7	48.5
1950	40.9	43.1	-2.2	257.4
Unified Budget				
1960	92.5	92.2	+0.3	290.5
1970	192.8	195.7	-2.9	380.9
1975	279.1	332.3	-53.2	541.9
1978	399.6	458.7	-59.2	776.6
1979	463.3	503.5	-40.2	828.9
1980	517.1	590.9	-73.8	908.5
1981	599.3	678.2	-78.9	994.3
1982	617.8	745.7	-127.9	1,136.8
1983	600.6	808.3	-207.8	1,371.2
1984	666.5	851.8	-185.3	1,564.1
1985	734.1	946.3	-212.3	1,817.0
1986	769.1	990.3	-221.2	2,120.1
1987	854.1	1,003.8	-149.7	2,345.6
1988	909.0	1,064.4	-155.1	2,600.8
1989	990.7	1,142.6	-152.0	2,866.2
1990 est.	1,073.5	1,197.2	-123.8	3,113.3
1991 est.	1,170.2	1,233.3	-63.1	3,319.2

Source: The Budget of the United States Government—1991.

[1] In the 1987 Budget, expenditures and deficits of the Unified Budget were redefined to include what were previously off-budget outlays.

[2] Includes debt to government trust funds.

[3] Less than $50 million.

Public Debt of the United States

U.S. Treasury securities are sold to finance gaps between the government's receipts and expenditures. Deficits may be planned and foreseen in the budget, or they may arise unexpectedly from changes in economic and other circumstances. Some shortfalls are seasonal in nature, reflecting differences in timing of expenses and receipts. Tax collections, for example, peak in the April–June calendar quarter, which includes the major individual and corporate tax dates, while expenditures are spread more evenly throughout the year. In addition to financing budget deficits, Treasury securities also are issued to raise funds on behalf of "off-budget" federal programs with expenditures, revenues, and borrowings.

Treasury securities are issued under authority of the Second Liberty Bond Act of September 24, 1917, as amended. Section 21 of the Act limits, to an amount set by Congress, the outstanding total face value of obligations issued under authority of the Act or guaranteed as to principal and interest by the United States. Obligations issued on a discount basis and subject to redemption prior to maturity at the option of the owner are included in the statutory debt limitation at current redemption values. The debt limit has been raised many times, but for a long time Congress labeled such increases "temporary." However, on May 26, 1983, a new "permanent" limit was set at $1,389 billion and subsequently increased several times. As of November 1989, the debt limit was increased to $3,122.7 billion. Congress usually acts to change the limit only when the value of outstanding debt approaches the ceiling, threatening to restrict the government's ability to issue additional securities to finance the budget deficit. As of May 31, 1990, the outstanding debt subject to the statutory limit totaled $3,029 billion.

Under the Public Debt Act of 1942, the Treasury has wide discretion in determining the terms on marketable securities. They may be sold on a competitive or other basis, and they may be issued on an interest-coupon or discount basis, or some combination thereof, at whatever prices the Secretary of the

Major Types of Budget Receipts and Expenditures

(Fiscal years, in billions of dollars)

	1988 actual	1989 actual	1990 estimate	1991 estimate
Receipts:				
Individual income taxes	401.2	445.7	489.4	528.5
Corporation income taxes	94.5	103.6	112.0	129.7
Excise taxes	35.2	34.1	36.2	37.6
Social insurance taxes & contributions	334.3	359.4	385.4	421.4
All other receipts	43.7	47.9	50.5	53.0
Total receipts	909.0	990.7	1073.5	1170.2
Expenditures:				
National defense	290.4	303.6	296.3	303.2
International affairs	10.5	9.6	14.6	18.2
General science, space & technology	10.8	12.8	14.1	16.6
Agriculture	17.2	16.9	14.6	14.9
Natural resources & environment	14.6	16.2	17.5	18.2
Commerce & housing credit	18.8	27.7	22.7	17.2
Community & regional development	5.3	5.4	8.8	7.8
Energy	2.3	3.7	3.2	3.0
Transportation	27.3	27.6	29.3	29.8
Health	44.5	48.4	57.8	63.7
Education, training, employment & social services	31.9	36.7	37.7	41.0
Social Security & Medicare	298.2	317.5	345.1	363.4
Income security	129.3	136.0	146.6	153.7
Veterans' benefits & services	29.4	30.0	28.9	30.3
Administration of justice	9.2	9.4	10.5	12.6
Interest	151.7	169.1	175.6	173.0
General government	9.5	9.1	10.6	11.3
Allowances	–	–	–	-1.1
Undistributed offsetting receipts:				
Employer share, employee retirement	-33.4	-34.3	-33.8	-36.0
Rents & royalties on the outer continental shelf	-3.5	-2.9	-2.6	-3.0
Total expenditures	1064.0	1142.6	1197.2	1233.3
Budget deficit (-)	-155.1	-152.0	-123.8	-63.1

Source: The Budget of the United States Government—1991.

Treasury may prescribe. There is no statutory limit on the interest rate that may be paid on bills, certificates, or notes. There had been a long-standing limit of 4¼% on the coupon rate on Treasury bonds, with Congress providing exemptions from that limit in recent years. On November 10, 1988 legislation was enacted repealing the statutory limitation on Treasury's long-term bond authority.

The Treasury has outstanding several types of marketable and nonmarketable securities. All are described in the following pages. Marketable issues presently consist of bills, notes, and bonds. These differ mainly in the length of period to maturity at the time of issuance. In addition, bills are issued on a discount basis, while notes and bonds carry interest coupons. Nonmarketable issues consist mainly of savings bonds and special issues to Treasury trust funds, foreign monetary authorities, and state and local governments.

In the past, bearer and registered bonds were issued in paper form. Those still outstanding may be exchanged at any Federal Reserve Bank or branch for an equal amount of any authorized denomination of the same issue. Outstanding bearer bonds are interchangeable with registered bonds and bonds in "book-entry" form. That is, the latter exist as computer entries only and no paper securities are issued. New bearer and registered bonds are no longer being issued. Since August 1986, the Treasury's new issues of marketable notes and bonds are available in book-entry form only. All Treasury bills and more than 90% of all other marketable securities are now in book-entry form. Book-entry obligations are transferable only pursuant to regulations prescribed by the Secretary of the Treasury.

Since October 1984, new issues of Treasury marketable securities maturing in ten years or more may be "stripped" (i.e., the coupons and the principal separated), and components may be traded in book-entry form under the Treasury STRIPS (Separate Trading of Registered Interest and Principal of Securities) program. Reconstituting STRIPS components into the original note or bond is also permitted.

Treasury securities are callable when so provided in the official terms of the issue. Notice of call must be given four months before the call date. No callable bonds have been issued since November 1984.

Treasury marketable securities are acceptable to secure deposits of public monies. They are also acceptable as security for notes discounted or rediscounted at Federal Reserve Banks. Income is subject to all federal income taxes but is exempt from state and local income taxes.

Maturity Distribution of Privately Held U.S. Treasury Marketable Debt

As of December 31

(In billions of dollars; to date of earliest call or maturity)

	1940[1]	1960	1970	1980	1986	1987	1988	1989
Under 1 year								
Amount outstanding	3.9	57.0	84.0	220.1	472.7	483.6	524.2	546.8
Percent of total	10	37	50	47	40	33	34	33
1–5 Years								
Amount outstanding	16.3	59.2	57.1	156.2	402.7	526.7	553.0	578.3
Percent of total	41	39	34	34	34	36	35	35
5–10 Years								
Amount outstanding	8.9	15.9	12.7	38.8	159.4	209.2	232.5	247.4
Percent of total	23	10	8	8	13	15	15	15
Over 10 Years								
Amount outstanding	10.3	21.3	14.6	48.6	150.7	225.9	245.6	282.1
Percent of total	26	14	9	11	13	16	16	17
Total marketable debt privately held	39.5	153.5	168.5	463.7	1,185.7	1,445.4	1,555.2	1,654.7
Average maturity [2]	n.a.	4 yr. 7 mo.	3 yr. 4 mo.	3 yr. 9 mo.	5 yr. 3 mo.	5 yr. 9 mo.	5 yr. 9 mo.	6 yr. 0 mo.

Source: Treasury Bulletin.
n.a. Not available.
[1] Pre-War June 30.
[2] Average maturity through December 1970 based on total marketable public debt, thereafter only on privately held public debt.
Note: Percentage breakdowns may not add to 100% due to rounding.

World War II brought major growth of United States government debt, from $55 billion at the end of fiscal 1941 to $280 billion by February 1946. Subsequent budget surpluses brought the figure down to $251 billion in April 1949, but since then the trend in the federal debt has been largely upward. In the environment of the last several years of tax reduction and continuing high defense and entitlement expenditures, government debt has grown by unprecedented amounts. By the end of May 1990, total marketable debt amounted to $2.025 *trillion*.

From the end of World War II until 1953, financing operations involved only issues maturing in less than 10 years. Several issues of bonds maturing in over 10 years were offered from 1953–1959, but the total sold was only $10 billion. Although concentration of Treasury debt in short-term issues was a matter of concern, it proved difficult to achieve any major extension into long-term securities. Funds for investment in long-term government securities were available only in limited amounts, and economic and market conditions generally were not favorable to large-scale sales of long-term bonds for cash. In the late 1950s and thereafter, moreover, market yields moved above the statutory limit of a 4¼% coupon rate for Treasury bonds, confining the Treasury to the issuance of notes (then subject to a statutory maximum maturity of five years), certificates, and bills.

Although refusing to relax the 4¼% ceiling, Congress did enact legislation in 1959 that facilitated a series of advance refundings by the Treasury beginning in 1960. In these the Treasury offered holders of issues, most of which were far from maturity, the opportunity to exchange them for longer dated bonds at a higher rate of return. Massive amounts, for that time, of long-term obligations were placed with the public with little impact upon market prices. A total of $67.8 billion was placed in 11 such advance refundings during 1960–65; $54.4 billion represented issues in maturities of over five years. These operations lengthened the average maturity of the marketable debt significantly. After mid-1965, however, market interest rates rose so far above the 4¼% coupon rate ceiling that further long-term refunding became impossible.

Subsequent legislation further eased the restrictions on the Treasury's issuance of long-term debt. In 1967, Congress lengthened the maximum maturity of notes from five years to seven years. Since notes are not subject to the 4¼% ceiling, this in effect permitted the Treasury to sell securities of up to a seven-year maturity freely, and it made active use of the privilege. The maximum maturity of new note issues was extended to 10 years by legislation enacted in March 1976. In 1971, the Treasury was authorized to issue up to $10 billion in bonds exempt from any coupon interest rate limitation. This was raised in several steps to $270 billion. On November 10, 1988 Congress repealed the coupon rate limit on long-term Treasury bonds. The average maturity of the privately held debt, mainly falling from 1965 until the end of 1975 but rising since then, is charted below and tabulated on page 46.

The table on pages 49–55 lists the Treasury debt outstanding as of March 31, 1990. A table showing the denominations of Treasury and agency securities appears on page 92.

Average Length of the Marketable Debt

(Privately held)

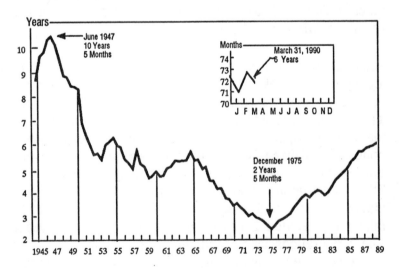

*Reproduced by courtesy of the U.S. Treasury.

48

Public Debt of the United States

March 31, 1990

Issue	Rate of interest (percent)	Date of initial issue	Amount outstanding (in millions of dollars)
Treasury bills	Various	Various	453,077
Treasury notes due:			
Apr. 1990	7 5/8	May 2, 1988	11,260
Apr. 1990	10 1/2	Apr. 4, 1983	5,054
May 1990	7 7/8	May 15, 1987	12,000
May 1990	8 1/8	May 31, 1988	9,677
May 1990	11 3/8	Mar. 1, 1985	7,029
June 1990	7 1/4	June 30, 1986	8,037
June 1990	8	June 30, 1988	11,115
July 1990	8 3/8	Aug. 1, 1988	10,971
July 1990	10 3/4	July 5, 1983	5,013
Aug. 1990	7 7/8	Aug. 17, 1987	11,128
Aug. 1990	8 5/8	Aug. 31, 1988	10,596
Aug. 1990	9 1/8	June 4, 1985 [1]	600
Aug. 1990	9 7/8	June 4, 1985	7,597
Aug. 1990	10 3/4	Aug. 15, 1980	3,762
Sept. 1990	6 3/4	Sept. 30, 1986	8,194
Sept. 1990	8 1/2	Sept. 30, 1988	10,770
Oct. 1990	8 1/4	Oct. 31, 1988	10,710
Oct. 1990	11 1/2	Oct. 5, 1983	5,044
Nov. 1990	8	Nov. 16, 1987	13,407
Nov. 1990	8 7/8	Nov. 30, 1988	10,605
Nov. 1990	9 5/8	Sept. 3, 1985	7,843
Nov. 1990	13	Nov. 17, 1980	5,701
Dec. 1990	6 5/8	Dec. 31, 1986	8,395
Dec. 1990	9 1/8	Jan. 3, 1989	11,007
Jan. 1991	9	Jan. 31, 1989	11,191
Jan. 1991	11 3/4	Jan. 4, 1984	5,512
Feb. 1991	7 3/8	Feb. 16, 1988	11,592
Feb. 1991	9 1/8	Dec. 3, 1985	7,687
Feb. 1991	9 3/8	Feb. 28, 1989	11,062
Mar. 1991	6 3/4	Mar. 31, 1987	8,555
Mar. 1991	9 3/4	Mar. 31, 1989	12,147
Apr. 1991	9 1/4	May 1, 1989	11,350
Apr. 1991	12 3/8	Apr. 4, 1984	5,377

Public Debt of the United States (continued)

March 31, 1990

Issue	Rate of interest (percent)	Date of initial issue	Amount outstanding (in millions of dollars)
May 1991	8 ⅛	Mar. 5, 1986	20,591
May 1991	8 ¾	May 31, 1989	11,218
May 1991	14 ½	May 15, 1981	2,047
June 1991	7 ⅞	June 30, 1987	8,368
June 1991	8 ¼	June 30, 1989	10,737
July 1991	7 ¾	July 31, 1989	9,833
July 1991	13 ¾	July 9, 1984	5,461
Aug. 1991	7 ½	June 3, 1986	7,778
Aug. 1991	8 ¼	Aug. 31, 1989	11,113
Aug. 1991	8 ¾	Aug. 15, 1988	13,490
Aug. 1991	14 ⅞	Aug. 17, 1981	2,812
Sept. 1991	8 ⅜	Oct. 2, 1989	11,452
Sept. 1991	9 ⅛	Oct. 15, 1987	7,919
Oct. 1991	7 ⅝	Oct. 31, 1989	12,322
Oct. 1991	12 ¼	Oct. 23, 1984	5,745
Nov. 1991	6 ½	Sept. 3, 1986	8,346
Nov. 1991	7 ¾	Nov. 30, 1982	12,583
Nov. 1991	8 ½	Nov. 15, 1988	11,542
Nov. 1991	14 ¼	Nov. 16, 1981	2,886
Dec. 1991	7 ⅝	Jan. 2, 1990	12,002
Dec. 1991	8 ¼	Dec. 31, 1987	8,083
Jan. 1992	8 ⅛	Jan. 31, 1990	11,311
Jan. 1992	11 ⅝	Jan. 4, 1985	5,759
Feb. 1992	6 ⅝	Dec. 3, 1986	8,537
Feb. 1992	8 ½	Feb. 28, 1990	11,841
Feb. 1992	9 ⅛	Feb. 15, 1989	11,512
Feb. 1992	14 ⅝	Feb. 16, 1982	2,813
Mar. 1992	7 ⅞	Mar. 31, 1988	8,140
Apr. 1992	11 ¾	Apr. 2, 1985	5,868
May 1992	6 ⅝	Mar. 3, 1987	8,415
May 1992	9	May 15, 1989	12,679
May 1992	13 ¾	May 17, 1982	10,798
June 1992	8 ¼	June 30, 1988	7,796
July 1992	10 ⅜	July 2, 1985	6,299
Aug. 1992	7 ⅞	Aug. 15, 1989	13,523
Aug. 1992	8 ¼	June 3, 1987	8,497

Public Debt of the United States (continued)

March 31, 1990

Issue	Rate of interest (percent)	Date of initial issue	Amount outstanding (in millions of dollars)
Sept. 1992	8 ¾	Sept. 30, 1988	8,000
Oct. 1992	9 ¾	Nov. 1, 1985	6,287
Nov. 1992	7 ¾	Nov. 15, 1989	14,311
Nov. 1992	8 ⅜	Sept. 3, 1987	8,549
Nov. 1992	10 ½	Nov. 15, 1982	4,331
Dec. 1992	9 ⅛	Jan. 3, 1989	8,287
Jan. 1993	8 ¾	Jan. 15, 1986	6,515
Feb. 1993	8 ¼	Dec. 1, 1987	8,256
Feb. 1993	8 ⅜	Feb. 15, 1990	14,744
Feb. 1993	10 ⅞	Feb. 15, 1983	5,162
Mar. 1993	9 ⅝	Mar. 31, 1989	9,204
Apr. 1993	7 ⅜	Apr. 3, 1986	6,511
May 1993	7 ⅝	Mar. 3, 1988	8,096
May 1993	10 ⅛	May 16, 1983	5,100
June 1993	8 ⅛	June 30, 1989	8,393
July 1993	7 ¼	July 7, 1986	6,757
Aug. 1993	8 ¾	June 1, 1988	7,370
Aug. 1993	11 ⅞	Aug. 15, 1983	6,593
Sept. 1993	8 ¼	Oct. 2, 1989	8,745
Oct. 1993	7 ⅛	Nov. 3, 1986	7,013
Nov. 1993	9	Sept. 1, 1988	7,518
Nov. 1993	11 ¾	Nov. 15, 1983	12,478
Dec. 1993	7 ⅝	Jan. 2, 1990	8,974
Jan. 1994	7	Jan. 5, 1987	7,295
Feb. 1994	8 ⅞	Dec. 1, 1988	7,806
Apr. 1994	7	Apr. 1, 1987	7,336
May 1994	9 ½	Mar. 3, 1989	8,532
May 1994	13 ⅛	May 15, 1984	5,669
July 1994	8	July 6, 1987	7,221
Aug. 1994	8 ⅝	June 2, 1989	7,842
Aug. 1994	12 ⅝	Aug. 15, 1984	6,300
Oct. 1994	9 ½	Oct. 15, 1987	7,074
Nov. 1994	8 ¼	Sept. 1, 1989	8,272
Nov. 1994	11 ⅝	Nov. 15, 1984	6,659
Jan. 1995	8 ⅝	Jan. 15, 1988	7,343
Feb. 1995	7 ¾	Dec. 1, 1989	8,344

Public Debt of the United States (continued)

March 31, 1990

Issue	Rate of interest (percent)	Date of initial issue	Amount outstanding (in millions of dollars)
Feb. 1995	11 ¼	Feb. 15, 1985	6,934
Apr. 1995	8 ⅜	Apr. 15, 1988	7,018
May 1995	8 ½	Mar. 1, 1990	8,293
May 1995	11 ¼	May 15, 1985	7,127
July 1995	8 ⅞	July 15, 1988	6,805
Aug. 1995	10 ½	Aug. 15, 1985	7,956
Oct. 1995	8 ⅝	Oct. 17, 1988	7,195
Nov. 1995	9 ½	Nov. 15, 1985	7,319
Jan. 1996	9 ¼	Jan. 17, 1989	7,421
Feb. 1996	8 ⅞	Feb. 15, 1986	163
Feb. 1996	8 ⅞	Feb. 15, 1986	8,412
Apr. 1996	9 ⅜	Apr. 17, 1989	7,782
May 1996	7 ⅜	May 15, 1986	20,086
July 1996	7 ⅞	July 17, 1989	7,725
Oct. 1996	8	Oct. 16, 1989	7,989
Nov. 1996	7 ¼	Nov. 15, 1986	20,259
Jan. 1997	8	Jan. 16, 1990	7,852
May 1997	8 ½	May 15, 1987	9,921
Aug. 1997	8 ⅝	Aug. 15, 1987	9,363
Nov. 1997	8 ⅞	Nov. 15, 1987	9,808
Feb. 1998	8 ⅛	Feb. 15, 1988	9,159
May 1998	9	May 15, 1988	9,165
Aug. 1998	9 ¼	Aug. 15, 1988	11,343
Nov. 1998	8 ⅞	Nov. 15, 1988	9,903
Feb. 1999	8 ⅞	Feb. 15, 1989	9,720
May 1999	9 ⅛	May 15, 1989	10,047
Aug. 1999	8	Aug. 15, 1989	10,164
Nov. 1998	7 ⅞	Nov. 15, 1989	10,774
Feb. 2000	8 ½	Feb. 15, 1990	10,673
Total notes			1,169,364
Treasury bonds due:			
May 1990	8 ¼	Apr. 7, 1975	1,203
Aug. 1992	4 ¼	Aug. 15, 1962	1,360
Aug. 1992	7 ¼	July 8, 1977	1,504
Feb. 1993	4	Jan. 17, 1963	66
Feb. 1993	6 ¾	Jan. 10, 1973	627

Public Debt of the United States (continued)

March 31, 1990

Issue	Rate of interest (percent)	Date of initial issue	Amount outstanding (in millions of dollars)
Feb. 1993	7⅞	Jan. 6, 1978	1,501
Aug. 1993	7½	Aug. 15, 1973	1,814
Aug. 1993	8⅝	July 11, 1978	1,768
Nov. 1993	8⅝	Oct. 10, 1978	1,509
Feb. 1994	9	Jan. 11, 1979	3,010
May 1994	4⅛	Apr. 18, 1963	436
Aug. 1994	8¾	July 9, 1979	1,506
Nov. 1994	10⅛	Oct. 18, 1979	1,502
Feb. 1995	3	Feb. 15, 1955	135
Feb. 1995	10½	Jan. 10, 1980	1,502
May 1995	10⅜	July 9, 1980	1,504
May 1995	12⅝	Apr. 8, 1980	1,503
Nov. 1995	11½	Oct. 14, 1980	1,482
May 1998	7	May 15, 1973	692
Nov. 1998	3½	Oct. 3, 1960	315
May 1999	8½	May 15, 1974	2,378
Feb. 2000	7⅞	Feb. 18, 1975	2,749
Aug. 2000	8⅜	Aug. 15, 1975	4,612
Feb. 2001	11¾	Jan. 12, 1981	1,501
May 2001	13⅛	Apr. 12, 1981	1,750
Aug. 2001	8	Aug. 16, 1976	1,485
Aug. 2001	13⅜	July 2, 1981	1,753
Nov. 2001	15¾	Oct. 7, 1981	1,753
Feb. 2002	14¼	Jan. 6, 1982	1,759
Nov. 2002	11⅝	Sept. 29, 1982	2,753
Feb. 2003	10¾	Jan. 4, 1983	3,007
May 2003	10¾	Apr. 4, 1983	3,249
Aug. 2003	11⅛	July 5, 1983	3,501
Nov. 2003	11⅞	Oct. 5, 1983	7,260
Aug. 2004	13¾	July 10, 1989	4,000
Nov. 2004	11⅝	Oct. 30, 1984	8,302
May 2005	8¼	May 15, 1975	4,224
May 2005	12	Apr. 2, 1985	4,261
Aug. 2005	10¾	July 2, 1985	9,270
Feb. 2006	9⅜	Jan. 15, 1986	4,756
Feb. 2007	7⅝	Feb. 15, 1977	4,234

Public Debt of the United States (continued)

March 31, 1990

Issue	Rate of interest (percent)	Date of initial issue	Amount outstanding (in millions of dollars)
Nov. 2007	7 ⅞	Nov. 15, 1977	1,495
Aug. 2008	8 ⅜	Aug. 15, 1978	2,103
Nov. 2008	8 ¾	Nov. 15, 1978	5,230
May 2009	9 ⅛	May 15, 1979	4,606
May 2009	12 ⅞	Apr. 5, 1984	3,755
Nov. 2009	10 ⅜	Nov. 15,1979	4,201
Feb. 2010	11 ¾	Feb. 15, 1980	2,494
May 2010	10	May 15, 1980	2,987
Nov. 2010	12 ¾	Nov. 17, 1980	4,736
May 2011	13 ⅞	May 15, 1981	4,609
Nov. 2011	14	Nov. 16, 1981	4,901
Nov. 2012	10 ⅜	Nov. 15, 1982	11,032
Aug. 2013	12	Aug. 15, 1983	14,755
May 2014	13 ¼	May 15, 1984	5,007
Aug. 2014	12 ½	Aug. 15. 1984	5,128
Nov. 2014	11 ¾	Nov. 15, 1984	6,006
Feb. 2015	11 ¼	Feb. 15, 1985	12,668
Aug. 2015	10 ⅝	Aug. 15, 1985	7,150
Nov. 2015	9 ⅞	Nov. 15, 1985	6,900
Feb. 2016	9 ¼	Feb. 15, 1986	7,267
Nov. 2016	7 ½	Nov. 15, 1986	18,864
May 2016	7 ¼	May 15, 1986	18,824
May 2017	8 ¾	May 15, 1987	18,194
Aug. 2017	8 ⅞	Aug. 15, 1987	14,017
May 2018	9 ⅛	May 15, 1988	8,709
Nov. 2018	9	Nov. 15, 1988	9,033
Feb. 2019	8 ⅞	Feb. 15, 1989	19,251
Aug. 2019	8 ⅛	Aug. 15, 1989	20,214
Feb. 2020	8 ½	Feb. 15, 1990	10,229
Total bonds			357,858
Federal Financing Bank securities			15,000
Total marketable issues			1,995,299

Public Debt of the United States (continued)

March 31, 1990

Issue	Rate of interest (percent)	Date of initial issue	Amount outstanding (in millions of dollars)
Foreign government series:			
Dollar denominated:			
Bills	Various	Various	$ 4,285
Bonds	Various	Various	32,776
Domestic series[2]	Various	Various	10,093
State and local government series	8.280	Various	163,512
R.E.A. series	5.000	Various	33
Depositary bonds	2.000	Various	4
U.S. savings bonds	7.016	Various	117,979
U.S. savings notes	6.972	Various	315
U.S. individual retirement bonds	6.144	Various	17
U.S. retirement plan bonds	5.888	Various	78
Total public issues—nonmarketable			329,092
Total public issues			2,324,392
Special issues			705,145
Total interest-bearing debt			3,029,537
Matured debt on which interest has ceased			21,661
Debt bearing no interest			759
Total public debt outstanding			3,051,956
Guaranteed obligations			322
(-) Debt not subject to limitation			
Treasury			597
Federal Financing Bank			15,000
Total debt subject to statutory limitation			2,988,875
Balance of statutory debt limit			133,825

Source: Statement of the Public Debt, March 31, 1990.

[1] Foreign targeted Treasury note.

[2] Mainly zero coupon Treasury bonds purchased by REFCORP.

Yields on Treasury Securities of Various Maturities

% (Weekly averages)

Thirty years →

←Two years

Three-month bills

1988   1989   1990

5 6 7 8 9 10

* 365-day bond-equivalent basis.

56

The Treasury has substantially routinized the procedures for refunding existing debt and raising new money to finance the government's deficit. This has greatly reduced the market uncertainty and turmoil that prevailed when the nature of each Treasury financing was potentially a major surprise.

A brief outline of the Treasury's current procedures is given below. It should be understood, however, that the Treasury is not irrevocably committed to these procedures, and it deviates from them when deemed appropriate.

Treasury Bills

Three-Month and Six-Month Bills normally are auctioned weekly on Mondays, with payment due the following Thursday when issues sold three and six months earlier mature. The amounts auctioned can be greater than, less than, or equal to the amounts maturing, depending on the Treasury's cash needs. Tenders by foreign official accounts that exceed their holdings of the maturing issues are allotted in addition to the announced offerings to the public. The amounts to be auctioned are ordinarily announced late in the afternoon on the Tuesday preceding the auction.

52-Week Bills are auctioned every four weeks, presently on a Thursday, with payment due the following Thursday when the issue sold 52 weeks earlier matures. As with shorter maturity bills, the amounts of 52-week bills auctioned may exceed, fall below, or be the same as the amount maturing. The size of the offering is usually announced in the late afternoon on the Friday preceding the Thursday auction. Once every four weeks, the payment dates for the 52-week, three-month, and six-month bills coincide.

Cash Management Bills are issued at irregular intervals with maturities ranging from a few days to almost nine months. Typically they are issued early in the month when government spending tends to be heaviest, and they usually mature shortly after one of the major mid-month tax receipt dates in March, April, June, September, or December. The Treasury usually sets the maturities of cash management bills on a Thursday to coincide with those of some bills already outstanding so that once issued, they become interchangeable for market trading purposes. Cash management bills always raise new cash and are usually sold only in large blocks, with a minimum of $1 million. Cash management bills are announced a few days before sale, and on a few occasions an issue has been announced and sold on the same day, in which case the minimum tender was $10 million.

Coupon Issues

Two-Year Notes are auctioned about a week before the end of each month, usually on a Wednesday. They are dated and mature as of month end. The amount to be sold usually is announced, also most often on a Wednesday, about a week before the auction and may be greater than, less than, or equal to the amount maturing, depending on the Treasury's cash position. In the second month of each quarter the terms of sale of the two-year note are announced together with the terms of sale of the five-year note. In the final month of the quarter, the two-year note is announced together with the four-year note.

Three-Year Notes generally are included in the Treasury's regular mid-quarter refundings. These occur in February, May, August, and November. The terms of the offerings are usually announced on the first Wednesday of these months. Securities sold in the quarterly refundings, such as three-year notes, are dated on or near the 15th of the month of issue and mature on the 15th. Normally, the amount of new securities sold exceeds the amount that is maturing.

Four-Year Notes are offered for sale in the last month of each quarter and are dated and mature at month end. The amount sold may be greater than, less than, or equal to the amount maturing, depending on the Treasury's cash needs. For a time after September 1982, these notes had become part of a "mini" refunding along with seven-year notes and, until year-end 1985, 20-year bonds. Beginning in late 1986, the four-year note was no longer routinely announced as part of a package with the seven-year note. Most often since then the four-year note is announced together with the two-year note, and auctions generally take place on two consecutive days near the end of the month, most often the two-year note on a Tuesday and the four-year note on the following Wednesday.

Five-Year Notes were first offered regularly in 1976, alternating with the sale of 15-year bonds in the first month of each quarter until April 1978. The Treasury resumed the regular sale of five-year notes in September 1979, but for payment early in the final month of each quarter. The notes are scheduled to mature at a mid-quarter refunding date. Generally the five-year notes are auctioned on a Thursday, the day after the two-year note auction.

Private Holdings of Treasury Marketable Debt by Maturity

(As of December 31)

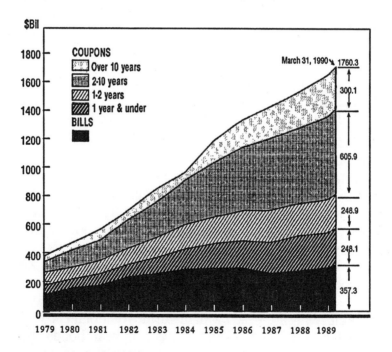

*Reproduced by courtesy of the U.S. Treasury.

Seven-Year Notes used to be part of the quarterly refunding package, but since February 1980 have been supplanted in that role by 10-year notes. Between September 1982 and late 1986, seven-year notes had been sold late in the last month of each quarter and issued early in the following month as part of the "mini" refunding. Lately, seven-year notes have most often been announced and sold in the beginning half of the first month of each quarter. They mature at mid-month.

Ten-Year Notes are now used in the mid-quarter refunding packages, along with a long-term bond and a note maturing in about three years. The notes generally are dated and mature on the 15th of the month.

Foreign Targeted Notes (FTNs) were sold at irregular intervals between October 1984 and May 1985. Only one note, maturing in February 1996, is still outstanding. FTNs were auctioned under competitive bidding and were companion issues to domestic notes offered for sale at the same time and with the same maturity. The coupon for both was established in the domestic auction. Interest on FTNs is paid annually, unlike that on the domestic notes, which is paid semiannually. Foreign Targeted Notes were sold entirely for new cash and only to foreign institutions, foreign branches of United States financial institutions, central banks or monetary authorities of foreign governments, or to certain international organizations of which the United States is a member. FTNs have been issued in book-entry and registered form and provide investors with some degree of anonymity since institutions do not have to disclose in whose name the securities are purchased. The notes may not be converted into the companion domestic issue or sold to United States persons for at least 45 days. With payment of an adjustment due to the difference between annual and semiannual interest payments, these notes may be exchanged for the companion domestic issues. Once converted, U.S. tax regulations requiring full information reporting apply.

Bonds currently are issued with maturities of around 30 years. From July 1978 until October 1980, 15-year bonds were offered for payment early in the first month of each quarter. Between January 1981 and the end of 1985, however, 20-year bonds were sold on that schedule and were dated to mature at a mid-quarter refunding. In April 1986, the Treasury announced the elimination of the 20-year bond offering because it became more cost-effective to issue instead larger amounts of 10-year notes and 30-year bonds in the mid-quarter refundings. Until November 1984, 30-year bonds were issued callable five years before maturity. Since then, 30-year bonds have been issued noncallable, primarily because the call feature interfered with stripping. (See pages 182–189 for a discussion of STRIPS.)

Since 1971, almost all Treasury offerings have been sold at auction. In earlier years, except for Treasury bills, fixed-price subscription offerings had been the general rule. Ordinarily, auction methods and rules are the same for Treasury bills and coupon issues. Since April 18, 1983, bids for both have been on a yield basis. Prior to that date, bids for Treasury bills had been on a price basis. Except in the case of bill sales, allotments to official foreign accounts are made in addition to the announced offerings to the public.

It has become the practice of the Treasury to announce ahead of each quarterly refunding its estimated cash needs for the balance of the quarter and the specific types of financing under consideration.

A list of Treasury notes and bonds issued during 1988 and 1989 begins on the next page.

Offerings of Marketable Treasury Securities Other than Regularly Auctioned Bills

(All offerings at auction; all amounts in millions of dollars)

Announcement date	Auction date	Issue date	Description of security	Maturity date	Average auction yield (%)	Total amount issued [1]		New cash raised or paydown (−) [2]
						To public	To foreign officials	
1/20/88	1/27/88	2/1/88	7⅜% 2-yr. Note	1/31/90	7.40	8,766	1,152	136
1/27/88	2/2/88	2/16/88	7⅜% 3-yr. Note	2/15/91	7.42	9,253	1,098	15,995
1/27/88	2/3/88	2/16/88	8⅛% 10-yr. Note	2/15/98	8.21	9,002	--	
1/27/88	2/4/88	2/16/88	8¾% 29¼-yr. Bond[3]	5/17/17	8.51	8,764	--	
2/17/88	2/24/88	2/29/88	7⅛% 2-yr. Note	2/28/90	7.16	8,780	1,210	8,144
2/17/88	2/25/88	3/3/88	7⅝% 5-yr., 2-mo. Note	5/15/93	7.65	7,252	830	
3/16/88	3/23/88	3/31/88	7⅜% 2-yr. Note	3/31/90	7.39	8,526	1,155	1,665
3/16/88	3/24/88	3/31/88	7⅞% 4-yr. Note	3/31/92	7.90	6,505	1,105	
4/5/88	4/12/88	4/15/88	8⅜% 7-yr. Note	4/15/95	8.44	6,257	--	6,257
4/20/88	4/27/88	5/2/88	7⅝% 2-yr. Note	4/30/90	7.64	8,526	1,235	−115

5/4/88	5/10/88	8⅛% 3-yr. Note	5/15/91	8.23	8,765	960	10,454
5/4/88	5/11/88	9% 10-yr. Note	5/15/98	9.06	8,751	--	
5/4/88	5/12/88	9⅛% 30-yr. Bond	5/15/18	9.17	8,505	--	
5/18/88	5/25/88	8⅛% 2-yr. Note	5/31/90	8.18	8,266	547	6,005
5/18/88	5/26/88	8¾% 5-yr., 2-mo. Note	8/15/93	8.77	7,001	335	
6/15/88	6/22/88	8% 2-yr. Note	6/30/90	8.05	8,539	1,115	518
6/15/88	6/23/88	8¼% 4-yr. Note	6/30/92	8.36	6,753	405	
7/5/88	7/12/88	8⅞% 7-yr. Note	7/15/95	8.91	6,505	200	3,323
7/20/88	7/27/88	8⅜% 2-yr. Note	7/31/90	8.41	8,782	605	-1,016
8/3/88	8/9/88	8¾% 3-yr. Note	8/15/91	8.77	11,097	635	14,998
8/3/88	8/10/88	9¼% 10-yr. Note	8/15/98	9.27	11,001	--	
8/3/88	8/11/88	248-day Cash Mgmt. Bills	4/20/89	8.19[4]	7,021	--	
8/17/88	8/23/88	8⅝% 2-yr. Note	8/31/90	8.72	8,779	820	6,475
8/17/88	8/24/88	9% 5-yr., 2-mo. Note	11/15/93	9.04	7,268	180	
9/21/88	9/27/88	8½% 2-yr. Note	9/30/90	8.53	8,782	740	-931
9/21/88	9/28/88	8¾% 4-yr. Note	9/30/92	8.76	7,025	420	1,046
10/5/88	10/12/88	8⅝% 7-yr. Note	10/15/95	8.73	6,754	--	3,556
10/19/88	10/26/88	8¼% 2-yr. Note	10/31/90	8.33	9,014	980	-910

Offerings of Marketable Treasury Securities Other than Regularly Auctioned Bills

(All offerings at auction; all amounts in millions of dollars)

Announcement date	Auction date	Issue date	Description of security	Maturity date	Average auction yield (%)	Total amount issued[1] To public	To foreign officials	New cash raised or paydown (-)[2]
11/2/88	11/8/88	11/15/88	8 1/2% 3-yr. Note	11/15/91	8.59	9,513	340	13,715
11/2/88	11/9/88	11/15/88	8 7/8% 10-yr. Note	11/15/98	8.94	9,593	--	
11/2/88	11/10/88	11/15/88	37-day Cash Mgmt. Bills	11/22/88	8.25[4]	11,025	--	
11/14/88	11/17/88	11/22/88[5]	9% 30-yr. Bond	11/15/18	9.10	9,026	--	9,026
11/16/88	11/22/88	11/30/88	8 7/8% 2-yr. Note	11/30/90	8.88	9,027	970	6,621
11/16/88	11/23/88	12/1/88	8 7/8% 5-yr., 2-mo. Note	2/15/94	8.97	7,504	260	
12/21/88	12/28/88	1/3/89	9 1/8% 2-yr. Note	12/31/90	9.23	9,030	765	665
12/21/88	12/29/88	1/3/89	9 1/8% 4-yr. Note	12/31/92	9.22	7,258	365	
1/4/89	1/11/89	1/17/89	9 1/4% 7-yr. Note	1/15/96	9.30	7,021	150	3,875
1/18/89	1/25/89	1/31/89	9% 2-yr. Note	1/31/91	9.08	9,289	860	-797
2/1/89	2/7/89	2/15/89	9 1/8% 3-yr. Note	2/15/92	9.18	9,761	465	14,106
2/1/89	2/8/89	2/15/89	8 7/8% 10-yr. Note	2/15/99	8.91	9,502	--	
2/1/89	2/9/89	2/15/89	8 7/8% 30-yr. Bond	2/15/19	8.91	9,508	--	
2/15/89	2/22/89	2/28/89	9 3/8% 2-yr. Note	2/28/91	9.49	9,263	760	7,859
2/15/89	2/23/89	3/1/89	9 1/2% 5-yr., 2-mo. Note	5/15/94	9.49	7,812	650	

3/22/89	3/31/89	9¾%	2-yr. Note	3/31/91	9.87	9,269	1,230 ⎫	2,192
3/22/89	3/31/89	9⅝%	4-yr. Note	3/31/93	9.70	7,510	710 ⎭	
4/5/89	4/17/89	9⅜%	7-yr. Note	4/15/96	9.39	7,020	600	4,382
4/19/89	5/1/89	9¼%	2-yr. Note	4/30/91	9.34	9,260	1,180	-439
5/3/89	5/15/89	9%	3-yr. Note	5/15/92	9.12	9,794	1,240 ⎫	13,056
5/3/89	5/15/89	9⅛%	10-yr. Note	5/15/99	9.18	9,530	300	
5/3/89	5/15/89	8⅞%	29¾-yr. Bond [6]	2/15/19	9.11	9,535	-- ⎭	
5/17/89	5/31/89	8¾%	2-yr. Note	5/31/91	8.84	8,769	1,330 ⎫	7,534
5/17/89	6/2/89	8⅝%	5-yr., 2-mo. Note	8/15/94	8.72	7,507	300 ⎭	
6/21/89	6/30/89	8¼%	2-yr. Note	6/30/91	8.26	8,759	955 ⎫	182
6/21/89	6/30/89	8⅛%	4-yr. Note	6/30/93	8.19	7,527	320 ⎭	
7/5/89	7/17/89	7⅞%	7-yr. Note	7/15/96	7.89	7,289	150	3,002
7/19/89	7/31/89	7¾%	2-yr. Note	7/31/91	7.75	9,007	--	-1,562
8/8/89	8/15/89	7⅞%	3-yr. Note	8/15/92	7.93	10,031	922 ⎫	14,564
8/9/89	8/15/89	8%	10-yr. Note	8/15/99	8.03	9,763	--	
8/10/89	8/15/89	8⅛%	30-yr. Bond	8/15/19	8.14	9,752	-- ⎭	
8/16/89	8/31/89	8¼%	2-yr. Note	8/31/91	8.37	9,501	650 ⎫	7,782
8/16/89	9/1/89	8¼%	5-yr., 2-mo. Note	11/15/94	8.26	7,800	450 ⎭	
9/20/89	10/2/89	8⅜%	2-yr. Note	9/30/91	8.39	9,754	980 ⎫	2,612
9/20/89	10/2/89	8¼%	4-yr. Note	9/30/93	8.35	7,787	620 ⎭	

Offerings of Marketable Treasury Securities Other than Regularly Auctioned Bills

(All offerings at auction; all amounts in millions of dollars)

Announcement date	Auction date	Issue date	Description of security		Maturity date	Average auction yield (%)	Total amount issued[1]		New cash raised or paydown (-)[2]
							To public	To foreign officials	
10/4/89	10/11/89	10/16/89	8%	7-yr. Note	10/15/96	8.08	7,531	160	3,580
10/18/89	10/24/89	10/31/89	$7\frac{5}{8}$%	2-yr. Note	10/31/91	7.74	10,039	720	1.471
11/1/89	11/9/89	11/15/89	$7\frac{3}{4}$%	3-yr. Note	11/15/92	7.77	10,023	645	11,090
11/1/89	11/13/89	11/15/89	$7\frac{7}{8}$%	10-yr. Note	11/15/99	7.94	10,071	300	
11/1/89	11/14/89	11/15/89	$8\frac{1}{8}$%	$29\frac{3}{4}$-yr. Bond[7]	8/15/19	7.87	10,061	--	
11/22/89	11/28/89	11/30/89	$7\frac{3}{4}$%	2-yr. Note	11/30/91	7.78	10,021	1,255	10,049
11/22/89	11/29/89	10/1/89	$7\frac{3}{4}$%	5-yr., 2-mo. Note	2/15/95	7.77	8,045	290	
12/13/89	12/19/89	1/2/90	$7\frac{5}{8}$%	2-yr. Note	12/31/91	7.71	10,014	735	2,771
12/13/89	12/20/89	1/2/90	$7\frac{5}{8}$%	4-yr. Note	12/31/93	7.65	8,052	270	

Source: Treasury Bulletin.

1 Other than to government and Federal Reserve for own account.
2 Estimates derived from holdings of maturing issues as of announcement dates.
3 Reopening of $8\frac{3}{4}$% 30-yr. bond issued 5/15/87.
4 Bond equivalent yield.
5 Issued 11/22/88, dated 11/15/88 with interest accrued from 11/15/88.
6 Reopening of $8\frac{7}{8}$% 30-yr. bond issued 2/15/89.
7 Reopening of $8\frac{1}{8}$% 30-yr. bond issued 8/15/89.

Treasury Bills

Treasury bills are issued on a discount basis. That is, they are sold at a dollar price less than their redemption value at maturity, with the difference, or discount, constituting the payment of interest. When Treasury bills are to be offered, the Treasury issues a notice with respect to the new offering, inviting tenders under competitive and noncompetitive bidding. In the case of competitive tenders, the bid must be expressed on a bank discount basis with not more than two decimals, e.g., 7.15%. Noncompetitive tenders (usually up to $1,000,000) without stated yield are accepted in full at the average yield of accepted competitive bids. Since April 1974, the Federal Reserve has been allowed to bid noncompetitively to "roll over" maturing bills owned by itself or its governmental customers (mainly foreign monetary authorities). Such holdings have averaged over $4 billion each week, a sizable amount when measured against the total of around $17 billion of bills offered in recent weekly auctions.

The Internal Revenue Code provides that a gain realized on the sale, exchange or retirement of Treasury bills is ordinary income to the extent of the ratable share, during the period the bill is held, of the difference between the cost or other tax basis of the obligation and the maturity value.

Bills are issued only in book-entry form and are paid at face amount without additional interest at maturity. They are issued in a variety of denominations from $10,000 up, as shown on page 92, and may be exchanged only for smaller denominations. As of May 31, 1990, there were 32 maturities of Treasury bills outstanding totaling $439.9 billion.

Computation of Discount and Price

Government securities dealers provide a market for Treasury bills in which purchases and sales are made at net prices expressed on a rate basis that, although often called "yield," is actually a rate of bank discount (or discount basis).

The computation of the discount and price is based on the actual number of days to maturity, using a 360-day year, according to the following formulas:

M — days to maturity
R — discount basis (in percent)
D — full discount per $100 maturity value
P — dollar price

$$D = \frac{M}{360} \times R$$

$$P = \$100 - D$$

The following example illustrates the computation:

Find the dollar price for a Treasury bill due in 147 days on a 7.75% discount basis:

$$D = \frac{M}{360} \times R$$

$$= \frac{147}{360} \times 7.75\%$$

$$= 3.16\% \text{ full discount}$$

$$= \underline{\$3.16} \text{ per } \$100 \text{ maturity value}$$

$$P = \$100 - D$$

$$= \$100 - \$3.16 \text{ per } \$100$$

$$= \$96.84 \text{ dollar price for } 7.75\% \text{ discount basis}$$

Bond-Equivalent Yield

The investment return or annualized "bond-equivalent" yield on a Treasury bill is at a higher rate than the discount basis. This may be illustrated as follows (365-day year):

In the example above the full discount (D) per $100 is $3.16. This discount is earned in 147 days. On a per annum basis the discount would be

$$\$3.16 \times \frac{365}{147} = \$7.8463$$

This amount is earned by the investment (P) of only $96.84. The bond equivalent yield (Y) would be

$$Y = \$7.8463 \times \frac{1}{\$96.84} \times 100$$

$$= \$8.10\% \text{ per year (approximate)}$$

This compares with the bank discount basis of 7.75%.

In terms of symbols:

$$Y = \frac{D}{P} \times \frac{365}{M} \times 100$$

or, alternatively, $\dfrac{36500 \times R}{36000 - (M \times R)} = Y$

When a bill is purchased with more than six months to maturity, it is necessary to take into account that no interest is paid on a bill until maturity, while on coupon issues the Treasury pays interest every six months. Therefore, a more complex formula must be employed to calculate the investment yield for these longer maturity bills.

$$Y = \frac{\sqrt{B^2 - (4 \times A \times C)} - B}{2 \times A} \times 100$$

where Y is the bond equivalent yield and

$$A = \frac{M}{2 \times 365} - 0.25$$

$$B = \frac{M}{365}$$

$$C = \frac{P - \$100}{P}$$

As before, M represents the number of days to maturity while P is the dollar price of the bill.

If the bill in our earlier example had been purchased with 347 days to maturity:

$$A = \frac{347}{730} - 0.25 = 0.2253$$

$$B = \frac{347}{365} = 0.9507; \ B^2 = 0.9038$$

$$D = \frac{347}{360} \times 7.75 = 7.4701$$

$$P = \$100 - 7.4701 = \$92.5299$$

$$C = \frac{\$92.5299 - \$100}{\$92.5299} = -0.0807$$

$$Y = \frac{\sqrt{0.9038 - (4 \times 0.2253 \times -0.0807) - 0.9507}}{2 \times 0.2253} \times 100$$

$$= 8.32\%$$

In the computation of bond-equivalent yield, 366 should be substituted for 365 whenever February 29 falls between the purchase date and the first anniversary of the purchase date.

A partial conversion table between discount and bond equivalent yields may be found on pages 228–229.

Formulas for Treasury Bill Returns
U.S. Treasury bills are frequently sold prior to maturity at a rate basis different from that at which they were purchased. Investors may desire to determine the annualized bond equivalent rate of return (Y) from bills under such conditions, or how long bills need to be held to avoid loss. We present the following formula as a means of facilitating calculations of the answers to such problems. The results are sufficiently accurate to meet the ordinary requirements of investors.

The formula utilizes the following data:

$N =$ the number of days held (days to maturity of Treasury bills when purchased minus days to maturity when sold)

$P =$ dollar price when purchased

$S =$ dollar price when sold

$Y =$ annualized bond-equivalent rate of return (investment yield)

The formula is as follows: $Y = \frac{S-P}{P} \times \frac{365}{N} \times 100$

Using the formula for computing the dollar price (P) (shown on page 68) and using the same formula for computing the dollar price (S), one can readily determine the annualized bond-equivalent (investment yield) rate of return (Y).

An illustration of the use of the formula is as follows:

Problem: 147-day bills are bought at 7.75%, held 45 days and sold at an 7.50% basis. What is the return for the period held?

In this problem:

$N = 45$

$P = \$96.84$

S is computed in the same way as P.

$$S = \$100 - D = \$100 - \frac{M}{360} \times R$$

$$M = 147 - 45 = 102$$

$$R = 7.50\%$$

$$D = \frac{102}{360} \times 7.50\% = 2.1250\%$$

$$S = \$100 - \$2.1250 = \$97.8750$$

$$Y = \frac{\$97.8750 - \$96.84}{\$96.84} \times \frac{365}{45} \times 100 = 8.67\%$$

With appropriate substitutions within this formula it is also possible to derive the number of days that bills must be held to achieve this (or some other) yield; or alternatively, to determine the price (S) or discount basis (R) needed to achieve a particular yield.

Table of Equivalents
On pages 232–233 is a table of 0.01% dollar equivalents for Treasury bills maturing from 1 to 366 days.

Ownership of U.S. Government Securities

As of December 31

(In billions of dollars)

	1979	1985	1986	1987	1988	1989
Total federal securities	845.1	1,945.9	2,214.8	2,413.7	2,684.4	2,953.0
Held by:						
U.S. government investment accounts	187.1	348.9	403.1	477.6	589.2	707.8
Federal Reserve Banks	117.5	181.3	211.3	222.6	238.4	228.4
Public	540.5	1,417.2	1,602.0	1,731.4	1,858.5	2,015.8
Commercial banks	96.4	198.2	203.5	201.5	193.8	180.6
Individuals:						
Savings bonds	116.1	79.8	92.3	101.1	109.6	117.7
Other	36.2	75.0	70.4	71.3	79.2	96.5
Insurance companies	16.7	78.5	105.6	104.9	107.3	107.9
Money market funds	4.7	25.1	28.6	14.6	11.8	14..4
Corporations	22.9	59.0	68.8	84.6	87.1	93.8
State & local gov'ts.	69.9	226.7	262.8	284.6	313.6	337.1
Foreign investors	123.7	224.8	263.4	299.7	362.2	393.4
Miscellaneous investors	90.1	450.1	506.6	569.1	593.9	674.3

Source: Treasury Bulletin and Federal Reserve Bulletin.

Coupon Issues

Current policy limits the maximum award to any single bidder in auctions of Treasury securities, bills or coupons, to 35% of the public amount of the offering. In addition, the maximum amount of tenders that may be submitted at any given yield by a single bidder is also limited to 35% of the public offering. The purpose of the limitations are to prevent a dealer or group of related entities from "cornering" a particular issue. In determining the total amount of an issue to be awarded to a single bidder, both competitive and noncompetitive tenders are considered. In addition, purchases of Treasury securities between the period of announcement and the auction of securities—"when-issued" transactions—are taken into account by the Treasury when applying the 35% maximum award limitation. Bidders are required to report on the tender form the par amount of such a "when–issued" position if it is over $200 million.

Private subscribers other than banks, federally insured savings and loan associations, primary dealers, and governmental entities and funds must submit full payment for their tenders for all Treasury issues.

Certificates, notes, and bonds may be offered to the public for cash subscription or in exchange for outstanding or maturing securities. Offerings are generally announced about one week in advance of the auction date. The announcement designates a deadline until which the books are to be open for entry of bids. The rules of such auctions generally parallel those of bill auctions. For denominations of Treasury coupon issues see page 92.

Treasury Notes

Treasury notes may be issued with a maturity of not less than one year nor more than 10 years. Many banks and other institutions prefer to arrange their government portfolios with maturities spread over a period of years to meet possible requirements for funds. Short-term notes are frequently purchased by nonfinancial corporations.

Maturity Schedule of Interest-Bearing Public Marketable Securities Outstanding on March 31, 1990

(In millions of dollars)

Year	Fixed maturity issues	Callable issues classified by		Publicly held [1]
		First call	Final maturity	
1990	206,716			186,482
1991	280,801			254,569
1992	185,057		1,360	167,993
1993	142,834	692	1,880	131,397
1994	86,024	2,378	436	82,810
1995	80,460	7,361		75,993
1996	79,837	1,485		76,129
1997	36,944			35,972
1998	39,885		692	38,962
1999	40,705		2,378	40,441
2000	10,673	4,224	7,361	14,815
2001	6,757		1,485	6,816
2002	4,512	5,729		4,243
2003	17,017	7,333		16,481
2004	16,057	8,807		15,754
2005	13,531	10,217	4,224	15,287
2006	4,756	9,510		4,756
2007		11,032	5,729	3,925
2008		14,755	7,333	4,923
2009		16,141	8,807	6,993
2010			10,217	7,275
2011			9,510	7,867
2012			11,032	10,010
2013			14,755	12,364
2014			16,141	14,323
2015	26,718			24,962
2016	44,955			43,402
2017	32,211			31,787
2018	17,742			17,522
2019	39,465			38,849
2020	10,229			10,003

Source: Treasury Bulletin.

[1] Includes fixed and final maturity issues.

Treasury Bonds

Treasury bonds may be issued with any maturity, but generally have original maturity of over 10 years. Treasury bonds outstanding and available in the market cover a wide range of maturities. New Treasury bonds are available only in book-entry form. Outstanding bearer bonds are interchangeable with registered bonds and bonds in book-entry form.

The following issues, when owned by a decedent and part of the estate, are redeemable at par plus accrued interest if the Secretary of the Treasury is instructed to apply the proceeds to federal estate taxes. This provision has given rise to a special demand for these deep-discount bonds, which are irreverently known in the market as "flower bonds."

4¼%	Aug. 15, 1987–92
4%	Feb. 15, 1988–93
4⅛%	May 15, 1989–94
3%	Feb. 15, 1995
3½%	Nov. 15, 1998

Treasury STRIPS, available since February 1985, are zero coupon instruments derived from selected Treasury bonds and notes of 10 or more years to maturity. On request, the underlying Treasury bonds and notes are separated on the books of the Federal Reserve into their component parts of principal and coupon payments. The resulting "zero coupon" securities may be separately owned, trade at a deep discount, and pay no interest until maturity. They are direct obligations of the U.S. government and are maintained in book-entry form with a minimum $1,000 denomination. They are traded in terms of yield to maturity. STRIPS components can also be reconstituted into the original note or bond. See pages 182–189 for a more detailed discussion of STRIPS and their predecessors, such as Treasury Receipts (TRs), Physicals, and Proprietary Receipts.

Marketable and Nonmarketable Debt

As of December 31

(In billions of dollars)

	1941	1986	1987	1988	1989
Marketable debt	41.6	1,619.0	1,724.7	1,821.3	1,945.4
Nonmarketable debt					
Savings bonds	6.1	90.6	99.2	107.6	115.7
Special issues[1]	7.0	386.9	461.3	575.6	695.6
Other nonmarketable debt	2.8	115.6	143.7	158.6	175.1
Total interest-bearing debt	57.5	2,212.0	2,428.9	2,663.1	2,931.8
Marketable debt as % of interest-bearing debt	72%	73%	71%	68%	66%

Source: Treasury Bulletin.

[1] Also called "government account securities."

Nonmarketable Securities

United States Savings Bonds

United States savings bonds, designed principally for the savings of individuals, were first issued in 1935. During World War II, they became an important medium for absorbing the large increases in personal incomes. Since that time, the Treasury has promoted sales of savings bonds, particularly through payroll savings plans, as an important part of the debt-management program. Series EE and HH bonds are the only ones currently being issued by the Treasury.

Series EE and HH savings bonds are noncallable, nontransferable, and registered. Both series are available on a continuous basis, although Series HH bonds are no longer sold for cash. Partial redemption and reissue is permitted, but only in amounts corresponding to authorized denominations. Other details are shown in the table on page 79.

The current redemption value of all savings bonds and notes outstanding on May 31, 1990, was $121.3 billion.

In July 1989 the Treasury announced a schedule of final maturity dates for outstanding savings bonds and notes, as well as for new issues of savings bonds.

- Series E savings bonds issued before December 1965 will stop earning interest 40 years from their issue dates.

- Series E bonds issued after November 1965, as well as all Series EE bonds and Savings Notes (Freedom Shares), will stop earning interest 30 years from their issue dates. All outstanding H bonds, which were issued through December 1979, will also have a final maturity 30 years from their issue dates.

- Series HH savings bonds, which have been issued since January 1980, will reach final maturity after 20 years from their issue dates.

Savings bonds are sold with designated "original" maturity periods, and are then granted extended maturity periods. For example, Series EE bonds issued at the present time have an original maturity period of 12 years, and are granted one 10-year extended maturity period and one 8-year extended maturity period—for a total interest-bearing life of 30 years. Outstanding bonds and notes are granted extended maturity periods sufficient to provide a total interest-bearing life as indicated above.

Series EE Savings Bonds

Series EE savings bonds are designed to provide a safe, convenient investment medium for small investors and groups at a relatively attractive yield with protection against market price fluctuations. They are sold at 50% of face value in denominations from $50 to $10,000 (effective October 1, 1990, $100 will be the minimum denomination available to enrollees in payroll savings plans) and are subject to an annual purchase limit of $15,000 (issue price) per investor. Interest on Series EE bonds accrues through periodic increases in redemption value.

A market-based interest rate formula has been in effect since November 1, 1982, for accrual-type savings bonds. All Series

EE bonds purchased on and after November 1, 1982 and held at least five years earn at least 85% of the average yield during the holding period on outstanding Treasury marketable securities with approximately five years remaining to maturity. They have a guaranteed minimum rate if held five years or more. Bonds held less than five years earn interest on a fixed, graduated scale. Outstanding Series E and EE savings bonds and savings notes also receive the benefit of the new market-based rate. The market-based variable investment yield is used for determining the redemption value of a bond, unless its applicable minimum investment yield produces a higher value.

The Treasury announced that, effective November 1, 1986, new issues of Series EE bonds and accrual-type bonds extended in maturity will have a guaranteed minimum rate of 6%. Redemption values during the original maturity period, which reflect the minimum guaranteed investment yield for Series EE bonds issued on and after that date, are shown in the table on page 81. Series EE bonds may be exchanged for Series HH current income bonds.

A new education benefit is in effect for Series EE savings bonds issued on or after January 1, 1990. Interest on these Series EE bonds is tax exempt, subject to certain limitations, if the taxpayer uses the proceeds of the bonds to pay for tuition and fees associated with the post-secondary education of the taxpayer, the taxpayer's spouse, or a dependent. The full interest exclusion is available only for married couples filing joint returns with incomes of $60,000 or less (modified adjusted gross income) and for single filers with incomes of $40,000 or less (modified adjusted gross income). The interest exclusion will phase out for joint filers with modified adjusted gross incomes of between $60,000 and $90,000 ($40,000 and $55,000 for single filers). After 1990 these income limits will be indexed for inflation. Bonds must be registered in the name of the taxpayer or in the name of the taxpayer and the taxpayer's spouse to exclude the bond interest from the taxpayer's gross income.

Series EE bonds issued before January 1, 1990 do not qualify for the education benefit. However, all accrual-type bonds

Comparison of Terms and Conditions
Series EE and HH Savings Bonds

	Series EE	Series HH
Denominations	$50 and $75 over-the-counter; $100, $200, $500, $1,000, $5,000 and $10,000 (face amount).	$500, $1,000, $5,000, $10,000.
Issue price	50% of face amount.	Face amount.
Final maturity	30 years.	20 years.
Yield curve	A fixed graduated rate increasing from 4.16% after six months to 6.0% after five years. Thereafter, the market-based variable investment yield will be used for determining the redemption value of a bond, unless the minimum investment yield of 6.0% produces a higher value.	6.0%.
Retention period	Redeemable any time after six months from issue date.	Same.
Annual limitation	$15,000 issue price.	No limit.
Tax status	Interest on bonds issued on or after January 1, 1990 may, if certain conditions are met, be eligible for Federal income tax-exemption. If interest is not excluded from Federal taxable income it may be reported (1) as it accrues or (2) in the year in which the bond matures, is redeemed, or is exchanged. Interest is also subject to estate, inheritance and gift taxes—Federal and State—but exempt from State and local income taxes.	Interest is subject to federal income tax reporting in year it is paid. Bonds subject to federal and state estate, inheritance and gift taxes. Exempt from state and local income taxes.
Registration	In name of individuals—in single, co-ownership of beneficiary form; in names of fiduciaries or organization—in single ownership only.	Same.
Transferability	Not eligible for transfer or pledge as collateral.	Same.
Rights of owners	Co-ownership: either owner may redeem; both must join reissue request. Beneficiary: only owner may redeem during lifetime; consent of beneficiary to reissue not required.	Same.
Exchange privilege	Eligible, alone or with Series E bonds or savings notes, for exchange for Series HH bonds in multiples of $500, with tax deferral privilege.	Issued only in exchange for Series E, EE, and savings notes in multiples of $500, with continued tax deferral privilege.

issued before that date, as well as Series EE bonds issued on or after January 1, 1990, (the interest on which is not excluded from taxable income) are eligible to receive a different tax benefit. Interest on such bonds may be deferred until maturity, redemption or exchange, or may be paid currently. Bondholders who have deferred the Federal income tax liability for their accrued interest may continue the tax deferral, by exchanging their accrual-type bonds for Series HH bonds, until the HH bonds are redeemed or reach final maturity.

Series EE bonds may not be used as collateral for a loan or as security for the performance of an obligation and may be transferred only under limited specified conditions such as in case of death. Series EE bonds are subject to regulations in Treasury Department Circular No. 3–80, as amended.

Series HH Current Income Bonds

Beginning November 1, 1982, Series HH savings bonds, which pay interest semiannually, are available only in exchange for Series E and EE savings bonds and savings notes with a total redemption value of $500 or more, or through the reinvestment of the redemption proceeds of matured Series H bonds. They are issued at face value in denominations from $500 to $10,000, and have a maturity period of 10 years with a 10-year extended maturity period. For HH bonds issued on or after October 1, 1989, semiannual interest payments will be made by direct deposit to the registered owner or coowner's account at a financial institution designated by the bondowner. Owners of Series H and HH bonds issued prior to that date may continue to receive interest payments by check or may elect to receive them by direct deposit.

For Series HH savings bonds issued on or after November 1, 1986, as well as older Series H and HH bonds entering an extended maturity period on or after that date, the interest rate is 6.0%. Interest on Series H and HH bonds is taxable in the year in which it is received.

Retirement Plan Bonds

Retirement plan bonds were issued by the Treasury from January 1, 1963, to April 30, 1982. The bonds were available for

Redemption Values and Investment Yields on Series EE Savings Bonds Bearing Issue Dates Beginning November 1, 1986

(Based on a $1,000 denomination bond)

Period after issue date[1]	Redemption values during each half-year period [2]	Approximate Investment Yield (percent)	
		On purchase price from issue date to beginning of each half-year period	On current redemption value from beginning of each half-year period to maturity
Issue date	$ 500.00		
½ year	510.40	4.16	6.08
1 year	521.60	4.27	6.16
1½ years	534.00	4.43	6.22
2 years	548.00	4.64	6.27
2½ to 3 years	563.20	4.82	6.31
3 to 3½ years	580.00	5.01	6.33
3½ to 4 years	599.60	5.26	6.31
4 to 4½ years	621.20	5.50	6.25
4½ to 5 years	645.60	5.76	6.14
5 to 5½ years	672.00	6.00	6.00
5½ to 6 years	692.40	6.01	5.99
6 to 6½ years	713.20	6.01	5.99
6½ to 7 years	734.40	6.00	6.00
7 to 7½ years	756.40	6.00	6.00
7½ to 8 years	779.20	6.00	5.99
8 to 8½ years	802.40	6.00	6.00
8½ to 9 years	826.80	6.01	5.99
9 to 9½ years	851.60	6.01	5.98
9½ to 10 years	876.80	6.00	6.00
10 to 10½ years	903.20	6.00	5.99
10½ to 11 years	930.40	6.00	5.98
11 to 11½ years	958.40	6.00	5.96
11½ to 12 years	986.80	6.00	6.00
Minimum value at the end of original maturity period	1,016.40	6.00	

[1] The redemption values and investment yields shown for interest accrual dates five years after issue and thereafter represent the minimum guaranteed investment yield. These redemption values will apply unless the application of the market-based variable rate produces a higher redemption value.

[2] Maturity value reached at twelve years after issue.

purchase only in connection with bond purchase plans and pension and profit-sharing plans under the Self-Employed Individuals Tax Retirement Act of 1962. Under the act, self-employed persons who qualified could deduct from income subject to tax amounts contributed to such plans up to a maximum limit determined by statute.

The bonds were registered only in the names of individuals in single ownership and beneficiary form. They cannot be transferred, sold, or used as collateral, but may be redeemed at any time. Interest ceases five years after the death of the registered owner.

Retirement plan bonds are subject to federal income, inheritance, and other taxes. Income tax liability becomes payable, for interest earned and for the amount of deduction taken when the bonds were purchased, when bonds are redeemed by the owner, unless the redemption proceeds are rolled over into an individual retirement account or qualified employee plan within 60 days after the receipt of such proceeds, in which case the tax liability for the retirement plan bonds may continue to be deferred. The Treasury discontinued selling retirement plan bonds April 30, 1982. As of May 31, 1990, the amount outstanding was $82 million.

Individual Retirement Bonds

Individual retirement bonds were issued by the Treasury from January 1, 1975, to April 30, 1982. These bonds were specially designed for investment by persons not covered by a retirement plan. Investment in these bonds was one of several investment options available under the Employee Retirement Income Security Act of 1974, which permitted employees not covered by a pension plan to set aside a part of their income for retirement and deduct the amount from their income subject to tax.

The bonds may be cashed at any time up to maturity without a tax penalty for the purpose of changing to another investment option available under the 1974 act, or in the event of death or disability. The bonds mature when the owner reaches age 70½ years, at which time the amount deducted to purchase the securities and the earned interest become reportable for federal income tax purposes. As of May 31, 1990, the amount outstanding was $18 million.

Government Account Series

These securities are sold by the Treasury directly to government agencies, trust funds, and accounts. They may be redeemed whenever funds are needed. The interest rate on these obligations is generally regulated by legislation and based on average market yields on outstanding Treasury obligations. As of May 31, 1990, the amount outstanding was $733.6 billion.

Depositary Bonds

Depositary bonds originally were issued in two series to designated depositaries and financial agents of the Treasury for the purpose of providing an offset to the cost of handling operations conducted as an otherwise free service to the government. The bonds pay interest at the rate of 2% and mature 12 years from the issue date.

The bonds are issued in registered form and are nontransferable, but may be redeemed at the option of the U.S. government or the owner, in whole or in part at par plus accrued interest at any time on written notice of from 30 to 60 days. They are acceptable as collateral to secure deposits of Treasury funds. They may be obtained only by special application to the Treasury. Acceptance of a subscription and its amount are dependent upon the Treasury's appraisal of services rendered.

Bonds of the first series, the only ones now outstanding, are issued to recompense banks for the cost of rendering essential government services. They were outstanding in the amount of $4 million on May 31, 1990.

State and Local Government Series

Since August 1972, the Treasury has issued nonmarketable certificates, notes and bonds to state and local governments wishing to reinvest the proceeds of "advance refundings" of their tax-exempt debt, termed "time-deposit securities." In such refundings, the state or local authority issues its own tax-exempt securities and temporarily reinvests the proceeds in taxable securities bearing a higher rate of interest. The Internal Revenue Service has established certain guidelines regulating this practice, and the interest rates and maturities on state and local government series securities are set so as to assure compliance with the guidelines. In February 1987, the Treasury began offering an overnight investment for proceeds of a tax-exempt issue to which arbitrage rebate provisions of the Tax Code apply. On May 31, 1990, there were $163.9 billion of state and local government series Treasury obligations, also known as SLUGS, outstanding.

Foreign Series

Two types of special nonmarketable securities have been issued by the Treasury to foreign governments and monetary authorities. One is a dollar-denominated security designated "Foreign Series." The other is the "Foreign Currency Series," which is denominated in the currency of the country or institution making the purchase. Issues in each series may be in the form of bills, certificates of indebtedness, notes or bonds. Foreign Series and Foreign Currency Series securities were issued beginning January 1962, in connection with transactions with foreign countries or involving foreign currencies. The number and amount of foreign series issues grew rapidly during 1971–73, representing reinvestment of some of the dollars absorbed by the world's central banks in supporting the foreign exchange value of the dollar. The total amount of Foreign Series (dollar-denominated) obligations outstanding on May 31, 1990, was $36.8 billion. The last Foreign Currency Series held by foreign governments and monetary authorities were redeemed in April 1979. Since December 1978, the Treasury from time to time offered foreign currency denominated securities to the residents of foreign countries. The last of these were redeemed in July 1983.

Securities of Government-Sponsored Enterprises, Agencies and International Institutions

The volume of securities that are not direct obligations of the Treasury but do involve federal sponsorship or guarantees continues to increase. The enlarged supply has been readily absorbed by the investing public, which recognizes the investment quality of these obligations and their sizable secondary markets. Agencies currently issuing securities to the public are listed below. However, the sections that follow also describe the status of unmatured securities of agencies that were issuers in the past but are so no longer.

Agencies currently issuing securities to the public:

Ordinary debt issues:
Asian Development Bank (ADB)
Farm Credit System
Farm Credit System Financial Assistance Corporation (FCSFAC)
Federal Home Loan Banks (FHLB)
Federal National Mortgage Association (FNMA)
Financing Corporation (FICO)
Inter-American Development Bank (IADB)
Maritime Administration
Resolution Funding Corporation (REFCORP)
Student Loan Marketing Association (SLMA)
World Bank

Mortgage-backed issues:
Federal Home Loan Mortgage Corporation (FHLMC)
Government National Mortgage Association (GNMA)
Federal Agricultural Mortgage Corporation (FAMC)

Like Treasury obligations, these securities generally are issued under the authority of an act of Congress and are exempt from registration with the Securities and Exchange Commission. (The securities of the Federal Agricultural Mortgage Corporation are not exempt from registration.) Most are eligible collateral for Federal Reserve advances and discounts to depository institutions, are legal investments for federally chartered institutions, and may be purchased and held without limit by national banks. A few are backed by the full faith and credit of the U.S. government and many are guaranteed by the Treasury or supported by the issuing agency's right to borrow from the Treasury, but some lack any formal governmental backing. In several cases, the interest earned on the securities is exempt from state and local taxation; a few still outstanding but no longer being issued are exempt from federal income tax. Some entities are privately owned; others are wholly governmental.

Outstanding Securities of Government Agencies and Sponsored Corporations

(In millions of dollars)

Issuer	Amount outstanding on December 31				
	1985	1986	1987	1988	1989
Banks for Cooperatives	220	--	--	--	--
Defense Department:					
Family housing and homeowners assistance notes	72	36	21	16	13
Farm Credit Banks	65,136	58,939	52,652	52,737	54,577
Federal Deposit Insurance Corporation:					
Bank Insurance Fund	--	--	56	1,879	2,130
FSLIC Resolution Fund	--	--	--	19,210	18,426
Federal Home Loan Banks	188,366	276,015	349,738	393,599	444,062
Federal Housing Administration	115	138	183	150	328
Federal Intermediate Credit Banks	926	565	--	--	--
Federal Land Banks	2,773	2,773	2,023	1,559	1,554
Federal National Mortgage Association	149,167	192,267	241,736	283,574	344,172
Government National Mortgage Association[1]	2,165	2,165	1,615	--	--
Postal Service	250	250	250	250	250
Student Loan Marketing Association	7,966	10,821	14,677	25,696	33,109
Tennessee Valley Authority	1,725	1,425	1,380	1,380	1,380
Other	25	21	13	13	13

Source: Treasury Bulletin.

[1] Participation certificates.

Securities of government-sponsored enterprises and federal agencies not eligible for purchase by the Federal Financing Bank (except for GNMA obligations arising from its special assistance programs) are eligible for purchase by the Federal Reserve in its open market operations in the secondary market. For longer-term issues to qualify under guidelines set by the Federal Reserve, at least $200 million must be outstanding. For short-term issues (with original maturity of five years or less), the cutoff is $300 million. The last time the Federal Reserve bought agency securities outright, however, was in 1981.

This chapter describes the specifics of the various securities and issuers and their relation to the U.S. government.

Federal Financing Bank

The Federal Financing Bank (FFB) was established by the Federal Financing Bank Act of 1973 to consolidate and reduce the government's cost of financing a variety of federal agencies and other borrowers whose obligations are guaranteed by the federal government. The FFB is authorized to purchase any obligation that is issued, sold, or guaranteed by a "federal agency" — defined in the act as an "executive department, an independent federal establishment, or a corporation or other entity established by the Congress which is owned in whole or in part by the United States." This definition excludes the government-sponsored agencies: the Farm Credit System, the Federal Home Loan Banks, the Federal Home Loan Mortgage Corporation, the Federal National Mortgage Association, and the Student Loan Marketing Association (Sallie Mae). It should be noted, however, that the FFB has purchased obligations from Sallie Mae when guaranteed by the Department of Education.

The FFB is under the general supervision of the Secretary of the Treasury, who is the chairman of a five-member board of directors. The other directors are Treasury officials appointed by the President of the United States. The bank is managed and staffed by Treasury employees.

Federal Financing Bank
Net Acquisitions of Obligations

(Fiscal years; in millions of dollars)

	1989 actual	1990 estimate	1991 estimate
Net Lending:			
Foreign military sales credit	-5,823	-2,031	-345
Rural Development Loans (USDA)	-1,225	–	–
Agricultural credit loans (USDA)	-3,960	-3,322	-1,975
Rural housing loans (USDA)	–	–	-1,415
Rural Electrification Administration (USDA)	113	-71	536
Navy Ship Leases	-38	-48	-48
Student Loan Marketing Assoc.	–	-30	-30
Health maintenance organizations (HHS)	-5	-6	-5
Medical facility loans (HHS)	-8	-7	-81
Geothermal resources development fund (DOE)	-50	–	–
Section 108 guaranteed loans (HUD)	-35	-55	-59
Low-rent public housing (HUD)	-42	-45	-47
Territories of Guam and the Virgin Islands (DOI)	-2	-2	-2
R.R. Revitalization and Regulatory Reform Act (DOT)	9	-14	-4
Federal buildings fund (GSA)	-9	-11	-12
Space, flight, control & data communications (NASA)	96	101	-1,096
Small business investment companies (SBA)	-77	-62	-54
Section 503 guaranteed loans (SBA)	-72	-92	-81
Development company loans (SBA)	-4	-5	-5
TVA	336	-2,730	-2,240
TVA-Seven States Energy Corporation	132	83	22
Export-Import Bank	26	57	77
Washington Metro Area Transit Authority	177	177	177
National Credit Union Administration	-7	-1	-1
Postal Service	603	1,503	1,500
Total	**-10,041**	**-6,788**	**-5,365**

Source: The Budget of the United States Government—1991.

Acronyms:
(DOE) Department of Energy
(DOI) Department of the Interior
(DOT) Department of Transportation
(GSA) General Service Administration
(HHS) Department of Health & Human Services
(HUD) Department of Housing & Urban Development
(NASA) National Aeronautics & Space Administration
(SBA) Small Business Administration
(TVA) Tennesssee Valley Authority
(USDA) U.S. Department of Agriculture

The FFB can finance its operations by issuing obligations (1) to the public — the volume outstanding is limited to $15 billion, or such additional amounts as are authorized in Appropriations Acts — and (2) to the Secretary of the Treasury. The FFB can require that the Secretary purchase up to $5 billion of its obligations, but the Secretary is authorized to purchase any amounts at his discretion. FFB obligations are general obligations of the U.S. government, identical in this respect to Treasury obligations. The FFB has usually financed itself by borrowing directly from the Treasury.

The Secretary of the Treasury has the authority under various statutes to approve the issuance, sale or guarantee of obligations by many federal agencies, and this authority has sometimes been used to require these agencies, which had previously borrowed in the private capital markets, to finance through the FFB.

However, the attraction of a lower interest rate is the main reason why the FFB has become the vehicle for financing most of the federal agency direct borrowing, fully guaranteed lending, and asset sale programs eligible for FFB financing. From June 1975 to the present (May 1990), the FFB lending rate has been set at ⅛% above the Treasury borrowing rate for comparable securities.

Pursuant to the Balanced Budget and Emergency Deficit Control Act of 1985, certain lending activities which were previously designated as "off-budget" have been moved on to the federal unified budget. Budget authority and outlays financed by FFB lending activities are attributed to the federal agency responsible for administration of the respective credit program.

Federal Status of U.S. Government Agency Securities

Agency	Full faith and credit of the U.S. Govt.	Authority to borrow from the federal Treasury	Interest on bonds generally exempt from state and local taxes
Farm Credit System	No	No	Yes
Farm Credit System Financial Assistance Corporation (FCSFAC)	Yes	Yes	Yes
Farmers Home Administration (FmHA) CBOs	Yes	Yes—Secretary of Agriculture has authority to issue notes to the U.S. Treasury.	No
Federal Financing Bank (FFB)	Yes	Yes—FFB can require the Treasury to purchase up to $5 billion of its obligations. The Treasury Secretary is authorized to purchase any amount of FFB obligations at his discretion.	Yes
Federal Home Loan Banks (FHLB)	No	Yes—the Treasury is authorized to purchase up to $4 billion of FHLB securities.	Yes
Federal Home Loan Mortgage Corporation (FHLMC) (Freddie Mac)	No	Yes—the Treasury may purchase up to $2.25 billion of Freddie Mac securities as a standby line of credit for Freddie Mac.	No
Federal National Mortgage Association (FNMA) (Fannie Mae)	No	Yes—at FNMA request the Treasury may purchase $2.25 billion of FNMA securities.	No
Financing Corporation (FICO)	No	No	Yes

Agency			
General Services Administration (GSA)	Yes	No	Yes
Government National Mortgage Association (GNMA)[1]	Yes	No	No
Maritime Administration Guaranteed Ship Financing Bonds issued after 1972	Yes	Yes	No
Resolution Funding Corporation (REFCORP)	No	Yes – the Treasury is the ultimate source of funds for interest payment, to the extent not obtainable from other sources.	Yes
Small Business Administration (SBA)	Yes	No	No, with exceptions
Student Loan Marketing Association (Sallie Mae)	Not since 1/9/82	Yes – at its discretion the Treasury may purchase $1 billion of Sallie Mae obligations.	Yes
Tennessee Valley Authority (TVA)	No	Yes – up to $150 million.	Yes
United States Postal Service	Guarantee may be extended if Postal Service requests and Treasury determines this to be in the public interest.	Yes – the Postal Service may require the Treasury to purchase up to $2 billion of its obligations.	Yes
Washington Metropolitan Area Transit Authority (WMATA) Bonds	Yes	No	No, with exceptions

[1] Fully modified pass-through mortgage-backed securities and certain mortgage-backed bonds of Fannie Mae are guaranteed as to timely payment of principal and interest by Ginnie Mae.

Denominations of U.S. Government and Agency Securities
December 31, 1989

	Bearer—B Registered—R Book-entry—E	$1	$500	$1,000	$5,000	$10,000	$25,000	$50,000	$100,000	$500,000	$1,000,000
Treasury bills[1]	E					•					
Treasury 2-yr. notes[2]	E					•					
Treasury 4-, 5-, 7-, 10-yr. notes[2]	E			•							
Treasury bonds[2]	E			•							
Asian Development Bank											
notes (US$)	B&R			•	•	•			•		
bonds (US$)[2]	R&E			•							
Department of Housing & Urban Development:											
Federal Housing Administration											
debentures[3]	R		•	•	•	•					
New housing authority bonds[4]	B&R				•						
Farm Credit System consolidated:											
bonds[5]	E			•	•						
discount notes[2]	E				•						
medium-term notes[6]	E				•				•		
Farmers Home Administration											
CBOs[7]	B&R&E						•	•	•	•	•
Federal Home Loan Banks											
consolidated bonds[8]	E				•						
consolidated discount notes[9]	E				•						
Federal Home Loan Mortgage Corporation											
real estate mortgage investment conduits											
regular class[10]	E	•		•							
residual class[11]	R			•							
collateralized mortgage obligations	E	•									
debentures[12]	E				•						
discount notes[13]	E	•									
participation certificates[14]	E	•									
Federal National Mortgage Association											
debentures[12]	E					•					
residential financing securities	E					•					
short-term notes	E					•					
master notes[15]	E										
Financing Corporation[12]	E					•					
General Services Administration											
participation certificates[16]	R					•	•	•			
Government National Mortgage Association											
participation certificates	R					•	•	•		•	•
pass-through securities[17]	R					•					
mortgage-backed bonds	R							•		•	•
Inter-American Development Bank[18]	B&R&E			•							
Maritime Administration											
notes	R			•							
bonds	R			•							
Resolution Funding Corporation bonds[2]	E			•							
Short-term tax-exempt notes[19]	B				•						•
Small Business Administration											
debentures[20]	R						•				
pool certificates	R							•			
Student Loan Marketing Association											
discount notes[21]	E								•		
floating-rate notes[12]	E				•						
Tennessee Valley Authority bonds[2]	E&R			•							
United States Postal Service	B&R							•	•	•	•
Washington Metropolitan Area Transit Authority bonds[22]	B&R						•	•	•	•	•
World Bank											
bonds (US$)[2]	R&E			•							
notes (US$)[2]	R&E			•							

Farm Credit System

The Farm Credit System is a cooperatively owned nationwide system of banks and associations that provides mortgage loans, short- and intermediate-term credit and related services to farmers, ranchers, producers or harvesters of aquatic products, rural homeowners and agricultural and rural cooperatives.

The banks and associations of the Farm Credit System are federally chartered instrumentalities of the United States and operate under authorities contained in the Farm Credit Act of 1971, as amended. The Farm Credit System is the oldest of the government-sponsored enterprises, dating back to 1916 when Congress established the Federal Land Banks. After identifying additional agricultural credit needs, Congress expanded the System with the creation of the Federal Intermediate Credit Banks in 1923 and the Banks for Cooperatives in 1933. In 1987 Congress provided for the mergers of the Federal Land Banks and the Federal Intermediate Credit Banks to create the Farm Credit Banks.

Footnotes refer to table on the previous page.

1 Minimum order $10,000, then multiples of $5,000. Cash management bills minimum order $1 million.
2 Available in this single denomination or in multiples thereof.
3 $50 and $100 denominations also available.
4 There have been no new issues of these bonds since 1974.
5 For maturities less than 13 months issued in multiples of $5,000; for longer maturities issued in multiples of $1,000.
6 Fixed-rate notes are issued in minimum denominations of $100,000 with $1,000 increments. Floating-rate notes are issued in multiples of $5,000.
7 There have been no new issues of CBOs since 1975.
8 New issues available in book-entry form only. Minimum $10,000, thereafter in multiples of $5,000.
9 Minimum $100,000, then in multiples of $5,000.
10 Regular, non-retail classes are issued in principal amounts of $1.00 and additional increments of $1.00. Retail classes are issued in denominations of $1,000 and integral multiples thereof. FHLMC utilizes the book-entry and payment system maintained by the Federal Reserve Bank of New York for regular, non-retail classes and the book-entry and payment system of the Depository Trust Company for retail classes.
11 Texas Commerce Bank National Association acts as registrar and paying agent for the residual classes, which are issued in minimum original principal amounts of $1,000 and additional increments of $1,000.
12 Minimum purchase $10,000, thereafter in multiples of $5,000.
13 Minimum purchase $25,000, then in increments of $1.00.
14 Minimum purchase $1,000, then in increments of $1.00.
15 Denominations are individually negotiated.
16 There have been no new issues of PCs since 1974.
17 Minimum purchase $25,000, then in multiples of $5,000.
18 New issues available in book-entry form only, in multiples of $1,000.
19 Most issues also have denominations that fall in between.
20 Available in this single denomination or in multiples thereof up to a maximum of $750,000.
21 Minimum purchase $100,000.
22 Registered bonds available in multiples of $5,000.

The Farm Credit Banks provide funds for long-term loans, secured by first mortgages on farm and rural real estate, made through Federal Land Bank Associations. The Farm Credit Banks also provide short- and intermediate-term loan funds to Production Credit Associations, which have direct lending authority, and to other financing institutions serving agricultural producers. As authorized by the Agricultural Credit Act of 1987, Federal Land Bank Associations and Production Credit Associations that have similar geographic territory may merge into a single Agricultural Credit Association. The Agricultural Credit Associations have direct lending authority in their territories as to real estate and to short- and intermediate-term loans. Federal Land Bank Associations that do not merge, but assume direct lending authority, are known as Federal Land Credit Associations.

Effective January 1, 1989, the Central Bank for Cooperatives and ten of the 12 district Banks for Cooperatives merged to form the National Bank for Cooperatives (CoBank), which makes loans to agricultural and aquatic cooperatives and to rural utilities on a nationwide basis, and also handles international transactions of borrowing cooperatives. The remaining two Banks for Cooperatives, headquartered in Springfield, Massachusetts, and St. Paul, Minnesota, are also authorized to make loans nationwide. CoBank may participate in loans that exceed the individual lending capacities of the other Banks for Cooperatives. The three Banks for Cooperatives may also participate with one another in filling the credit needs of their respective borrowers.

The banks and associations of the Farm Credit System are not depositary institutions and consequently rely on the money and credit markets to raise lendable funds. The banks maintain the Federal Farm Credit Banks Funding Corporation in New York City through which public offerings of their securities are made. The Funding Corporation manages a nationwide selling group of approximately 115 dealers, including First Boston, that sell Farm Credit Securities in the United States and abroad.

Responsible for supervising the Farm Credit System in the public interest is the Farm Credit Administration, which is an independent agency of the U.S. government. Each of the banks, their related associations, and the Funding Corporation is audited and examined periodically by Farm Credit Administration examiners.

Farm Credit consolidated systemwide obligations finance the Banks for Cooperatives and the Farm Credit Banks. Bonds previously issued by the combined Federal Land Banks, which are now obligations of the Farm Credit Banks, will continue to be available in the secondary market until maturity. As of December 31, 1989, outstandings were $1,554 million.

The Agricultural Credit Act of 1987 established the Farm Credit System Insurance Corporation primarily to insure timely payment of the principal and interest on consolidated or Systemwide debt securities issued on behalf of one or more of the System banks. The Insurance Corporation is managed by a board of directors consisting of the Farm Credit Administration's Board. Each System bank became insured effective January 1989 and contributes to the Insurance Fund through an annual assessment amounting to 0.15 percent on accruing loans and 0.25 percent on nonaccrual loans. The Insurance Corporation may begin expending funds for insurance and related purposes in January 1993.

Farm Credit Consolidated Systemwide Discount Notes. Consolidated systemwide discount notes are the secured joint and several obligations of the banks of the Farm Credit System. The discount note program became operational in January 1975. The notes are issued in book-entry form in amounts of $5,000 and multiples thereof.

Discount notes are used to complement borrowings from commercial banks, to provide a source of interim financing between bond sales, and to supply the banks with additional flexibility in securing funds during periods of unexpected demand. On December 31, 1989, discount notes outstanding totaled $16,452 million.

The discount notes are secured in the same manner, are eligible as investments for the same institutions, and share the same tax status as consolidated systemwide bonds, described below.

Federal Farm Credit Banks Consolidated Systemwide Bonds. The Farm Credit System introduced the Federal Farm Credit Banks Consolidated Systemwide Bonds in August of 1977. These bonds are secured joint and several obligations of the banks. Bonds are presently issued each month with three-month, six-month and one-year maturities. Longer-term bonds are issued approximately eight times a year. They are issued in book-entry form, in multiples of $1,000 for maturities of over 13 months and in multiples of $5,000 for shorter maturities. On December 31, 1989, bonds outstanding totaled $34,345 million.

Systemwide bonds sold to the public are secured by collateral consisting of notes or other obligations of borrowers, obligations of the U.S. government or any agency thereof, other readily marketable securities approved by the Farm Credit Administration, or cash, in an aggregate value equal to the bonds outstanding. Although the government assumes no direct or indirect liability for them, the bonds are secured obligations of banks operating under federal charter with governmental supervision.

The bonds are considered eligible investments for national banks and state member banks of the Federal Reserve System. They are lawful investments for all federal credit unions and federal savings and loan associations and all fiduciary and trust funds under the jurisdiction of the U. S. Government, and they may be accepted as security for all public deposits, including Treasury tax and loan accounts. The bonds are also legal investments for banks, trust companies, insurance companies, fiduciary funds, savings banks, and trust funds in various states. Savings and loan associations that are members of the Federal Home Loan Banks may include bonds maturing in five years or less as part of their required liquidity. Regulation A of the Board of Governors of the Federal Reserve System provides that the bonds may be accepted by Federal Reserve Banks as collateral security for advances to depository institutions under Section 13 of the Federal Reserve Act. The bonds are eligible for purchase and sale by the Federal Reserve System in its open market operations. National banks may invest in Federal Farm Credit Bank bonds without regard to statutory limitations generally applicable to investment securities.

The bonds and the interest derived from them are exempt from state, municipal, and local income taxation. Gain from the sale or other disposition of the bonds and transfer by inheritance and gift are subject to federal and state taxation.

Federal Farm Credit Banks Consolidated Systemwide Medium-Term Notes. Introduced in 1989, Federal Farm Credit Banks Consolidated Systemwide Medium-Term Notes are also the joint and several obligations of the banks. These medium-term notes, which have maturities of not less than one year or more than 30 years from the date of issue, have various interest rates, interest rate formulas, selling prices, and other terms as determined from time to time. Generally, interest on fixed-rate notes is payable semiannually each January 20 and July 20 and interest on floating-rate notes is payable quarterly each January 20, April 20, July 20, and October 20. The medium-term notes are available in book-entry form only. Fixed-rate medium-term notes are issued in minimum denominations of $100,000, then in multiples of $1,000. Floating-rate notes are issued in minimum denominations of $5,000, then in multiples of $5,000. On December 31, 1989, medium-term notes outstanding totaled $2,917 million.

Farm Credit System Financial Assistance Corporation

The Financial Assistance Corporation (FCSFAC), pursuant to the Agricultural Credit Act of 1987, was established on January 11, 1988, to carry out a program of providing capital, as directed by the Assistance Board, to institutions of the System that are experiencing financial difficulty. The Assistance Board may authorize assistance only to System institutions that it has certified as eligible for such assistance. The requesting institution must agree to the terms and conditions for assistance specified by the Assistance Board. A board of directors, consisting of the Secretary of the Treasury, the

Secretary of Agriculture, and one agricultural producer appointed by the President with the consent of the Senate, directs the activities of the Assistance Board.

The Financial Assistance Corporation funds the provision of financial assistance through the issuance, with the approval of the Assistance Board, of up to $2.8 billion of uncollateralized debt, which is guaranteed as to the payment of principal and interest by the Secretary of the Treasury as provided in the 1987 act. The ceiling on such debt issuances may be increased to $4.0 billion if the initial $2.8 billion has been issued and the Assistance Board determines that additional funds are required and so reports to Congress. The guaranteed debt securities have maturities of 15 years and may be issued no later than September 30, 1992. On December 31, 1989, bonds outstanding totaled $847 million.

Interest on obligations issued by the Financial Assistance Corporation will be funded by the Secretary of the Treasury during the first five years, will be allocated between the Secretary of the Treasury and System institutions during the second five years, and is to be paid entirely by System institutions during the final five years of each obligation's term.

The principal balance of bonds issued to provide financial assistance to certified institutions may be repaid by such institutions, the Financial Assistance Corporation, the Farm Credit System Insurance Corporation, or the Secretary of the Treasury under criteria set forth in the 1987 Act.

Federal Agricultural Mortgage Corporation

The Agriculture Credit Act of 1987 established the Federal Agricultural Mortgage Corporation (FAMC or Farmer Mac), a federally chartered institution within the Farm Credit System, to facilitate the development of a secondary market for farm mortgage loans. Farmer Mac is intended to be operational during 1990. In developing and maintaining the secondary market for farm loans, Farmer Mac will play a role similar to that of Fannie Mae and Ginnie Mae in the secondary market for home mortgages.

Under this legislation, Farm Credit System banks, commercial banks, thrifts, insurance companies, and other qualified originators of agricultural real estate loans will be able to sell their loans to certified "poolers." The poolers will package the loans, in accordance with statutory and Farmer Mac requirements, into pools that will serve as collateral for securities sold to the investing public. Farmer Mac will examine the pools of farm mortgages, place its guarantee on principal and interest payments on the loans for a fee, and permit underwriters to sell them to the public. The Farmer Mac guarantee will be backed by a cash reserve or subordinate interest initially equal to 10% of each loan pool and by a $1.5 billion line of credit to the Treasury. Farmer Mac sold stock to banks, insurance companies, System institutions and other financing entities to raise initial capital. Ongoing operations will be financed through fees for its guarantees on participating institutions and occasional additional stock offerings.

Federal Home Loan Banks

The Federal Home Loan Bank system (FHLB) was organized under the Federal Home Loan Bank Act and opened for business in October 1932. The Financial Institutions Reform, Recovery, and Enforcement Act of 1989 (FIRREA) changed the regulatory framework of the Federal Home Loan Bank System. The twelve District Banks comprising the system are distributed geographically around the country similarly to the Federal Reserve Banks. They operate as a credit reserve system for the thrift industry to stabilize the flow of mortgage credit to the public and to provide funds for low- and moderate-income housing programs. The District Banks are wholly owned by their member institutions but operate under the supervision of the Federal Housing Finance Board, an independent federal agency. Since FIRREA, the supervisory and regulatory functions with respect to thrift institutions and their holding companies and the FHL Banks' former supervisory and examination functions now reside in the Office of Thrift Supervision, an office within the Department of the Treasury.

FIRREA permits any institution whose deposits are federally insured, including any state-chartered bank, national bank, or credit union, to become a member of the FHL Bank serving its district, if the institution meets certain criteria, which include holding at least 10% of its assets in residential mortgage loans. State-chartered thrift institutions, including savings and loan associations, savings banks, cooperative banks, and homestead associations, continue to be eligible to become members, provided they meet specific requirements for membership. Some insurance companies may also be eligible for membership. To join the System a qualified institution must purchase capital stock in its regional District Bank in the amount that would be required under the Federal Home Loan Bank Act if at least 30% of the member's assets were home mortgage loans. This provides the System with a solid equity base to support debt issues. Debt is issued as consolidated obligations which are the joint and several obligations of the 12 Federal Home Loan Banks. Consolidated obligations consisting of bonds and discount notes are limited by statute to an amount not to exceed 12 times the total paid-in capital stock and legal reserves of all the Banks. Although System debt is not guaranteed by the U.S. government, the Banks do operate under federal charter and government supervision. At all times the District Banks must maintain secured advances, guaranteed mortgages, U.S. government securities, or cash in an amount at least equal to the consolidated bonds and discount notes outstanding. Also, the Bank Act (as amended) authorizes the Secretary of the Treasury to purchase up to $4 billion of the Banks' obligations.

System consolidated obligations are lawful investments and may be accepted as security for all fiduciary, trust, and public funds, including Treasury tax and loan accounts, under the authority or control of the U.S. government. Savings banks, insurance companies, trustees and other fiduciaries may legally invest in consolidated obligations under the laws of many states. National banks may invest in Federal Home Loan Banks' obligations without regard to the statutory limitations and restrictions generally applicable to investment securities. Income from the obligations is exempt from state, municipal and local income taxation, but is subject to federal taxation. Gain from the sale or other disposition of the obligations and transfer by inheritance and gift are subject to federal and state taxation.

Consolidated Bonds. Consolidated bonds are issued only in book-entry form for a minimum of $10,000 with multiples of $5,000 thereafter. Bond financings are scheduled once a month, and the System enters the market if funds are needed. Bonds are for longer-term funding requirements with maturities generally ranging from one to ten years. During 1989, bonds issued totaled over $47.96 billion resulting in an outstanding balance of $119.49 billion at year end. Primary distribution of bonds is conducted through a group of approximately 100 bank and nonbank firms, including First Boston.

Consolidated Discount Notes. Consolidated obligations issued on a discount basis to mature in one year or less are designated consolidated discount notes. They were first issued in mid-1974 and have become an important financing tool to enhance the flexibility of cash management and to integrate asset and liability management. At the time of the sale the buyer may select maturities within the 30- to 360- day range, subject to the general limitations prescribed by the system. They are issued in book-entry form only and are available in multiples of $5,000, with a minimum purchase of $100,000. Consolidated discount notes are distributed by eight major dealers, including First Boston.

The payment of face value at maturity is made at the Federal Reserve. Consolidated discount notes are acceptable as collateral at the discount window of the Federal Reserve and for open market repurchases executed by the Federal Reserve. At the end of 1989 the par value outstanding was approximately $16.7 billion. The dealer community maintains an active secondary market to provide liquidity to investors.

The liabilities (consolidated obligations and member deposits) and capital (capital stock, legal reserves, and undivided profits) of the System are used to fund advances (or loans) to members. Advances may have maturities up to 20 years. A District Bank is required to obtain and maintain a security interest in eligible collateral at the time of origination or renewal of an advance. Home mortgages, obligations of the U.S. government, and certain marketable investments in which members may invest are acceptable as collateral. Outstanding advances to a member may not exceed 20 times its capital stock in the District Bank. In certain cases, this ratio may be reduced significantly.

Medium-Term Bonds. Medium-term bonds are issued only in book-entry form with a minimum purchase of $10,000 and multiples of $5,000. Issues of $100,000 or less yield five basis points below the posted rate. Bonds are offered in maturities of one to ten years, with daily postings reflecting specific financing needs of the Federal Home Loan Bank System. The medium-term bonds were first offered in October 1988. During 1989, bonds issued totaled $450 million, resulting in an outstanding balance of $939 million at year-end 1989. The selling group for medium-term bonds consists of eight dealers.

Financing Corporation

The Financing Corporation (FICO) was chartered on August 28, 1987, under the provisions of the Competitive Equality Banking Act of 1987 as a mixed-ownership government corporation with status as an agency of the U.S. government. FICO's sole purpose was to recapitalize the Federal Savings and Loan Insurance Corporation (FSLIC) through the transfer of proceeds from FICO public debt offerings to FSLIC for use in resolving problems of insolvent thrift institutions. The Financial Institutions Reform, Recovery, and Enforcement Act of 1989 (FIRREA) transferred substantially all of the assets and liabilities of FSLIC to the newly-created FSLIC Resolution Fund, a separate fund managed by the FDIC. Transfer of proceeds from future FICO public debt offerings will be to the FSLIC Resolution Fund. FIRREA also established the Savings Association Insurance Fund (SAIF) to insure deposits at thrift institutions and the Bank Insurance Fund (BIF) to insure commercial banks. Both funds are under the supervision of the FDIC. FICO is managed by a three-member Directorate comprised of two Federal Home Loan Bank presidents and the Director of the Office of Finance of the Federal Home Loan Banks. FICO operates under the supervision of the Federal Housing Finance Board.

The Act authorizes the issuance of nonvoting capital stock, not to exceed $3.0 billion, for purchase by the Federal Home Loan Banks and borrowing authority of $10.825 billion. The net proceeds of the obligations may be used only to purchase nonredeemable capital certificates issued by FSLIC Resolution Fund, or to refund any previously issued obligations. Through December 31, 1989, FICO had borrowed $8.17 billion in the capital markets, leaving $2.655 billion of authorized but unissued FICO obligations.

No obligations may be issued with a maturity greater than 30 years or with a maturity date beyond December 31, 2026. Legislation states that FICO bonds will not have the explicit guarantee of the U.S. government, the Federal Home Loan Banks, or the FSLIC Resolution Fund. The Act requires that the capital contributions of the FHLBs will be used only to purchase high-quality zero coupon debt instruments in amounts equal to the amount of FICO debt outstanding to effectively guarantee the repayment of principal of FICO's long-term bonds. These zero-coupon bonds are not pledged to bondholders, but rather are held by FICO in a segregated account at the Federal Reserve Bank of New York. Repayment of interest on the debt and related costs will be serviced by several sources, including FICO and SAIF assessments on SAIF-insured thrifts and exit fees payable by institutions transferring to the FDIC system, as well as investment income of FICO accounts.

Like the debt of other government-sponsored agencies, FICO securities are eligible for investment by the investors able to purchase the consolidated obligations of the Federal Home Loan Banks, are accepted as collateral for open market operations, are eligible as collateral for advances at the discount window of the Federal Reserve System, and are exempt from SEC registration and from local and state taxation. Obligations are sold as needed subject to Treasury approval. They are offered in book-entry form only and are available in a minimum denomination of $10,000 and additional increments of $5,000.

Resolution Funding Corporation

The Resolution Funding Corporation (REFCORP) is a mixed-ownership government corporation established by Title V of the Financial Institutions Reform, Recovery, and Enforcement Act of 1989 (FIRREA). The sole purpose of the corporation is to provide financing for the Resolution Trust Corporation (RTC). REFCORP is under the management of a three-member directorate comprised of the Director of the Office of Finance of the Federal Home Loan Banks and two members selected by the Oversight Board from among the presidents of the twelve Federal Home Loan Banks. The Oversight Board is charged with the general oversight and direction of the Resolution Funding Corporation, and is comprised of the Secretary of the Treasury, the Chairman of the Federal Reserve Board of Governors, the Secretary of Housing and Urban Development and two independent members appointed by the President. The Resolution Trust Corporation was created by the 1989 FIRREA legislation to help the government in the sale and disposition of failed thrifts and their assets.

The Resolution Funding Corporation is authorized to issue up to $30 billion in debt obligations. Payment of principal on the debt comes from funds transferred from the Federal Home Loan Banks. These funds are used to purchase zero coupon Treasury bonds matching the maturity of REFCORP bonds. The legislation authorized several sources of funds to make the interest payments; the ultimate source is the Secretary of the Treasury, who will pay to the Resolution Funding Corporation an amount equal to all interest payable on the bonds to the extent not paid from other sources. FIRREA contains language that appropriates any funds needed for this fiscal year and all future fiscal years. In addition, the Justice Department has concurred with the general counsel of Treasury and the acting general counsel of the Office of Management and Budget that these Treasury payments are exempt from reductions under the Gramm–Rudman deficit reduction legislation.

FIRREA provides most of the elements of "agency status" for securities issued by the Resolution Funding Corporation, including: exemption of both principal and interest from all direct taxation (except surtaxes and estate, inheritance and gift taxes) now or hereafter imposed by any state, county, municipality or local taxing authority; eligibility as security for fiduciary, trust, and public funds under the control of the U.S.; and eligibility as collateral at the Federal Reserve window. An exception is that the securities are not specifically exempted from registration with the Securities and Exchange Commission (SEC). However, the legislation provided for the SEC to make an exemption by rule or order consistent with the public interest and protection of investors. Accordingly, the SEC has exempted the securities from registration.

Federal Home Loan Mortgage Corporation

The Federal Home Loan Mortgage Corporation (FHLMC) known as Freddie Mac, is a government-sponsored enterprise chartered on July 24, 1970, pursuant to Title III of the Emergency Home Finance Act of 1970, as amended, 12 U.S.C. §§ 1451–1459 (the Freddie Mac Act). Freddie Mac was established to increase the availability of mortgage credit for residential housing, primarily through developing and maintaining an active, nationwide secondary market in conventional residential mortgages. Freddie Mac's statutory mission is to provide ongoing assistance to the secondary market for home mortgages, to respond appropriately to the private capital market, and to provide ongoing assistance to the secondary market for home mortgages (including mortgages securing housing for low and moderate income families involving a reasonable economic return to Freddie Mac) by increasing the liquidity of mortgage investments and improving the distribution of investment capital available for home mortgage financing. Freddie Mac accomplishes this mission by purchasing residential mortgages from individual lenders (primarily conventional mortgages that are not insured or guaranteed by any agency of the United States), grouping the purchased mortgages into pools and subsequently selling mortgage-backed pass-through securities backed by such mortgages. Freddie Mac also holds a relatively small portfolio of retained mortgages (currently less than eight percent of its securitized mortgage portfolio), which it funds primarily with general obligation debt. Freddie Mac contracts with outside institutions (usually the loan originators from which it has purchased the mortgages) to service the purchased mortgages. As of December 31, 1989, Freddie Mac had securitized or purchased for its retained portfolio approximately $300 billion in mortgages.

Mortgage Purchases. Freddie Mac purchases a variety of whole residential mortgages and participations in mortgages from authorized financial institutions whose deposits or accounts are insured by agencies of the U.S. government (primarily savings associations and banks) and from other HUD-approved mortgagees (primarily mortgage bankers). The mortgages purchased by Freddie Mac include single-family, fixed- and adjustable-rate first lien mortgages; second mortgages on single-family owner-occupied properties; and multifamily mortgages.

Freddie Mac is subject to statutory limits, which may be adjusted annually, on the maximum original principal amounts of the single-family and multifamily mortgages it purchases. In addition to the maximum loan purchase amounts, Freddie Mac's charter prohibits it from purchasing loans with loan-to-value ratios exceeding 80 percent unless the seller retains at least a 10 percent participation in the mortgage, provides private mortgage insurance, or agrees to repurchase such mortgages in the event of default. During 1989, Freddie Mac purchased 992,542 mortgages for a total of $78.6 billion, an average of $79,191 per mortgage.

Purchases are made through Freddie Mac's Cash and Guarantor Programs for standard mortgages (i.e., mortgages that meet Freddie Mac's underwriting standards), and its Structured Transactions Department for mortgages that do not meet the normal criteria. Under the Cash Program, Freddie Mac purchases mortgages for cash, assembles the purchased mortgages into pools and sells Mortgage Participation Certificates (PC) representing interests in such pools. Under the Guarantor Program, a seller originates and pools a group of loans in accordance with Freddie Mac's pooling standards. In exchange for the pool of mortgages, Freddie Mac issues (or swaps) directly to the lender PCs backed by the same mortgages.

New types of mortgages or significant variations to existing mortgages are purchased through Freddie Mac's Structured Transactions Department. Structured transactions are tailored to meet the specific needs of the customer and Freddie Mac, and are negotiated at Freddie Mac's corporate headquarters.

Corporate Governance. The Financial Institutions Reform, Recovery, and Enforcement Act of 1989 (FIRREA) modified Freddie Mac's capital structure and the composition of Freddie Mac's Board of Directors. Prior to the enactment of FIRREA, Freddie Mac's Board of Directors consisted of the three members of the Federal Home Loan Bank Board (FHLBB). FIRREA abolished the FHLBB and provided for Freddie Mac to be governed by a permanent Board of Directors consisting of 18 members. Freddie Mac was governed by an interim Board of Directors until its first annual stockholders' meeting on February 6, 1990 during which thirteen persons were elected to the Board of Directors. FIRREA provides for five additional directors to be appointed to the Board by the President of the United States; three such directors had been appointed as of June 1, 1990.

Capital Structure. FIRREA authorized the conversion of Freddie Mac's publicly held senior participating preferred stock into voting common stock. Subject to approval by the Secretary of HUD, new shares of voting common stock may be issued in such manner and amount, and with such limitations on concentration of ownership as may be prescribed by the Board of Directors. Until February 1990, Freddie Mac also had outstanding 100,000 shares of nonvoting common stock held by the twelve Federal Home Loan Banks. The new Board of Directors subsequently authorized the retirement of the nonvoting common stock at par, as provided in Freddie Mac's charter, effective February 7, 1990, and paid to each Federal Home Loan Bank its proportionate share of the aggregate $100,000,000 retirement price of the stock. As a result, the capital stock of Freddie Mac consists exclusively of voting common stock, par value $2.50 per share, of which approximately 60,000 shares were outstanding at June 1, 1990.

Market Value Accounting. Freddie Mac publishes annually and quarterly a Consolidated Market Value Balance Sheet, which presents the assets and liabilities of Freddie Mac on a "mark-to-market" basis (that is, at their estimated current market values) rather than on the historical cost basis utilized in financial statements prepared in accordance with generally accepted accounting principles (GAAP). Currently, the most significant difference between these two bases of accounting as applied to Freddie Mac is that market value accounting includes as an asset the present value of Freddie Mac's future rights to receive income from the management and guarantee fees generated by its sold mortgage portfolio. The net market value of Freddie Mac's assets and liabilities was approximately $5.1 billion before tax and approximately $4.0 billion after tax as of December 31, 1989. Its GAAP stockholders' equity at that date was approximately $1.9 billion.

Mortgage Participation Certificates. The principal activity of Freddie Mac currently consists of the purchase of first lien, conventional, residential mortgages, including participation interests in such mortgages, and the resale of the mortgages so purchased in the form of single-class guaranteed mortgage securities, primarily various types of PCs. PCs represent undivided interests in pools of mortgages purchased by Freddie Mac and provide for the monthly payment of interest and the pass-through of principal based on collections with respect to the underlying mortgages. Freddie Mac guarantees to PC holders payment of interest on and principal of the mortgages. Freddie Mac purchases a variety of single-family and multifamily fixed-rate and adjustable-rate mortgages primarily through its Cash and Guarantor Programs. The majority of Freddie Mac's mortgage purchases and PC sales volume occurs through the Guarantor Program. As of December 31, 1989, originally issued PCs having an aggregate unpaid principal balance of approximately $272.9 billion were outstanding, including approximately $195.3 billion attributable to the Guarantor Program.

108

Freddie Mac has announced plans to begin issuing enhanced PCs, called Gold PCs, in October 1990. Investors will have the option to convert their existing PCs to Gold PCs once issuance of the enhanced securities begins. Freddie Mac expects to issue Gold PCs in phases, beginning with securities backed by 15- and 30-year, fixed-rate, single-family mortgages (including balloon resets, second mortgages and fixed-rate Giant PCs). These will be followed by Gold PCs backed by other mortgage types. Implementation dates for each phase will be announced separately.

These enhanced securities will pass through a first payment to investors 45 days after issuance, compared to 75 days after issuance currently. The faster pass-through is expected to command higher security prices. Gold PCs will also offer investors a guarantee of timely payment of interest and scheduled principal, the pass through of actual rather than predicted prepayments, one payment cycle for all Gold PCs, and immediate eligibility for use in REMICs, Giants and other types of derivative securities.

Giant Mortgage Participation Certificates. Freddie Mac also issues Giant Mortgage Participation Certificates (Giant PCs), which represent beneficial ownership interests in a pool consisting of two or more (1) PCs (either all fixed-rate or all ARM PCs) formed under either the Guarantor or Cash Programs, and/or (2) other Giant PCs. Payments of principal and interest with respect to Giant PCs are passed through monthly, on the same date as payments are made on the underlying PCs and/or Giant PCs. Freddie Mac's guarantees with respect to Giant PCs are economically equivalent to those on the underlying PCs. Giant PCs generally are single-class passthrough securities, although Freddie Mac may form Giant PC pools with more than one class. Multiple-class Giant PCs may include Giant Principal Only PCs and Giant Interest Only PCs entitling holders thereof to principal or interest payments, respectively, received on the underlying PCs. Giant PCs having an aggregate unpaid principal balance of approximately $17.1 billion were oustanding as of December 31, 1989.

Multiclass Securities. Freddie Mac issues securities having multiple classes. Between 1983 and 1986, Freddie Mac issued Collateralized Mortgage Obligations (CMOs) and Mortgage Cash Flow Obligations (MCFs), which are general debt obligations of Freddie Mac secured by (in the case of CMOs) or based upon (in the case of MCFs) specified mortgages. CMOs and MCFs were issued in series, with different classes of a series having different maturities, and provide for semiannual payments of principal and interest. As of December 31, 1989, the outstanding principal balances, net of discount, were approximately $2.3 billion and $262.6 million for CMOs and MCFs, respectively.

Since February 1988, Freddie Mac has issued Multiclass Mortgage Participation Certificates (Multiclass PCs) backed by Multiclass PC pools, for which treatment as a Real Estate Mortgage Investment Conduit (REMIC) has been elected under the United States Internal Revenue Code of 1985, as amended. Multiclass PCs sold to date represent beneficial ownership interests in a pool typically consisting of PCs and/or Giant PCs, but have also consisted of other assets such as multifamily mortgages or installment sales contracts for manufactured housing. The Multiclass PCs are issuable in series, and each series consists of two or more classes of Multiclass PCs. Interest, if any, on each class of Multiclass PCs is usually passed through monthly at an applicable interest rate. Principal, if any, is typically paid monthly, in accordance with a formula which allocates principal among the classes in each series. Interest and principal generally are passed through on the same date as payments are made on the underlying PCs.

Freddie Mac has issued Multiclass PCs with fixed and variable interest rate classes, classes (designed to appeal to foreign investors) that pay principal and interest on an annual or semiannual basis rather than monthly, principal only and interest only classes with principal allocation formulas that would, under certain prepayment assumptions, provide for relative stability in the payment of principal (so-called Planned Amortization PCs and Targeted Amortization PCs). In late 1988 and early 1989, Freddie Mac also issued several series of Multiclass PCs carrying a mandatory purchase obligation

110

(MPO), which gives the holder of such Multiclass PCs the right (during a specified two-week "tender period") to require Freddie Mac to repurchase the PCs for their full unpaid principal balance.

General Obligation Debt. Freddie Mac began issuing notes and debentures in 1981. These debt instruments are unsecured general obligations of Freddie Mac issued in book-entry form. Debentures have a specified term of at least one year and generally pay interest semi-annually at a fixed coupon rate, although Freddie Mac has also issued floating-rate debentures that pay interest quarterly. Debentures are issued in minimum denominations of $10,000 with additional increments of $5,000 and usually are issued at par or a slight discount. As of December 31, 1989, there were approximately $2 billion in debentures outstanding.

Freddie Mac notes are short-term debt instruments, usually two years or less, that generally pay a fixed interest rate on a quarterly basis, although floating rate notes have been issued. Of Freddie Mac's short-term debt instruments, the most frequently offered are so called "discount notes," which do not pay interest and are sold at a discount. Discount notes are issued in minimum denominations of $25,000 with additional increments of $1. As of December 31, 1989, there were approximately $17 billion in notes of all types outstanding.

Federal National Mortgage Association

The Federal National Mortgage Association (FNMA, often called Fannie Mae) is the sixth largest corporation in the United States, based on assets, and the nation's largest supplier of funds for home mortgages. Fannie Mae supports the housing market by purchasing mortgages and, since 1981, by issuing and guaranteeing mortgage-backed securities (MBSs).

Fannie Mae was incorporated in 1938 as a corporation wholly owned by the federal government pursuant to Title III of the National Housing Act. In 1954, Title III was revised as the Federal National Mortgage Association Charter Act (the Charter Act). Under the Charter Act, Fannie Mae became a mixed-ownership corporation owned partly by private share-holders. In 1968, Congress split the original entity into two separate corporations: the Government National Mortgage Association (Ginnie Mae) and the Federal National Mortgage Association. Ginnie Mae is a wholly owned corporate instrumentality of the United States within the Department of Housing and Urban Development (see page 124). The legislation enabled Fannie Mae to raise capital to repay the U.S. government's financial investment in the corporation. By 1970, Fannie Mae completed the transition and officially became a private corporation.

The Secondary Mortgage Market. FNMA and other secondary market entities support primary institutions — savings and loan associations, mortgage bankers, commercial banks, and other lenders around the country — primarily by buying mortgages from them. In purchasing the mortgage loans that lenders originate, the secondary market institutions help replenish the lenders' supply of funds — enabling them to make additional loans to home buyers.

Lenders' sales of loans in the secondary market accomplish several objectives. If there is a limited capital base to finance housing in their geographic area, sales in the national secondary market help keep capital flowing to that area to finance new mortgage originations. The secondary market outlet also allows lenders to originate mortgages they do not want to put in their portfolios. In addition, this market, in standardizing the products it will buy from lenders, has helped attract nontraditional investors to mortgages.

Fannie Mae's mortgage purchases are made under terms specified in a commitment. Under mandatory delivery commitments, Fannie Mae agrees in advance to purchase a specified dollar amount of loans at a predetermined yield. The servicing of Fannie Mae-owned mortgages is handled primarily by the lenders who originate the loans. Lenders earn a fee from Fannie Mae for this service.

With the exception of certain mortgage-backed bonds guaranteed by Ginnie Mae, obligations of Fannie Mae,

112

together with any interest thereon, are not guaranteed by the U.S. government and do not constitute a debt or obligation of the U.S. government or any agency thereof.

All obligations issued by the corporation are, by statute:

- Acceptable as security for deposit of public monies subject to control of the U.S. government or its officers.

- Among those which, under federal law, national banks may deal in, underwrite, and purchase for their own accounts without limitation.

- Eligible as security for advances to member banks by Federal Reserve Banks.

- Legal investments for surplus funds and reserve funds of Federal Home Loan Banks.

- Legal investments for any portion of the assets of federal savings and loans associations and, when having a remaining maturity of five years or less, may be counted as part of the liquidity requirements prescribed by the Office of Thrift Supervision (successor agency to the Federal Home Loan Bank Board) for these institutions.

- Eligible for purchase by the Open Market Committee of the Federal Reserve Bank in its day-to-day implementation of monetary policy.

- Legal investments for federal credit unions.

The Internal Revenue Service has ruled that Fannie Mae is an instrumentality of the United States for purposes of Section 7701(a)(19) of the Internal Revenue Code of 1986. Therefore, domestic building and loan associations and savings banks are permitted to invest in the corporation's securities to meet the percentage of total assets required to be invested in, among other things, "stock or obligations of a corporation which is an instrumentality of the United States."

Fannie Mae's primary debt instruments—short-term notes and debentures—typically have offered 10 to 100 basis points more in yield than Treasuries of comparable maturity. There exists a liquid secondary market for short-term notes and debentures, aided by the large size of the individual debenture issues, which generally have ranged between $500 million and $1 billion.

Debentures. Fannie Mae's debentures are unsecured general obligations of the corporation and do not contain provisions permitting the holders to accelerate their maturity. Debentures generally are issued in book-entry form in minimum denominations of $10,000, then in multiples of $5,000. Except for certain special issues of debentures described below, debentures issued on or after March 10, 1978, are available only in book-entry form, i.e., in the form of an entry made on the records of a Federal Reserve bank. Debentures issued prior to March 10, 1978, are available in both definitive form and book-entry form, with conversions from one form to the other allowed upon application to the Federal Reserve Bank of New York. Principal and interest on the corporation's securities issued in book-entry form are payable through any member of the Federal Reserve System. In most cases, interest payments are made semiannually.

Fannie Mae usually offers its debentures (except for certain special issues) at the beginning of each month for delivery on or around the 10th day of each month. Debenture offerings may be announced on any business day. Most Fannie Mae debenture offerings are placed through a nationwide group of securities dealers and dealer banks (the "Selling Group"), including First Boston. The corporation also issues debentures with special features through a group of underwriters or a single underwriter.

Since 1984, the corporation also has issued debentures targeted to foreign investors. These debentures have certain characteristics different from those described in this section, and Fannie Mae generally makes available circulars describing the specific terms of these special offerings.

Examples of Nontraditional Fannie Mae Debt

- Dual currency debenture–a bond that pays initial proceeds and interest in one currency and principal in another.

- Domestic yen debenture–a yen-denominated bond issued in the U.S. by an American borrower.

- Eurodollar debenture–a dollar-denominated bond issued in the Eurobond market. With an exchangeable Eurodollar bond, holders have the option to exchange the bond for another specified domestic debenture issued by the same issuer.

- Euroyen debenture–a yen-denominated bond issued in the Eurobond market. To avoid exchange rate fluctuations, frequently the issuer will arrange a currency swap with a third party.

- Samurai debenture–a yen-denominated bond issued in the domestic Japanese bond market by a non-Japanese borrower.

- Yen syndicated loan–a loan in yen typically given by a consortium of banks and insurance companies.

- Shogun debenture–a dollar-denominated bond issued in the domestic Japanese bond market by a non-Japanese borrower.

Short-Term Notes. Maturities are tailored to the investors' needs, up to 360 days. The corporation announces rates for its short-term notes, which usually provide a yield higher than Treasury bills with similar maturity. The minimum original amount of purchase is $10,000 although additional amounts can be purchased in increments of $5,000. Short-term notes are distributed through a group of dealers and dealer banks, which maintain a secondary market for the notes. Short-term notes are available in discount form and payment for the notes must be made in federal funds. All Fannie Mae short-term notes are issued in book-entry form through the Federal Reserve System and are payable at maturity at the Federal Reserve Bank of New York.

Fannie Mae Short-Term Notes

Issued	Face amount ($millions)	Average term in days	Average cost
1989	29,258	141	8.88%
1988	34,034	172	7.77%
1987	18,248	149	7.23%
1986	13,440	191	6.33%
1985	14,882	229	8.55%

Residential Financing Securities. RFS are six-month, one-year, or two-year securities. They are issued in minimum amounts of $10,000 with $5,000 increments. These securities, offered through a group of securities dealers and dealer banks, are issued in book-entry form and are offered every business day at rates publicly announced by the corporation. During 1989, Fannie Mae issued $9.323 billion in RFSs at an average cost of 9.16%. The average maturity of these issues was 280 days.

Master Notes. Fannie Mae also issues individually negotiated variable principal amount notes. Such notes have been issued to banks, pension funds, savings and loan associations, insurance companies, and others under its master note program. Master notes, which have varying maturities, carry a floating interest rate tied to 91-day U.S. Treasury bill rates. The interest rate on these notes is adjusted weekly on the day following the 91-day Treasury bill auction.

Investors have the option of increasing or decreasing the principal amount outstanding on these notes on a daily basis, usually within a range of 80% to 120% of an agreed amount. Master notes are thus particularly useful investment vehicles for institutions whose liquidity fluctuates daily. Most master notes have a specific maturity.

Investment Agreements. Investment agreements are individually negotiated agreements that provide for the investment of a variable principal amount. In an investment agreement, Fannie Mae agrees to pay a negotiated fixed or variable rate of interest on funds invested with the corporation. Investment agreements have been used largely by tax-exempt issuers to invest bond proceeds during project construction. They are also used by issuers of collateralized mortgage obligations and other mortgage-backed bonds to deposit monthly cash flow pending distribution to bondholders.

Medium-Term Notes. MTNs are continuously offered securities with maturities that range from one day to 30 years. Investors have the flexibility of purchasing fixed-rate, floating-rate, zero coupon, amortizing, or foreign currency-denominated notes. In 1989 Fannie Mae issued $1.233 billion of MTNs at 8.70%.

Mortgage-Backed Securities. At the end of 1989, the corporation had $228.2 billion of MBSs outstanding. Most MBSs are issued through lender swap transactions, whereby participating lenders place pools of mortgages in trust in exchange for securities.

Since 1986, Fannie Mae also has been issuing stripped mortgage-backed securities (SMBSs). An SMBS consists of two or more classes of securities. There may be separate classes for principal and interest; alternatively, each class may represent a specified percentage of undivided ownership interest in the principal payments made on a pool of mortgage loans or MBS certificates and a different specified ownership interest of the interest payments on such a pool. Under the traditional MBS program, an investor has an undivided interest in the entire pool of underlying mortgage loans. The issuance of an SMBS provides an opportunity to tailor the underlying mortgage flows more closely to the needs of different types of investors. The corporation had $17.3 billion of SMBSs outstanding as of December 31, 1989.

Fannie Mae had $47.6 billion of real estate mortgage investment conduit securities (REMICs) outstanding as of December 31, 1989. A REMIC is a mortgage pass-through entity that allows multiple classes of securities and is authorized by the Tax Reform Act of 1986. REMIC certificates represent beneficial ownership interests in pools of mortgage loans or MBSs. REMICs enable the corporation to structure securities with differing principal and interest payments and maturities.

Summary of MBS Activity
(Dollars in millions)

	1987		1988		1989	
	$	%	$	%	$	%
Issuances of MBS:						
Lender originated	57,078	90	48,942	89	64,396	92
Fannie Mae originated	6,151	10	5,936	11	5,368	8
Total	63,229	100	54,878	100	69,764	100
Securities outstanding:						
Lender risk	62,402	45	84,143	47	94,343	41
Fannie Mae risk	77,558	55	94,107	53	133,889	59
Total	139,960	100	178,250	100	228,232	100

The table above summarizes MBS activity, including SMBSs and REMICs, for the three-year period ended December 31, 1989. Sellers of pools of mortgage loans may retain the primary default risk on loans comprising the pools or they may elect to transfer this risk to Fannie Mae and, in return, pay a higher guaranty fee. However, because the corporation guarantees timely payment of principal and interest on the MBS to the investors, it bears the ultimate risk of default on all MBS pools.

Student Loan Marketing Association

Student Loan Marketing Association (Sallie Mae) is a stockholder-owned corporation established by the Higher Education Act of 1965 (as amended). Sallie Mae has broad statutory authority to provide liquidity for banks, savings and loan associations, educational institutions, state agencies and other lenders engaged in the federal Guaranteed Student Loan Program (GSLP) comprising the Stafford (formerly GSL) loan programs, the supplemental PLUS and SLS loan programs, and the Health Education Assistance Loan (HEAL) program, and to otherwise support the credit needs of students. Stafford and PLUS/SLS loans are either insured directly by the U.S. government or guaranteed by state or nonprofit private agencies and reinsured by the U.S. government. Loans originated under HEAL are insured directly by the federal government.

118

Sallie Mae offers lenders loan purchases, warehousing advances and forward commitments for both instruments, as well as automated student loan management systems and services. In addition to making its other products and services available to state student loan agencies, Sallie Mae offers to issue letters of credit to back their student loan revenue bond issues. Sallie Mae letters of credit impart the highest (both Standard & Poor's and Moody's) investment grade rating to issues they back. Sallie Mae also provides financing to post-secondary educational institutions for academic plant and equipment and offers loan consolidation for student borrowers. In addition, Sallie Mae is authorized to offer participations or pooled interests in loans and to assist in financing student loans where there is a shortage of capital, either as a direct lender, if requested by the Secretary of Education, or as a source of funds to eligible guarantee agencies or direct lenders. Sallie Mae is also authorized to deal in uninsured student loans, to purchase and underwrite student loan revenue bonds, to serve as a guarantee agency or direct lender if requested by the Secretary of Education and to engage in such other activities as its Board of Directors determines to be in furtherance of meeting the credit needs of students.

Sallie Mae's voting common stock may be held only by financial institutions eligible to participate in the GSLP and by higher educational institutions. Sallie Mae's nonvoting common stock is not subject to ownership restrictions.

Sallie Mae finances its activities primarily from the sale of its debt securities in the domestic and international capital markets. From 1974 through 1982, Sallie Mae financed its activities principally through the issuance of debt obligations to the Federal Financing Bank (FFB). As of September 30, 1989, Sallie Mae had $4.91 billion in outstanding obligations to the Federal Financing Bank.

In May 1981, Sallie Mae began to finance its operations in part through the public issuance of nonguaranteed discount notes. These notes are unsecured debt obligations, mature within one year and are issued on a daily basis in minimum denominations of $100,000, and multiples of $50,000 above that amount. Issuance and delivery of these definitive securities are through Bankers Trust in New York City. In February 1984, Sallie Mae also began issuing short-term floating rate notes, at a spread to the bond-equivalent yield on the 91-day Treasury bill. These notes are offered monthly and generally have maturities of three years or longer. From time to time, Sallie Mae also offers to the public long-term floating-rate securities and fixed-rate securities, on which the corporation frequently converts interest payment stream to floating rate through interest rate swaps. Other debt issued by Sallie Mae includes master notes, medium-term notes, zero coupon notes, indexed currency option notes, yield curve notes, exchange rate-linked notes, and various foreign currency-related securities.

As provided for by the Higher Education Act, securities issued by Sallie Mae are lawful investments and may be accepted as security for all fiduciary, trust and public funds, the investment or deposit of which is under authority or control of the U.S. government. Sallie Mae securities are eligible as collateral for Federal Reserve Bank "discount window" transactions and for Treasury tax and loan accounts. National banks and state member banks may deal in, underwrite and purchase for their own account, Sallie Mae's debt obligations. SLMA securities are legal investments for federal savings and loan associations, federal mutual savings banks, and federal credit unions and for surplus and reserve funds of Federal Home Loan Banks. Sallie Mae securities are eligible to be purchased by the Federal Reserve in its day-to-day implementation of monetary policy.

The Internal Revenue Service has ruled that Sallie Mae is an instrumentality of the U.S. government for purposes of Section 7701 (a)(19)(C)(ii) of the Code. As a result, domestic building and loan associations and federal and domestic savings and loan associations are permitted to include Sallie Mae obligations among those assets defined as "stock or obligations of a corporation which is an instrumentality of the United States." The Internal Revenue Service has also ruled that Sallie Mae obligations constitute "obligations of the United States or of any agency or instrumentality thereof" within the meaning of section 895 of the Code, relating to foreign central banks of issue.

The Secretary of the Treasury is authorized in his discretion to purchase obligations of Sallie Mae in the aggregate principal amount of $1.0 billion. These obligations are in addition to any guaranteed obligations that may then be outstanding to the FFB. To date, no borrowings have been made under this provision. In addition, Sallie Mae is authorized to sell or issue student loan-backed obligations to the FFB.

United States Postal Service

The United States Postal Service was created as an independent establishment in the executive branch of the U.S. government pursuant to the Postal Reorganization Act (39 USC 201). On July 1, 1971, the Postal Service succeeded to the business of the Post Office Department, which had been charged with the responsibility of operating a postal system in the United States. The Postal Service has, subject to certain exceptions, the exclusive right to deliver letter mail in the United States.

The act granted the Postal Service certain powers not vested in the Post Office Department, including the power to issue debt obligations to finance capital expenditures and current operations. The Postal Service is authorized to borrow funds as may be necessary to carry out the objectives of the act, either through the FFB or the Department of the Treasury, or at the discretion of the Secretary of the Treasury, through direct offerings to the public. The aggregate amount of borrowings outstanding at any one time may not exceed $15 billion, an enlargement from $10 billion that becomes effective in 1992, and in any one fiscal year the net increase in borrowings may not exceed (1) $2.0 billion to finance capital improvements and (2) $1.0 billion to defray operating expenses. The Postal Service is authorized to pledge its assets and to pledge and use its revenues and receipts to secure its obligations.

The Postal Service may require the Secretary of the Treasury to purchase its obligations as long as the Secretary's holdings from such required purchases do not exceed $2 billion at any one time. Under a trust indenture made in connection with a bond offering of February 1, 1972, the Postal Services must (1) reserve an amount available under the $2 billion mandatory purchase authority at least equal to the aggregate principal amount of bonds outstanding under the trust indenture (currently $250 million) and (2) exercise such authority to the extent necessary to meet principal, premium, if any, and interest payments on such obligations.

Obligations of the Postal Service may be fully guaranteed as to timely payment of principal and interest by the U.S. government if the Postal Service so requests, and the Secretary of the Treasury determines that the guarantee is in the public interest.

As of December 31, 1989, the Postal Service had outstanding $250 million in Series A Bonds, due February 1, 1997, which are not guaranteed by the U.S. government. These bonds were issued in registered or coupon form in denominations of $10,000, $25,000, $100,000, and $500,000 and carry an interest rate of $6\frac{7}{8}\%$. At the option of the Postal Service, they are redeemable at par after February 1, 1982. Postal Service bonds are lawful investments and may be accepted as security for all fiduciary, trust, and public funds under the control and authority of the U.S. government. The bonds are eligible as security for 90-day advances to depository institutions by the Federal Reserve System and as collateral for Treasury tax and loan accounts. They are exempt from all state and local taxes except estate, inheritance, and gift taxes.

In addition, the Postal Service had outstanding $6,445 million in unsecured notes payable to the Federal Financing Bank and approximately $31 million in mortgage notes secured by land and buildings payable to various holders.

Department of Housing and Urban Development

Federal Housing Administration

The Federal Housing Administration (FHA) was established on June 27, 1934, under the National Housing Act, subsequently amended from time to time, to encourage improvement in housing standards and conditions, to provide a system of mutual mortgage insurance as an aid to builders and buyers of homes and to mortgage-lending institutions, and for other purposes. FHA is authorized to insure mortgage loans made for a variety of purposes, mostly related to residential housing.

A major purpose of the National Housing Act is to encourage the flow of private capital into residential financing on a protected basis. FHA does not make loans and does not plan or build housing. Its operating costs and a substantial part of insurance losses are paid from current income from fees, premiums and interest, together with appropriated funds. Any surplus or deficit is credited or charged to the reserves of its insurance funds.

FHA Debenture Obligations. Under the Housing and Urban Development Act of 1965, the FHA has the option of paying claims in cash, in debentures, or in some combination thereof. All multifamily claims paid since January 25, 1966, except Title X and some others under multifamily programs, have been settled by the issuance of debentures. All home claims except Section 221 (g) (4) have been and will continue to be paid in cash at the option of FHA.

Outstanding debentures, as of December 31, 1989, amounted to $324.8 million. When excess cash is available in the various insurance funds, the FHA may call debentures for redemption prior to maturity, with the approval of the Secretary of the Treasury.

All debentures are registered and transferable. They are available in denominations of $50, $100, $500, $1,000, $5,000, and $10,000.

Although the debentures are primarily the liabilities of the insurance funds under which they are issued, they are fully and unconditionally guaranteed as to principal and interest by the U.S. government.

Federal Housing Administration obligations are lawful investments and may be accepted as security for all fiduciary, trust, and public funds under the authority and control of the U.S. government. They are eligible collateral for Treasury tax and loan accounts. National banks may invest in them without regard to the statutory limitations and restrictions generally applicable to investment securities.

Reference should be made to Chapter 13 of *Mortgagees' Guide: Home Mortgage Insurance Fiscal Instructions* (HUD Handbook 4110.2) for additional information concerning the payment of mortgage insurance premiums with FHA debentures and the various interest rate, redemption, maturity, and tax provisions of FHA debentures.

Government National Mortgage Association

The Government National Mortgage Association (GNMA, often called Ginnie Mae) was created in 1968 through amendment of Title III of the National Housing Act. Under the provisions of the Housing and Urban Development Act of 1968, the Federal National Mortgage Association (FNMA), originally established in 1938, was rechartered as a private corporation to provide secondary support for the private residential mortgage market; GNMA was established as a government corporation within the Department of Housing and Urban Development (HUD) to administer mortgage support programs which could not be carried out in the private market.

GNMA securities enjoy an active and well-established secondary market. With $369.9 billion of securities outstanding through December 1989 and an estimated $622.8 billion traded or re-registered, GNMA securities were the most widely held and traded mortgage-backed securities in the world in 1989.

Mortgage-Backed Securities Program. The Government National Mortgage Association's Mortgage-Backed Securities (MBS) programs have been instrumental in the development and expansion of the nation's secondary mortgage market. The MBS programs serve to increase and stabilize the overall supply of mortgage credit and to reduce its cost by making it possible for the residential lending industry to acquire an increasing amount of funds from the nation's securities markets. Consequently, funds that normally circulate in the securities and bond markets now flow into the mortgage market as well.

As of December 31, 1989, GNMA had guaranteed over $576 billion in securities collateralized by approximately 232,565 mortgage pools, which are composed of mortgages insured by the Federal Housing Administration (FHA) or guaranteed by the Veteran's Administration (VA), or the Farmers Home Administration (FmHA). These securities, issued by some 1,100 mortgage lenders, have helped finance over 11.5 million housing units. Some 58% of the approved issuers of GNMA securities are mortgage bankers and approximately 27% are savings institutions. The remainder are commercial banks and other types of financial intermediaries.

GNMA administers two mortgage-backed securities programs, each of which in turn has several subprograms. The GNMA I program was initiated in 1970. The GNMA II program was introduced in July 1983 and takes advantage of many technological improvements that have emerged since the first GNMA I securities were introduced. The key features of the GNMA II program include the use of a central paying agent and the availability of larger geographically dispersed multiple-issuer pools. The central paying agent provides consolidated monthly payments (one check for all GNMA II holdings) to investors. GNMA II multiple-issuer pools provide investors with improved prepayment consistency.

Through the MBS programs, GNMA guarantees privately issued securities backed by pools of mortgages. Security holders receive a "pass-through" of the principal and interest payments on the pool of mortgages, less amounts to cover servicing costs and certain GNMA fees. GNMA guarantees that the securities holders will receive timely payments of scheduled monthly principal and interest, as well as unscheduled recoveries of principal. If homeowners fail to make timely payments on their mortgages, the securities issuers, using their own resources, must advance the scheduled payments to the registered securities holders.

A Comparison of GNMA I and GNMA II Mortgage-Backed Securities

	GNMA I	GNMA II
Underlying mortgages	FHA, VA, & FmHA loans	FHA, VA, & FmHA loans
Pools	Single issuer	Custom (single issuer) & multiple issuer
Central paying agent	None – multiple monthly checks to investors	Chemical Bank – single monthly check to investors
Transfer agent	Chemical Bank	Chemical Bank
Interest rate	All mortgages in a pool have the same interest rate (except manufactured home pools)	Mortgages in a pool may have interest rates that vary within a one percentage point range
Guarantor	GNMA (full faith and credit of the U.S. government)	GNMA (full faith and credit of the U.S. government)
Guarantee	Full and timely payment of principal and interest, plus prepayments	Full and timely payment of principal and interest, plus prepayments
Payment date	Check received by the 15th	Check mailed on the 19th

Because of the federal guarantee (pledge of full faith and credit of the U.S. government) and uniformity of securities, the GNMA securities become as safe, as liquid, and as easy to hold as Treasury securities. Underlying the securities are mortgages, which are used by GNMA as collateral for the guarantee. The issuer is responsible for acquiring and servicing the mortgages, and marketing the securities it issues.

GNMA securities, colloquially known as Ginnie Maes, provide investors monthly payments, rather than the customary semiannual payment associated with most bonds. They also provide a relatively high yield. The holder of a Ginnie Mae also has a readily marketable, highly liquid instrument. All

126

securities are issued in registered form and are fully and easily transferable.

GNMA mortgage-backed securities have been ruled by the Internal Revenue Service to represent an undivided interest in real property and thus may be purchased by thrift institutions and real estate investment trusts as qualifying real-property loans. Mortgage-backed securities are also legal investments for federally chartered credit unions.

Activity in GNMA Securities
(Dollars in billions)

Calendar Year	1985	1986	1987	1988	1989
New securities issued	45.9	98.2	98.3	56.5	57.5
Cumulative issuances	267.4	365.6	463.9	519.1	546.6
Securities outstanding	212.1	260.9	316.9	340.5	369.9
Re-registrations (transfers)	270.8	405.1	516.6	427.6	622.8

Public Housing Bonds
In the past, the Department of Housing and Urban Development (HUD) administered a program of assistance to local public housing and urban renewal agencies that involved the public issuance of federally guaranteed securities.

New Housing Authority Bonds. Under this program local authorities typically obtained permanent financing for low-income housing projects by issuing long-term bonds at or near completion of new construction or modernization. These bonds usually were 40-year serial issues designed to provide level annual debt service and were sold to the public. They were secured by the federal government's full faith and credit pledge to pay annual contributions to the local authorities in sufficient amounts to meet principal and interest payments. Bonds were issued in $5,000 denominations, in bearer or registered form at the option of the original purchaser. They may be reissued subsequently in alternative forms at the expense of the holder. They are typically callable after 15 years at specified premiums.

Public participation in federally secured new housing authority bonds began in 1951. There have been no new issues of these bonds since 1974, but $5.6 billion of them were still outstanding as of December 31, 1989.

Farmers Home Administration

The Farmers Home Administration (FmHA) in the Department of Agriculture extends loans in rural areas for farms, homes, and community facilities. Currently the Farmers Home Administration finances its programs through borrowing from the U.S. Treasury. The sale of certificates of beneficial ownership (CBOs) to the public was discontinued in March 1975, but as of December 31, 1989, $222 million remained outstanding.

During late 1977, holders of note insurance contracts with 10- and 15-year maturities were given the option to exchange the contracts for CBOs. Holders of over $1.1 billion of the outstanding contracts accepted the exchange offer. CBOs offer no principal paydown, are available in registered, Federal Reserve Bank book-entry, and bearer form, and are eligible for denominational exchanges. Contracts are available in registered form only, are not eligible for denominational exchange, and a small amount of principal may be paid on each annual settlement date.

As obligations secured by the full faith and credit of the U.S. government, CBOs are acceptable security for deposits of public moneys such as Treasury tax and loan accounts and are eligible collateral for advances not exceeding 90 days within the meaning of Paragraph 8, Section 13 of the Federal Reserve Act. Interest on FmHA obligations is subject to federal income tax. The statutory exemption of federal agency securities from income tax imposed by states or localities has not applied to FmHA obligations.

During fiscal year 1987 FmHA sold $2.9 billion in rural housing loans and $1.9 billion in community loans without recourse to the government in the event of borrower default. The sales were to private sector trusts which then issued pass-through certificates and bonds were sold to the public by underwriters.

A mix of maturities was used to match maturities on the underlying loans.

General Services Administration

The General Services Administration (GSA), an agency in the executive branch of the federal government, was established by the Federal Property and Administrative Services Act of 1949 (63 Stat. 379). Its purpose is to provide for the federal government economical and efficient management of its property and records, including construction and operation of buildings, procurement and distribution of supplies, disposal of surplus property, traffic and communications management, stockpiling of strategic and critical materials, and creation, preservation, and disposal of records.

The Public Buildings Amendments of 1972, P.L. 92-313 (86 Stat. 216) provided authority through July 1, 1975, for the GSA to undertake a purchase contract program for the construction of a number of public buildings projects and their long-term purchase by the government.

Utilizing this legislation, GSA financed 14 projects through the issuance of participation certificates under three separate public buildings purchase contract and trust indentures. Series A through E, due November 1, 2002, were issued on November 15, 1972, in the aggregate principal amount of $196,500,000. Participation certificates, Series F, due December 15, 2002, were issued on December 21, 1972, in the aggregate principal amount of $200,000,000. Participation certificates, Series G, due March 1, 2003, were issued on March 22, 1973, in the aggregate principal amount of $126,000,000. The financing of 17 additional projects was accomplished through a fourth public buildings purchase contract and trust indenture dated August 1, 1973, which permitted the issuance of participation certificates in one or more series. The first series of participation certificates, Series H due July 31, 2003, was issued on August 2, 1973, in the aggregate principal amount of $71,000,000. The second such series, Series I due July 31, 2003, was issued on January 24, 1974, in the aggregate principal amount of $98,000,000. Subsequent issues of securities have been sold

129

wholly to the Federal Financing Bank. The coupon rates on the Series A through I certificates ranged from 7⅛% to 8⅛%.

The proceeds from the sale of participation certificates are required by the indentures to be held by a trustee initially in a construction fund and, to the extent directed by GSA, a debt service fund, and to be applied toward the payment of interest, project construction costs, and other related expenses. In the interim, monies in these funds may, subject to certain limitations, be invested as GSA directs.

Participation certificates are acceptable for banks to pledge as collateral for deposits of public money subject to the control of the U.S. government or its officers, agents, or employees, and for Treasury tax and loan accounts. Certificates are eligible for purchase, dealing in, underwriting, and unlimited holding for national banks under federal law, and for state banks which are members of the Federal Reserve System. Certificates are eligible as security for advances to depository institutions by Federal Reserve Banks.

In the opinion of special counsel for GSA, participation certificates constitute "obligations of the United States" within the meaning of Title 31, Section 742, of the United States Code, as amended, and accordingly the participation certificates and interest thereon are exempt from local taxation by or under state or municipal or local authority, except nondiscriminatory franchise or other nonproperty taxes in lieu thereof imposed on corporations and except estate taxes or inheritance taxes. The interest paid on participation certificates is not exempt from federal income taxes.

The full faith and credit of the U.S. government is pledged to pay to the trustee the purchase price (as defined) under the indentures for the public building projects covered thereby; and the participation certificates evidence undivided interest in such obligation.

Merchant Marine obligations are issued and guaranteed in accordance with the provisions of the Merchant Marine Act, of 1936, as amended, under the auspices of the Maritime Administration, U.S. Department of Transportation. Formerly, ship mortgages were insured by the U.S. government under Title XI of the Act. However, the Ship Financing Act of 1972 (Public Law 92–507) changed the concept of Title XI from the insurance of a mortgage to the direct guarantee of the obligation itself by the U.S. government acting by and through the Secretary of Transportation. Applications for Title XI made after October 18, 1972, must be financed under the new guarantee form. The obligations guaranteed by the U.S. government under P.L. 92–507 provide as follows: "The full faith and credit of the United States is pledged to the payment of all guarantees made under this title with respect to both principal and interest, including interest, as may be provided for in the guarantee, accruing between the date of default under a guaranteed obligation and the payment in full of the guarantee."

Previously, the mortgages themselves had been insured by the U.S. government under Title XI as follows: "The faith of the United States is solemnly pledged to the payment of interest on and the unpaid balance of the principal amount of each mortgage and loan insured under this title." Mortgages securing bonds issued prior to the aforementioned changes in the Merchant Marine Act continue to be insured.

Title XI bonds and notes are issued by shipowners and are marketed by investment banking firms. Usually these obligations are issued in multiples of $1,000 and pay interest semiannually. The interest rate is fixed at the time of issuance in accordance with the current market conditions.

Each issuance of Merchant Marine bonds or notes is secured by a first preferred ship or fleet mortgage, which currently may finance as much as 75% of the actual cost. In the event of default of payments due under the obligations, Title XI of the Act provides for steps to be taken by the trustee of the bonds, as a result of which bondholders would be entitled to receive cash payment from the U.S. government equal to the unpaid principal amount of the bonds and accrued interest.

Various series of bonds, notes, and obligations have been offered since 1958. As of December 31, 1989, $3.481 billion of Merchant Marine bonds, notes, and obligations were outstanding. This amount leaves an unobligated balance from the total $12.0 billion authorization of $6.019 billion, after allocating $1.650 billion to be utilized for the financing of ocean thermal energy conversion (OTEC) vessels and $850 million to the National Marine Fisheries Services.

Small Business Administration

The Small Business Administration (SBA) was created in 1953 and derives its present authority from the Small Business Act of 1958, as amended (15 U.S.C. 661), the Small Business Investment Act of 1958 (15 U.S.C. 661), and various other laws. SBA provides financial, procurement, and management assistance to small business concerns and also assists victims of natural and other disasters. SBA financial aid to small business firms includes both direct loans and guaranteed loans.

Small Business Investment Company Program. As part of its financial assistance functions, SBA guarantees loans to small business investment companies (SBICs), which are privately owned, SBA-licensed and regulated, companies that supply venture capital and long-term financing to small firms. SBA loans to SBICs may have terms of up to 15 years and may be made in amounts of up to $35 million. SBA is also authorized to purchase at subsidized rates the preferred stock and debentures of SBICs that invest exclusively in small concerns owned by persons whose participation in the free enterprise system is hampered by social or economic disadvantages. The subsidized stock and debentures have not served as the basis for any sale of securities by SBA. As of December 31, 1989, there were $870.5 million SBA-guaranteed SBIC debentures outstanding.

From 1974 to 1986 all such sales of debentures were made to the Federal Financing Bank, which is subject to the general supervision and direction of the United States Treasury.

132

Currently, SBIC and CDC (see below) debentures are pooled, and participation certificates in such pools are sold to the public on an underwritten basis. The pool certificates have a timely payment and full faith and credit guaranty.

SBA-guaranteed debentures are acceptable as security for deposit of public funds under the control of the U.S. government, are eligible as collateral for Treasury tax and loan accounts, and may serve as security for advances to depository institutions by Federal Reserve Banks. Income from SBA debentures is subject to federal income taxes.

The Internal Revenue Service has ruled that SBA-guaranteed debentures are considered "Government securities" where that term is used in the relevant sections of the Internal Revenue Code of 1954, as amended.

Regular Business Loan Program. The guaranteed portion of SBA Section 7(a) loans can be sold by lenders to broker/dealers or directly to investors. The majority of SBA-guaranteed loans sold into the secondary market are regular business loans in the 7(a) program. Only the entire guaranteed portion ("Guaranteed Interest") may be sold.

Although it is legally permissible that there be multiple owners of the Guaranteed Interest, there can be only one registered holder on the books of SBA's fiscal and transfer agent (FTA). The registered holder of a guaranteed interest may be an individual, joint tenants, tenants in common, or tenants in the entirety. Effective on February 15, 1985, all primary and secondary sales of SBA-guaranteed loans must use the FTA.

Single Loan Sales. Investors may purchase SBA-guaranteed interests on an individual basis. These instruments have a full faith and credit guarantee of the U.S. government but do not have a timely payment guarantee. Single Guaranteed Interests may be purchased in amounts ranging up to $750,000. The owner of an individual Guaranteed Interest receives a certificate from SBA's fiscal and transfer agent representing the ownership of the instrument. Borrower payments of principal and interest are apportioned between the lender and investor according to their respective ownership interests and the servicing fee of the lender. Monthly payments made by the borrower are forwarded to the FTA by the lender on the 30th of the month and forwarded to the investor by the FTA on the 15th of the following month.

SBA Loan Pools. On March 31, 1985, SBA implemented final regulations for the SBA Loan Pooling Program. The purpose of the pooling program is to provide an investment vehicle that is attractive to institutional investors not interested in investments under $1,000,000. Approved pool assemblers are able to form and market pools of SBA-guaranteed interests. The pool certificates have a timely payment and a full faith and credit guarantee. Unlike single loan sales, there is no maximum size for a pool certificate. The minimum size is $25,000. The FTA forwards a payment to pool holders on the 25th of the month, regardless of whether payments were received on the underlying loans.

Fiscal and Transfer Agent. Both the individual and pool certificates are registered with SBA's fiscal and transfer agent. Transfers are arranged between the seller and buyer and must be reregistered with the FTA in order to insure receipt of payments by the new holder.

Further printed information is contained in the "Secondary Market Program Guide," obtainable by calling (212) 264-5877 or writing to Mr. James Hammersley, Director, Secondary Market Activities, Small Business Administration, 1441 L Street, NW, Room 800C, Washington, DC 20416.

Certified Development Company Program. Another of SBA's financial assistance programs is delivered by certified development companies (CDC). This program was authorized on July 21, 1980. The majority of CDCs are not-for-profit, local private/public corporations which are certified and regulated by the SBA to provide financing for the acquisition or construction of fixed assets (e.g., plant, heavy machinery, and equipment). With SBA approval, a CDC may sell an SBA-guaranteed debenture with a maturity of 10 or 20 years, using the sale proceeds to fund a loan to a small business. The maximum amount of a debenture is $750,000. Debentures have a self-amortizing, semiannual repayment schedule.

For the first five years of the program, all debentures were sold to the Federal Financing Bank. Beginning in 1986, debentures have been sold publicly, on an underwritten basis. SBA guarantees the timely payment of principal and interest. The guarantee is secured by the full faith and credit of the U.S. government. As of December 31, 1989, there are more than $1.4 billion worth of debentures outstanding.

Tennessee Valley Authority

The Tennessee Valley Authority (TVA) was established by an Act of Congress in 1933 to develop the resources of the Tennessee Valley region in order to strengthen the regional and national economy and the national defense. Power operations are segregated from nonpower activities. Assets of the power program amounted to $27 billion in 1989. TVA was authorized to issue debt up to $30 billion in October 1979. Under this authorization, TVA also may obtain advances from the Treasury of up to $150 million.

TVA bonds are not obligations of, nor are they guaranteed by, the United States. The bonds are secured by a first charge upon net power proceeds (in essence, net income before interest and noncash expenses including depreciation). Interest and principal due on bonds rank ahead of annual payments due to the Treasury, which aggregated over $87 million in fiscal year 1989. From October 1974, through early 1989, TVA sold long-term bonds to the Federal Financing Bank (FFB). In October 1987, TVA resumed sale of bonds in the public market; these bonds were issued with original maturities of five, seven, ten, thirty, and forty years. The bonds were issued in book entry form in minimum denominations of $1,000. The proceeds of the bonds were used to refund certain high interest rate long-term debt and to reduce short-term debt. In addition, the TVA sells short-term power bonds to the FFB several times each month.

Bonds sold to the public in 1974 and earlier were issued in coupon form in denominations of $1,000 and $5,000 and in registered form in denominations of $1,000 or any multiple thereof. Income on bonds and notes is subject to federal income taxes. Principal and interest are exempt from all state or local taxes except estate, inheritance, and gift taxes. TVA obligations have been declared legal for fiduciary, trust, and public funds under control of the U.S. government. National banks are permitted to underwrite these obligations and to invest in them up to 10% of capital stock and surplus. TVA obligations are approved by the Treasury as collateral security for the deposit of public monies.

The amount of TVA bonds and notes outstanding on December 31, 1989, was $19,149 million—$9,380 million in bonds payable to the public, $9,425 million in bonds and $194 million in notes payable to the FFB, and $150 million in a note payable to the Treasury.

Washington Metropolitan Area Transit Authority

The Washington Metropolitan Area Transit Authority was created, effective February 20, 1967, by interstate compact between Maryland, Virginia, and the District of Columbia pursuant to Public Law 98–774, approved in 1966; Maryland Acts of General Assembly, 1965, Chapter 869; and Virginia Acts of Assembly, 1966, Chapter 2. The authority is a federally assisted regional public body and is characterized as a common agency and instrumentality of its three signatory states. The principal purpose of the authority is to plan, develop, finance, and provide for the operation of mass transit facilities, including rapid rail transit and bus systems, in the greater Washington, D.C. metropolitan area.

Construction of rapid rail transit facilities is financed through contributions from the federal government and the surrounding local governments, and by issuance of federally guaranteed transit bonds. Current legislation (Public Law 96–184) continues an eight-to-two federal matching of money contributed by the local jurisdictions. Further, this legislation requires local jurisdictions to develop a stable and reliable source of revenue to provide for retirement of existing Metro bonds, and for future projected operating deficits. The Authority has issued $820 million in bonds to the public and $177 million to the Federal Financing Bank.

The Guarantee Act authorizes the appropriation to the Secretary of Transportation without fiscal year limitation the necessary amounts to enable the Secretary to discharge responsibilities under the guarantee. If at any time the monies available to the Secretary of Transportation are insufficient to discharge responsibilities under the guarantee, the Guarantee Act provides that notes or other obligations shall be issued by the Secretary of Transportation and purchased by the Secretary of the Treasury in a sufficient amount.

The bonds are issued in either coupon or full registered form. Coupon bonds are issuable in denominations of $5,000, $10,000, $25,000, $100,000, and $500,000. Registered bonds are issuable in denominations of $5,000 and any integral multiples of $5,000 and are interchangeable. The bonds may be subject to redemption prior to maturity. Interest income on the bonds is subject to federal income taxes and carries no special exemption from taxes imposed by state or local taxing authorities. However, 22 states in addition to the parties involved in the interstate compact which created the Authority have exempted the bonds from state income taxes.

Pursuant to the Guarantee Act, the bonds are lawful investments, and may be accepted as security for the deposit of fiduciary, trust, and public funds under authority or control of the U.S. government. It also provides that building and loan associations, any savings and loan association organized and operating under the laws of the District of Columbia, or any federal savings and loan association may invest funds in the bonds. Under the provisions of the compact, the bonds are securities in which all public officers and public agencies of Virginia, Maryland, or the District of Columbia and their political subdivisions, and within such jurisdictions all banks, trust companies, savings and loan associations, investment companies, insurance companies, administrators, executors, guardians, trustees and other fiduciaries, and all other persons may legally and properly invest funds, including capital in their control or belonging to them.

Asian Development Bank

The Asian Development Bank is an international institution created in 1966 when 31 countries signed the Agreement Establishing the Asian Development Bank (the "charter"). As of December 31, 1989, the Bank had 47 members. The principal purpose of the Bank is to foster economic growth and cooperation in Asia and the Pacific region by lending funds, promoting investment and providing technical assistance. The Bank pays special attention to the needs of the smaller or less-developed member countries in the region. The United States participated actively in the formation of the Bank and is one of the largest subscribers to the Bank's capital stock. The principal office of the Bank is located in Metropolitan Manila, Philippines.

The percentage of voting power in the Bank's affairs held by the respective members is related to their capital subscriptions. The aggregate voting power of the developed member countries, the United States, Japan, Australia, the United Kingdom, Canada, New Zealand, and 12 continental European countries represents about 55% of the total.

The capital stock of the Bank is defined in the charter in terms of the United States dollar of the weight and fineness in effect on January 31, 1966 ("1966 dollar"). The capital stock had historically been translated into current United States dollars (the Bank's unit of account) on the basis of its par value in terms of gold. Since April 1, 1978, when the Second Amendment to the Articles of Agreement of the International Monetary Fund (IMF) came into effect, currencies no longer have par values in terms of gold. Pending a decision on the implications of this change on the valuation of its capital stock, the Bank's capital stock has been valued for purposes of its financial statements in terms of the Special Drawing Right (SDR), at the value in current United States dollars as computed by the IMF.

As of December 31, 1989, the authorized capital stock of the Bank was equivalent to about $22,111.0 million, of which

$21,137.6 million had been subscribed. The Bank's initial capital was $1,560.5 million (1,100.0 million 1966 dollars) of which the United States and Japan subscribed to $283.7 million (200.0 million 1966 dollars) each. This subscription made the United States and Japan the two largest subscribers, and each was then entitled to cast about 17.1% of the total votes. As of December 31, 1989, the United States had subscribed to $3,165.5 million of the capital stock, entitling it to cast 12.4% of the total votes of all members of the Bank. The paid-in portion of the United States subscription is equivalent to $380.0 million and the callable portion is equivalent to $2,785.4 million.

The subscribed capital is presently divided into paid-in and callable portions, with approximately 12% being paid-in and 88% callable at the end of 1989. The callable portion of the Bank's subscribed capital may be called only when required to meet obligations on borrowings and guarantees given in the course of the Bank's ordinary operations. No calls have been made on the callable portion of the subscriptions. At the end of 1989, the subscribed paid-in capital and callable capital of the Bank were $2,551.9 million and $18,585.7 million, respectively.

Under its charter, the Bank has accepted nonnegotiable, noninterest-bearing demand obligations in lieu of part of the required payments in national currencies where the national currencies were not required for the Bank's operations. At the end of 1989, 86% of the Bank's paid-in capital was paid or payable in gold or convertible currencies and 14% in the currencies of members with nonconvertible currencies.

The Bank's primary activity is to make loans for projects within the territories of its developing members. The loans are made only for projects of high developmental priority, including those for energy, agriculture and agro-industry, transport and communication, national development banks, water supply, industry and nonfuel minerals, urban development, education, and health. At the end of 1989, the Bank had approved 536 loans aggregating $19,015.1 million in its ordinary operations for projects in 18 developing member countries. The Bank's ordinary operations are financed from its ordinary capital resources, which consist of its subscribed capital stock, the proceeds of borrowings, the sale of participations in its loans, and funds derived from operations.

Special operations of the Bank are financed from special funds administered by the Bank. The Bank's special funds resources, most of which are contributed by members, are completely segregated from ordinary capital resources and are used to provide loans and grants to members whose economic positions require more lenient terms. At the end of 1989, the Bank had approved 468 loans in its special operations aggregating $9,581.6 million for projects in 29 member countries and technical assistance grants totaling $420.4 million to 28 member countries.

The Bank's charter requires separate financial statements for ordinary operations and for special operations and provides that the ordinary capital resources shall under no circumstances be charged with, or used to discharge, losses or liabilities arising out of special operations or other activities for which special funds were originally used or committed.

Loans may be made to developing member countries or their governments, to any of their agencies or political subdivisions, and to public or private entities and enterprises operating in such countries, and to international or regional agencies concerned with economic development in the region. The Bank may require member countries or their governments to guarantee loans not made directly to member countries or their governments.

During 1986, the Bank began direct lending to private enterprises and financial institutions in developing member countries without government guarantees. These loans are made on terms comparable to similar loans from commercial sources, with generally shorter maturities and different interest rates from those typically offered by the Bank. As of December 31, 1989, the Bank had approved such loans totaling $180.7 million, of which $172.2 million are to be financed from ordinary capital resources and $8.5 million from the Asian Development Fund.

In November 1987, the Bank decided to expand its program lending activities, which are designed to provide financial resources to meet medium-term development issues as well as traditional short-term goals of its developing member countries. The ceiling on program lending as a percentage of total lending, interpreted flexibly over a three-year moving average centered on the current year, is currently 15%.

The Bank is empowered by charter to guarantee, as primary or secondary obligor, loans for economic development projects in which the Bank also participates as lender. The Bank extended its first guarantee, under the Bank's Complementary Financing Scheme, on March 13, 1989. As of December 31, 1989, outstanding guarantees amounted to $16.6 million.

The Bank is also empowered by the Charter to make equity investments under certain conditions. As of December 31, 1989, the Bank had approved 36 such equity investments aggregating $107.4 million and had been involved, to the extent of $36.2 million, in underwriting five equity funds. Included in the Bank's equity activities for 1989 was a $35 million investment in the Asian Finance and Investment Corporation, Ltd., a new regional institution designed to channel funds to private enterprises in the region.

The Bank follows a policy of not taking part in debt rescheduling agreements. The Bank had outstanding borrowings of $6,872.4 million as of December 31, 1989. The average cost of these outstanding borrowings, weighted by amount and after adjustment for swap transactions, was 7.22%. The Bank's publicly issued bonds are rated AAA by both Moody's and Standard & Poor's. It is the Bank's policy to diversify its borrowings by currency and market to avoid becoming too dependent on any one currency or market for funds.

Inter-American Development Bank

The Inter-American Development Bank is owned by the governments of 27 regional and 17 nonregional countries. Its purpose is to further the economic and social development of its regional developing member countries, individually and collectively.

The Bank operates under an agreement that became effective on December 30, 1959. Its present subscribed ordinary capital resources are $61 billion of which $3.3 billion is paid-in and $57.7 billion is callable. In 1987 the Bank merged its former interregional capital stock into its ordinary capital, thus leaving the Bank with one capital source.

The subscription of the U.S. government to the ordinary capital resources is $888 million paid-in and $11 billion subject to call.

The Bank separately administers a Fund for Special Operations amounting at present to the equivalent of $10 billion. Since 1976, the Bank has admitted 17 nonregional countries to membership. They are Austria, Belgium, Denmark, Finland, France, West Germany, Israel, Italy, Japan, the Netherlands, Norway, Portugal, Spain, Sweden, Switzerland, the United Kingdom, and Yugoslavia.

The Bank also administers funds entrusted to it by several member and nonmember countries. Foremost among these funds are the Social Progress Trust Fund, whose resources of $525 million provided by the U.S. government have already been committed in loans, and the $500 million Venezuelan Trust Fund established in 1975 under an agreement between the Bank and the Venezuelan Investment Fund to help finance projects in economically less-developed countries, those with limited markets, and those of intermediate development. In addition, the Bank administers other funds established by Argentina, Canada, West Germany, Japan, Norway, Spain, Sweden, Switzerland, the United Kingdom, the Vatican, and the InterGovernmental Committee for European Migration to help foster the economic and social development of the Bank's member countries in Latin America. As of the end of 1989, the Bank had extended loans, from all of its sources of funds, aggregating $41.6 billion, net of cancellations and exchange adjustments.

On December 31, 1989, the Bank had an outstanding funded debt of $14,630.1 million, of which $21.0 million equivalent is payable in Austrian schillings, $2,477.3 million in Deutsche marks, $119.7 million in European Currency Units (ECUs), $3,897.5 million in Japanese yen, $1,057.6 million in Netherlands guilders, $636.9 million in British pounds sterling, $2,609.3 million in Swiss francs, $2.4 million in Trinidad and Tobago dollars, and $3,808.4 million in United States dollars.

The proceeds have been incorporated into the ordinary capital resources available for lending. It is the Bank's present policy to limit the amount of its borrowings and guarantees chargeable to its capital resources, less the special reserves kept for meeting liabilities on such borrowings and guarantees, to the subscribed callable capital of the nonborrowing members of the Bank, which are the United States, Canada, and the nonregional members. Such subscriptions are callable only when required to meet the Bank's obligations on borrowings of funds for inclusion in the Bank's respective capital resources or on guarantees chargeable to such resources, and may be used only for these purposes.

Interest paid to nonresident aliens and foreign corporations on obligations of the Bank generally is not subject to federal tax because such income is treated as derived from sources outside the United States.

International Bank for Reconstruction and Development (World Bank)

The World Bank, officially known as the International Bank for Reconstruction and Development, began operations in 1946. It is the oldest and largest of the multilateral development banks. The Bank's capital stock is owned by its 152 member countries, of which the United States is the largest shareholder, owning 16.14% of its capital stock and 15.57% of the total voting power. (All numerical data for the World Bank are as of December 31, 1989, and are unaudited.) The uncalled portion ($18 billion) of the U.S. subscription to the capital of the Bank is an obligation backed by the full faith and credit of the U.S. government. The U.S. Secretary of the Treasury represents the United States on the Bank's Board of Governors, and the U.S. Executive Director is appointed by the President with the advice and consent of the Senate.

The principal purpose of the Bank is to promote the economic development of its member countries. The Bank provides loans and related technical assistance for specific projects and for programs of economic reform in developing member countries, aiming to promote long-term growth of international trade and improved standards of living.

Liquid Assets. The Bank holds about $18.7 billion of actively managed investments in primarily government and agency securities and deposits in selected banks, equivalent to 22% of outstanding debt and 51% of debt placed with nongovernmental investors maturing within five years. Its policy is to maintain liquidity at a level that gives it the flexibility to decide when, where and how much to borrow.

Loan Portfolio. The Bank's loans are made to, or are unconditionally guaranteed by, member countries. Total loans made since 1946 amount to $178.8 billion, of which $85 billion is disbursed and outstanding and $48.2 billion is approved but undisbursed. The balance has been repaid, sold to third parties or canceled prior to disbursement. Most loans are for specific projects; these projects must produce acceptable rates of return and be of high priority in a country's development program. Projects are supervised until physical completion. Project loans, typically disbursed over six to nine years, primarily finance goods and services procured under international competitive bidding and average 30–40% of estimated project costs. The balance comes principally from borrowers' resources and external loans. The Bank reviews supporting documentation for project expenditures. The Bank also makes loans to support the introduction of basic reforms in economic, financial, and other policies of key importance for the economic development of member countries. Structural and sectoral adjustment loans are targeted at 25% of current and projected commitments. The Bank does not reschedule interest or principal payments on its loans or participate in debt rescheduling agreements in respect of its loans.

Borrowings. The Bank has outstanding $85.5 billion in borrowings denominated in 23 currencies or currency units. These borrowings carried an average cost of 7.39% during the

144

six months ended December 31, 1989. In the United States, the Bank's medium- and long-term publicly issued notes and bonds are rated AAA by Moody's and Standard & Poor's. The Bank's policy is to diversify borrowings by currency, country, source and maturity to provide maximum funding flexibility.

Capital and Reserves (Equity). The Bank's equity is $16.1 billion, of which $6.1 billion is paid-in capital available for lending and $10.0 billion is reserves and unallocated net income. The Bank's debt/equity ratio is 5.3, and the ratio of disbursed and outstanding loans to equity is 5.3. Its ratio of reserves to outstanding loans, particpations, and guarantees was 10.2% on June 30, 1989. The Bank also has $112.7 billion in callable capital, which is an obligation of member governments that may only be called to meet the Bank's obligations for borrowings or guarantees. Callable capital may not be used for lending operations or administrative expenses; it protects the Bank's lenders.

The Bank's total authorized capital on December 31, 1989 was about $171 billion. This includes a $74.8 billion general capital increase that became effective in April 1988, 3% of which is to be paid-in. Shares are being allocated among existing members on a pro rata basis and subscriptions are being accepted until September 1993. Another $1.7 billion of shares was authorized to provide for the admission of new members.

Limit on Lending and Foreign Exchange Exposure. Under the Bank's charter, the total amount outstanding of direct loans, participations in loans, and callable guarantees ($85.0 billion) may not be increased to an amount exceeding 100% of the sum of paid-in and callable capital, reserves, and unallocated net income ($133 billion). On December 31, 1989 this percentage was 64%. The Bank matches its liabilities in each currency with assets in the same currency.

Profitability. The Bank has earned a profit every year since 1947. Net income for the last three fiscal years averaged $1,070 million. For the second half of 1989, net income was $566 million. The Bank's profitability results from (1) its low cost of available funds compared to return on earning assets (6.24%

and 8.31%, respectively, on average for the six months ended December 31, 1989); (2) its return on liquid assets (9.18% for the six months ended December 31, 1989); and (3) its policy of pricing loans to cover borrowing and administrative costs and to earn a reasonable return on equity (loan charges currently include variable interest semiannually reset by the Bank at a ½% spread over the cost of a pool of its borrowings and a commitment fee of ¼% on undisbursed loan balances).

Securities — Availability, Eligibility for Investment, Taxation. The World Bank issues in domestic and international public markets medium- and long-term debt securities denominated in U.S. dollars and 22 other currencies.

In the dollar markets the Bank issues Global Bonds, which are offered in the U.S. domestic, Eurodollar, and Japanese markets via an international syndicate engaged in worldwide distribution and trading of U.S. dollar bonds. These global issues are usually about $1.5 billion in size, are noncallable, and are included in government sponsored and agency sectors of major bond indexes. The bonds are issued to Federal Reserve book-entry accounts, and holders have a choice of clearing and settlement systems (Fedwire, Euro-clear or Cedel). A stream-lined settlement process is in place for transfers between Euro-clear/Cedel users and Fedwire users, with procedures available to reduce associated costs.

Also available in U.S. dollars are bonds and notes, many of them noncallable. In addition, a series of zero coupon bonds and a variety of synthetic and specially engineered securities are available. In the medium-term note market, the Bank offers noncallable continuously offered longer-term securities (COLTS) in maturities of three to 30 years or longer, with fixed or floating rates, zero coupons or deep discounts, in definitive or book-entry form. The Bank also offers discount notes in maturities up to one year. These trade in the U.S. agency discount note sector of the U.S. money market. All of the Bank's securities issued in the United States trade nationwide on the Federal Reserve communications system.

The Bank offers a variety of debt instruments in other important currencies, with substantial issuance particularly in Japanese yen, Deutsche marks and Swiss francs.

Global bonds and other World Bank bonds are:

- "Exempted securities" under the Securities Act of 1933 and the Securities Exchange Act of 1934.

- Eligible as security for public monies of the U.S. and as collateral for Treasury Tax and Loan Accounts at their face amount. They are also eligible as collateral at the discount window of Federal Reserve Banks.

- Assigned a 20% risk asset weighting (the same as U.S. government-sponsored agencies) on the books of banks under Federal Reserve, Federal Deposit Insurance Corporation and Comptroller of the Currency regulations.

- Eligible for investment by commercial banks, savings banks, insurance companies, pension funds, trustees and other fiduciaries under pertinent federal and state law.

Under the Internal Revenue Code of 1986, as amended, a United States citizen or resident alien individual, as well as a United States domestic corporation, trust or estate, will be taxable on interest accrued or received on World Bank bonds depending on their respective method of accounting. The Treasury Department has issued rulings to the Bank dated May 4, 1988 and May 5, 1989 which provide that interest paid on World Bank securities, including payments attributable to accrued original issue discount, constitutes income from sources outside the United States. The rulings further determined that neither the Bank nor an agent appointed by it as principal for the purpose of paying interest on securities issued by the Bank is required to withhold tax on interest paid by the Bank. Under the rulings, interest paid by the Bank ordinarily would not be subject to United States Federal income tax, including withholding tax, if paid to a nonresident alien individual (or foreign partnership, estate or trust) or to a foreign corporation, whether or not such person is engaged in trade or business in the United States. However, absent any special statutory or treaty exception, interest would be subject to United States Federal income tax in the following cases: (a) interest is derived by the person in the active conduct of a banking, financing or similar business within the United States or is received by a corporation whose principal business is trading in stock or securities for its own account, and in either case the interest is attributable to an office or other fixed place of business of the person within the United States or (b) the person is a foreign corporation taxable as an insurance company carrying on a United States insurance business and the interest is attributable to its United States business.

Outstanding Publicly Issued Bonds and Notes of the World Bank

(As of December 31, 1989)

Coupon range	Maturity range	Currency in which payable		Outstanding *
0–16⅝%	1990–perpetuity	United States	$	22,043,443,000
0–14⅛%	1992–1994	Australia	A$	720,000,000
6⅝–8¼%	1990–1999	Austria	As	2,742,760,000
7¼–10¼%	1994–1996	Belgium	BF	15,000,000,000
0–12¾%	1990–2083	Canada	Can $	1,825,000,000
10–10¼%	1994	Denmark	DKr	800,000,000
7½–11%	1993–1997	ECU	ECU	1,025,000,000
9⅝–10%	1992–1996	Finland	Fmk	1,500,000,000
8¾–10.90%	1993–1998	France	F	3,200,000,000
0–10½%	1990–2016	Germany	DM	15,125,000,000
10⅛%	1995	Hong Kong	HKD	500,000,000
10⅜–12½%	1992–1997	Italy	Lit	899,670,000,000
4¼–8¾%	1990–2001	Japan	¥	1,522,400,000,000
7–7½%	1991–1994	Kuwait	KD	32,000,000
7–8%	1990–1997	Luxembourg	LuxF	4,000,000,000
6¼–11¾%	1990–2006	Netherlands	f	4,910,000,000
9½–11%	1991–1995	Norway	NKr	500,000,000
10⅜–12⅜%	1994–1998	Spain	Ptas	65,000,000,000
6–10½%	1992–1993	Sweden	SKr	1,342,500,000
0–7¼%	1990–perpetuity	Switzerland	SwF	5,804,020,000
9¼–11½%	1991–2010	United Kingdom	£	1,275,000,000

* Zero coupon securities are included at their par amounts.

Dealer Volume and Positions in Treasury and Agency Securities

(Daily averages; in millions of dollars)

	Dealer transactions			Dealer positions		
	Treasury securities		Agency	Treasury securities		Agency
	Bills	Coupons	securities	Bills	Coupons	securities
1988						
Jan.	31,884	75,937	18,159	2,293	-15,579	23,943
Feb.	28,003	76,463	17,767	3,156	-13,390	26,654
Mar.	28,277	62,360	15,674	3,290	-13,428	28,780
Apr.	29,291	65,092	14,702	5,536	-20,641	26,622
May	30,344	74,854	15,180	86	-26,494	26,785
June	28,059	82,949	15,657	1,719	-26,910	29,417
July	29,150	62,955	14,276	-90	-31,230	30,070
Aug.	29,548	70,568	13,948	1,658	-33,439	27,844
Sept.	27,398	71,822	15,474	6,816	-33,575	29,023
Oct.	29,616	80,142	17,651	3,690	-29,500	30,169
Nov.	32,553	82,254	17,541	331	-24,415	32,162
Dec.	28,522	61,432	14,801	-1,623	-31,442	27,287
1989						
Jan.	31,908	75,183	19,428	-3,563	-28,734	26,690
Feb.	33,886	87,574	17,209	-3,914	-27,962	30,007
Mar.	30,718	70,389	15,417	-2,056	-30,257	30,770
Apr.	29,330	78,695	17,238	1,445	-24,037	28,602
May	29,373	91,518	16,303	1,162	-15,919	27,123
June	30,774	98,498	19,893	365	-6,656	29,467
July	29,041	85,087	20,849	1,339	-1,505	31,289
Aug.	30,810	88,905	19,032	10,292	-6,551	35,268
Sept.	27,685	72,591	19,173	20,415	-8,246	36,097
Oct.	35,904	94,899	20,987	19,152	-8,512	36,270
Nov.	32,611	83,051	20,012	22,515	-5,376	35,453
Dec.	26,756	57,397	17,939	26,823	-1,599	35,928

Source: Federal Reserve Bulletin.

149

Yields on Three-Month Money Market Instruments

% (Weekly averages; all yields on 360-day coupon equivalent basis)

Certificates of Deposit

Commercial Paper

Treasury Bills

10.5

9.5

8.5

7.5

6.5

5.5

1988

1989

1990

Money Market Instruments

Bankers' Acceptances

A bankers' acceptance is a unique credit instrument used to finance both domestic and international self-liquidating transactions. By definition, it is "... a draft or bill of exchange, whether payable in the United States or abroad and whether payable in dollars or some other money, accepted by a bank or trust company, or a firm, company, or corporation engaged generally in the business of granting bankers' acceptance credits."[1]

Creation and Life of an Acceptance

Consider a coffee processor in the United States who wishes to finance the importation of Colombian coffee on an acceptance basis. The American importer, after negotiating with the exporter in Colombia, arranges for his American commercial bank to issue an irrevocable letter of credit in favor of the exporter. The letter of credit specifies the details of the shipment and states that the Colombian exporter may draw a time draft for a certain amount on the American bank. The Colombian exporter, in conformity with the terms of the letter of credit, draws a draft on the American bank and negotiates the draft with his local bank, receiving immediate payment. The Colombian bank then forwards the draft to the United States for presentation to the bank that issued the letter of credit. This bank stamps the draft "accepted," thus incurring an obligation to pay the draft at maturity. An acceptance has been created.

The new acceptance typically is discounted for the Colombian bank by the accepting bank and the proceeds credited to the account of the Colombian bank. The accepting bank in turn may either sell the acceptance to a dealer or hold it in its own portfolio. Whatever the case, the shipping documents are

---

[1] Advances and Discounts by Federal Reserve Banks, Regulation A, Board of Governors of the Federal Reserve System, p. 5.

released to the American importer against a trust receipt, thus allowing the importer to process and sell the coffee. The importer is obligated to deposit the proceeds of the coffee sales at the accepting bank in time to honor the acceptance. At maturity, the acceptance is presented for payment by its owner and the transaction is completed.

The cost of acceptance financing is the sum of the discount charged when the acceptance is discounted and the commission paid to the accepting bank. This cost may be paid by either of the commercial parties to the transaction, in accordance with the agreement made with the accepting bank.

Acceptances as an Investment

From the standpoint of security, a bankers' acceptance is an irrevocable primary obligation of the accepting bank, and a contingent obligation of the drawer and of any endorsers whose names appear upon it. The bank is protected by its customer's agreement to provide good funds by the time the acceptance matures and generally also by the pledge of documents such as invoices, bills of lading, independent warehouse or terminal receipts, trust receipts, and other papers evidencing ownership and insurance of the goods financed. In 76 years of usage in the United States, the bankers' acceptance has come through war and economic depression with no known principal loss to investors. Courts have held that the letter of credit agreement, from inception to conclusion, is based on the principle that the accepting bank holds the agreement not for its own benefit or that of its general creditors, but in trust for the holder of the acceptance. The landmark decision on this subject involved the failure of the Bank of the United States in New York in December 1930, with 403 acceptances outstanding.[2]

Acceptances with original maturities of 180 days or less and with 90 or fewer days remaining to maturity, which are owned by a member bank and which meet the other requirements of

---

[2] *Bank of the United States vs. Seltzer,* App. Div. 225, 251 N.Y. Supp. 637 (1937).

eligibility, are eligible collateral for borrowing from the Federal Reserve Banks.[3]

The gain or income realized on bankers' acceptances is subject to U.S. income tax for American investors, but generally is exempt when owned by foreign investors.

Historical Background

On September 14, 1914, shortly after the passage of the Federal Reserve Act, the National City Bank of New York accepted the first draft in the amount of $27,361.90.[4] An early peak in the volume outstanding of $1,732 million was reached in 1929. From then until the middle of World War II, the volume shrank to a low of $117 million in 1943. In the postwar years, with the tremendous expansion of international trade, acceptance volume once again grew rapidly, with the highest outstandings reaching $82.0 billion in June of 1984. Since that time overall outstandings have decreased to a current level of $53.8 billion as of April 1990.

The Dealer Market

Shortly after the enabling legislation provided by the Federal Reserve Act, the major banks encouraged the formation of acceptance dealers to provide a market for accepted drafts. The First Boston Corporation (then The First National Corporation, a wholly owned subsidiary of The First National Bank of Boston) was founded in 1918 and began dealing in acceptances and issuing letters of credit.

Bankers' acceptances are bought and sold at yields comparable to those on other actively traded money market instruments. The Federal Reserve is a frequent participant in the market on behalf of its foreign customers. Its earlier practice of buying acceptances for its own account was ended in 1977, and as of July 2, 1984, the Federal Reserve discontinued use of

[3] Detailed criteria as to such eligibility may be found in the Summer 1981 issue of the *Quarterly Review* of the Federal Reserve Bank of New York.

[4] *Bankers' Acceptance Volume and Rates in the Discount Money Markets* (New York, American Acceptance Council, 1928), p. 7.

repurchase agreements on bankers' acceptances in its open market operations.

Acceptances are available in a wide variety of principal amounts. Since acceptance dealers carry a stock of drafts purchased from the many prime commercial banks doing international business, acceptances are usually available in principal amounts suitable for both large and small investments and with a wide variety of maturity dates.

Foreign Acceptances

Foreign acceptances are U.S. dollar-denominated acceptances backed by the credit of foreign banks or agencies domiciled in the United States. Foreign acceptances have generally traded at a yield premium over acceptances issued by domestic banks. Historical spreads have ranged from a high of 100–125 basis points when the market was just getting established to the present yield spread of about five basis points, depending on market conditions. Many foreign banks of high quality, however, trade as well as or better than U.S. banks. Foreign bankers' acceptances are similar to domestic BAs in many respects. They face the same Federal Reserve eligibility requirements; usually have comparable maturity, settlement date, and delivery characteristics; have liquidity provided by an active secondary market; and have comparable safety, with no known principal loss to investors.

Foreign acceptances (primarily of Japanese banks) now account for more than half of the acceptances outstanding. Other foreign banks, realizing the advantages and profitability of the BA market, have also taken advantage of increased investor receptivity and have participated in this market. In addition to Japanese banks, French, English, German, Dutch, Swiss, Australian, and Canadian banks are now active, to varying degrees, in the foreign acceptance market.

Several primary dealers, including First Boston, are involved in the secondary trading of these foreign acceptances. The top 12 Japanese banks constitute what is called the "run" and all other foreign acceptances trade at varying spreads to the "run." As of

154

April 1990, there were approximately $34.2 billion foreign BAs outstanding, including $29.5 billion Japanese acceptances.

Finance Bills

Finance bills, or working capital acceptances, are unlike the usual acceptances, as there is no underlying collateral. Rather, a draft to finance general business activity is accepted by a bank which assumes the obligation to make payment at maturity. Once widely available, working capital acceptances have diminished sharply since the Federal Reserve imposed reserve requirements in mid-1973 on bank liabilities under such arrangements. These acceptances are not acceptable for discount or purchase by the Federal Reserve but are backed by the accepting bank's unconditional obligation to pay the acceptance at maturity.

Investment Yields and Computations

Bankers' acceptances are quoted, bought and sold on a discount basis, as are Treasury bills (see page 67).

Certificates of Deposit

Certificates of deposit, familiarly known as CDs, are negotiable certificates in denominations of $100,000 or more. They are issued by commercial banks and thrift institutions against funds deposited for specified periods of seven days or longer and earn specified rates of interest.

In early 1961, major New York commercial banks began to issue such interest-bearing negotiable certificates to domestic business corporations. Previously, only nonnegotiable certificates had been issued, but apparently were not actively solicited. Banks in other cities soon followed suit.

Negotiable certificates have developed into an important money market instrument. They give banks an opportunity to compete for corporate and other funds that in the past were invested in Treasury bills and other types of short-term marketable paper. They give corporations and others another money market instrument to invest in at competitive rates. CDs now bear rates of interest in line with money market rates at the time of issuance.

Major banks also issue variable-rate CDs with maturities of up to five years. The rate, which is adjusted every 30, 90, or 180 days, usually includes a fixed spread over or under the composite secondary market rate for major bank CDs, as compiled and published by the Federal Reserve Bank of New York. The federal funds, prime, and the London interbank rate are sometimes used as benchmark rates.

Issuing banks may not purchase their own certificates of deposit, nor may issuers redeem their outstanding certificates prior to maturity. Banks apparently will not lend funds against their own certificates, at least partly because in the event of default on the loan the bank might become the owner of the certificate, in effect redeeming it prior to maturity.

Unless otherwise agreed upon, certificates bought or sold in the secondary market are deliverable in New York on the business day following the date of the transaction. Payment is made in federal funds. CDs are issued in denominations from $100,000 to $1,000,000. The normal round-lot trading unit is $5,000,000. On CDs with maturities of up to one year, interest is calculated on a 360-day basis and is paid at maturity.

A market in CDs is maintained by First Boston and other dealers at rates related to those on bankers' acceptances, commercial paper, Treasury bills, and other short-term money market instruments. Trading volume in domestic bank CDs by dealers reporting to the Federal Reserve Bank of New York averaged about $2.8 billion daily in 1989.

Most CDs are issued for terms of a year or less. The minimum maturity permitted is seven days and there is no limit on the maximum maturity banks are permitted to offer.

Term CDs are those issued with a maturity in excess of one year. They normally pay interest semiannually.

Deposit Notes

Deposit notes, also referred to as medium-term deposit notes or certificate of deposit (CD) notes, are medium-term obligations issued by domestic banks (not bank holding companies) and foreign banks via their U.S. branches. Deposit notes are a hybrid of traditional bank term CDs and intermediate-term corporate bonds. They are senior to all obligations of the issuing bank, except deposit obligations — with which they are pari passu. Deposit notes issued by domestic banks are FDIC insured up to $100,000 per account. Because deposit notes of foreign banks are issued by their U.S. branches, they are obligations of the bank, as well as the branch. The market for deposit notes is expanding. In 1986, $3.6 billion of deposit note programs were established, while in 1989, $41.3 billion were established.

Deposit notes may be issued in a regular periodic offering program where the bank may from time to time post and issue a small amount of deposit notes to specific maturities. Deposit notes also may be offered daily. Offering levels are quoted either at a spread over Treasuries or floating-rate indices or at an absolute rate.

A deposit note program provides the maximum flexibility in accessing all maturities from 18 months to 30 years. There are reserve requirements for maturities 18 months and shorter. Deposit note programs allow issuers to take advantage of financing windows or reverse inquiry opportunities and offer a means to maximize cost-effective funding through derivative products (e.g., swaps, caps, futures and options). Deposit notes are exempt from registration with the Securities and Exchange Commission.

In addition to the traditional buyers of CDs such as money market funds, deposit notes are purchased by corporate bond buyers such as bank trust departments, insurance companies, investment advisers, corporations and pension funds. Certain Federal Home Loan Boards allow thrifts to purchase deposit notes for their liquidity portfolios.

Deposit note programs allow the investor to select daily from a wide range of credits, maturities and amounts, in either fixed-rate or floating-rate form, to fill targeted investment requirements for managed portfolios. Portfolio managers involved in rededication, in particular, find deposit note programs attractive because they represent assets that can be tailored to specific needs. First Boston is active as an agent for many issuing bank clients and as a major market maker in secondary trading of deposit notes.

Eurodollar CDs

Eurodollar CDs are negotiable dollar-denominated certificates of deposit issued by foreign (mainly London) branches of major American and foreign commercial banks.

Eurodollar CDs were originally introduced in 1966 as a marketable alternative to Eurodollar time deposits. Eurodollar CDs have the advantage of a secondary market which makes them more attractive to investors. The liquidity also allows banks to issue CDs at a rate slightly below the rates offered on time deposits of similar maturities. Initially Eurodollar CDs grew rapidly due to the higher yields the London branches of U.S. banks were able to offer investors, as compared with their home offices whose rates were then restricted by Regulation Q. Regulation Q was abolished in the early 1970s, but somewhat higher rates are still available because reserve requirements are levied on domestic but not offshore CDs and because of a perceived political risk in the offshore origination.

Recent years have seen an expansion in the issuance of Eurodollar CDs by smaller U.S. banks, major Canadian institutions, the top "clearing banks" of the United Kingdom, and, in particular, the largest Japanese banks. The CDs of these issuers trade well in the secondary market but generally must offer a yield premium relative to the top U.S. banks. The secondary market for Japanese paper rivals the liquidity of the U.S. Eurodollar CD market.

Normally, Eurodollar CDs are delivered in London on the second business day following the transaction, with payment in

New York in clearinghouse funds. Delivery and payment are not simultaneous as with other money market instruments due to the time difference between London and New York. The separate transfer of the CDs and cash is accomplished through the use of "agreements of understanding" that guarantee the payment in New York following delivery earlier in the day in London.

Floating-Rate CDs (FRCDs) were first issued in 1977. Essentially, these are medium-term CDs with maturities most often ranging from 18 months plus one day to five years. They can be issued in original denominations as small as $5,000,000 and can range up to more than $100,000,000. Incremental denominations are usually $1,000,000. Coupons are adjusted periodically according to a predetermined formula and generally carry a given premium over a chosen interest rate index. Coupons have been pegged to a one-, two-, three-, or six-month London interbank offered rate (LIBOR); the cost of funds index; a three- or six-month Treasury bill rate; the prime rate; a one-, three- or six–month CD composite rate; a one-, two-, or three-month commercial paper rate; and the daily or weekly federal funds rate. Interest on floating-rate CDs may be paid monthly, quarterly, or semiannually.

FRCDs can be issued by money center, regional, or foreign banks domiciled in the U.S. (Yankee banks) in either domestic or European markets. As a bank deposit, an FRCD is an obligation that is senior to holding company notes, and thereby offers investors greater credit protection. Moody's and S&P rate the long-term and short-term deposits of the aforementioned banks. The secondary market liquidity is excellent.

Yankee CDs

Yankee CDs are U.S. dollar-denominated CDs issued by foreign banks domiciled in the United States. They have maturities of seven days or longer and earn specified rates of interest. Maturities of 18 months or less are subject to reserve requirements set by the Federal Reserve. Japanese, Canadian, British, German, and Dutch banks are active participants.

Interest on maturities of one year or less is usually paid at maturity. Term Yankee CDs, usually with maturities of two to five years, pay interest either annually or semiannually.

Computation of Proceeds

For CDs with original maturities of one year or less, interest is normally calculated for the actual number of days held, on a 360-day per year basis, and paid at maturity. The dollar price is computed as shown below.

Example: Find the dollar price on a $1,000,000, 8.25%, 180-day certificate sold 45 days before the redemption date on an 8.00% basis.

(1) Compute gross proceeds on redemption date at issue rate. A = (a) + (b)	(a) Interest, 180 days at 8.25% $82,500 x $\frac{180}{360}$	= $ 41,250.00
	(b) Principal	1,000,000.00
	Gross proceeds at redemption	A = $1,041,250.00
(2) Compute accrued interest due seller at issue rate (B).	Interest for 135 days at 8.25% due seller $82,500 x $\frac{135}{360}$ =	B = $ 30,937.50
(3) Compute gross sales proceeds. C = A ÷ (c)	(c) = $1 + (8.00\% x \frac{45}{360})$ =	1.01
	Gross sales proceeds $\frac{\$1,041,250}{1.01}$	C = $1,030,940.59
(4) Compute principal dollar amount. D = C - B	Gross sales proceeds less interest due seller	$1,030,940.59 - 30,937.50
	Principal dollar amount (per $ million	D = $1,000,003.09
(5) Compute dollar price. E = D ÷ 10,000	Dollar price (per $100)	E = $ 100.000309

For Fixed-Rate Term CDs of over one year calculating proceeds is somewhat more complex than for short-term CDs. However, once the concept of a repeated rediscounting of maturity proceeds is grasped, the mechanics are fairly simple.

The next example follows the usual convention in the United States of semiannual interest payments. In the Eurodollar CD market, interest payments are usually made annually on the anniversary date of the issue. Those calculations are the same as shown below, but whole years (365 or 366 days) must be substituted for the half-years used here.

Example: Find the net proceeds on a $1,000,000 CD with an original maturity of five years and a coupon of 8.25% which is sold at a yield of 8.00% after 120 days.

(1) First calculate the 10 semiannual interest payments:

(coupon ÷100) × (principal) × (number of days in coupon period÷360)

Semiannual interest payments are:

Coupon period		
1 (182 days)		$41,708.33
2 (183 days)		41,937.50
3 (182 days)		41,708.33
4 (183 days)		41,937.50
5 (182 days)		41,708.33
6 (183 days)		41,937.50
7 (183 days — leap year)		41,937.50
8 (183 days)		41,937.50
9 (182 days)		41,708.33
10 (183 days)		41,937.50

Note: Semiannual coupon periods can vary from 181 to 184 days, depending on maturity and coupon dates.

(2) Maturity proceeds = principal + final interest payment =
$1,000,000 + $41,937.50 = $1,041,937.50

(3) Discount maturity proceeds as follows:

Coupon period 10 (183 days at 8.00%)
$$(\$1,041,937.50) \div \left(1+\frac{8.00\times183}{100\times360}\right) = \$1,001,221.17$$

Coupon period 9 (182 days at 8.00%)
$$(\$1,001,221.17+41,708.33) \div \left(1+\frac{8.00\times182}{100\times360}\right) = \$1,002,388.46$$

Coupon period 8 (183 days at 8.00%)
$$(\$1,002,388.46+41,937.50) \div \left(1+\frac{8.00\times183}{100\times360}\right) = \$1,003,516.30$$

Coupon period 7 (183 days at 8.00%)
$$(\$1,003,516.30+41,937.50) \div \left(1+\frac{8.00\times183}{100\times360}\right) = \$1,004,600.06$$

Coupon period 6 (183 days at 8.00%)
$$(\$1,004,600.06+41,937.50) \div \left(1+\frac{8.00\times183}{100\times360}\right) = \$1,005,641.47$$

Coupon period 5 (182 days at 8.00%)
$$(\$1,005,641.47+41,708.33) \div \left(1+\frac{8.00\times182}{100\times360}\right) = \$1,006,636.92$$

Coupon period 4 (183 days at 8.00%)
$$(\$1,006,636.92+41,937.50) \div \left(1+\frac{8.00\times183}{100\times360}\right) = \$1,007,598.75$$

Coupon period 3 (182 days at 8.00%)
$$(\$1,007,598.75+41,708.33) \div \left(1+\frac{8.00\times182}{100\times360}\right) = \$1,008,518.12$$

Coupon period 2 (183 days at 8.00%)
$$(\$1,008,518.12+41,937.50) \div \left(1+\frac{8.00\times183}{100\times360}\right) = \$1,009,406.43$$

Discount for 62 days (182 days less 120 days held) of 1st coupon period at 8.00%
$$(\$1,009,406.43+41,708.33) \div \left(1+\frac{8.00\times62}{100\times360}\right) = \$1,036,829.55$$

Net proceeds $= \$1,036,829.55$

For Floating-Rate CDs (FRCDs). The FRCD is traded on a dollar price rather than a yield to maturity basis.

To calculate the proceeds on a FRCD, the following information must be supplied:

a. The face value of the CD
b. The coupon for the present interest period
c. The number of days from last interest date to value date
d. Dollar price

Net proceeds can then be calculated using the following formula:

Net proceeds = proceeds + accrued interest

Proceeds = (a × d) ÷ 100

Accrued interest = (a× b × c) ÷ (360 × 100)

Example: A $1,000,000 FRCD originally issued for three years is bought with 15 months to run. Last interest date was 90 days prior to value date. Present coupon is 8.25%, and the purchase is at a dollar price of 99¾.

$$\text{Proceeds} = \frac{\$1,000,000 \times 99.75}{100} = \$997,500.00$$

$$\text{Accrued interest} = \frac{\$1,000,000 \times 8.25 \times 90}{360 \times 100} = \$20,625.00$$

Net proceeds = $997,500.00 + $20,625.00 = $1,018,125.00

Funds Raised in Credit Markets

(In billions of dollars)

	Net amount raised				Year-end level
	1986	1987	1988	1989	1989
Total	1,250.3	1,027.5	890.0	843.8	16,677.4
Corporate equities, market value	-68.5	-57.3	-117.2	-99.0	3,763.7
Investment company shares	159.0	71.6	-0.7	38.2	548.0
Debt instruments	1,159.8	1,013.2	1,007.9	904.7	12,365.7
U.S. Government securities	403.4	331.5	277.2	290.2	3,501.3
Treasury issues	214.7	143.4	140.0	150.0	2,245.2
Savings bonds	13.6	7.8	8.5	8.2	117.7
Sponsored agency issues	15.2	30.2	44.9	25.0	373.1
Mortgage pool securities [1]	173.1	156.4	74.9	115.4	860.7
State and local obligations	22.7	34.1	34.0	24.2	784.0
Corporate bonds	207.3	186.3	172.7	157.9	1,571.3
Foreign bonds	3.1	7.4	6.9	5.1	94.3
Open market paper	26.4	33.2	74.9	65.3	584.2
Commercial paper	32.2	26.8	78.5	66.1	523.4
Bankers' acceptances	-5.9	6.4	-3.6	-0.8	60.8
U.S. Government loans	9.0	-3.0	-8.8	-1.6	155.9
Sponsored credit agency loans	19.2	27.3	21.9	-3.4	188.1
Bank business loans	69.7	3.8	38.0	35.3	803.6
Consumer credit	58.0	32.9	51.1	46.1	797.9
Other loans	56.1	66.5	53.4	30.2	820.8
Mortgages	316.4	324.9	306.7	255.4	3,502.6
Residential	218.7	234.9	231.0	196.1	2,370.1
Commercial	73.7	71.9	61.0	43.8	742.5
Farm	-9.5	-6.4	-2.1	-0.3	86.5

Source: Federal Reserve Board, Flow of Funds Accounts.

[1] GNMA, FNMA, FHLMC, and FmHA pools. Excludes Federal Financing Bank holdings of pool securities.

"Commercial paper" is the market name for the short-term unsecured promissory notes issued by various economic entities in the open market to finance certain short-term credit needs. The Securities Act of 1933 contains several provisions that exempt commercial paper from the registration requirements of the Securities and Exchange Commission. The most commonly used exemption, called 3(a)3, applies to commercial paper sold with maturities not exceeding nine months, the proceeds of that are used to finance current transactions. Commercial paper ranks equally with the other unsecured debt of a borrower.

There are approximately 2,500 rated commercial paper programs. These represent a variety of industrial companies, utilities, commercial bank holding companies, finance companies, insurance companies, savings and loan associations, and a growing number of foreign corporations and government bodies. Traditionally, commercial paper—the lowest-cost source of short-term dollars—has been used to fund seasonal working capital requirements. However, more and more issuers use commercial paper in new ways: to provide the floating-rate component of an interest rate swap, the dollar-based component of a currency swap, or bridge financing for an acquisition. The institutional market for commercial paper is open only to borrowers with substantial liquidity and strong credit standing.

Commercial paper is generally backed by unused bank credit lines to repay the notes in the event the issuer is unable to roll the paper over in the market at maturity. Virtually all paper issued through dealers is rated by at least one of the independent rating agencies such as Moody's Investors Service, Inc. or Standard & Poor's Corp. Buyers of commercial paper include business corporations, insurance companies, public entities, commercial bank trust departments, mutual funds, and pension funds.

The volume of commercial paper outstanding has expanded from $33 billion in December 1970 to $545 billion in April

1990. Of the April 1990 outstandings, about $214 billion consisted of paper sold directly to investors, mainly by major finance companies and banks. The remainder, approximately $331 billion, consisted of paper sold through commercial paper dealers on behalf of a widely diversified group of issuers. First Boston is a major commercial paper dealer.

Commercial paper purchased from dealers such as First Boston is usually bought and sold on a discount basis, figured for the actual number of days to maturity on a 360-day basis, in the same manner as bankers' acceptances. Interest-bearing commercial paper also is available. Maturities range from one to 270 days.

The minimum round-lot transaction is $100,000, although some issuers sell commercial paper in denominations as small as $25,000. The notes are normally issued in bearer form. Payment at maturity is effected by presentation to the bank designated as paying agent on the face of the note.

Most issuers of commercial paper have designated New York City banks as issuing/paying agents, and trading is customarily for New York delivery with settlement on the same day in federal funds. State and local governments issue tax-exempt short-term notes that resemble commercial paper. In most respects this paper is comparable to its taxable counterpart except for the exemption of interest from federal income taxes, therefore it trades at a lower yield.

Repurchase and Reverse Repurchase Agreements

A repurchase agreement consists of two simultaneous transactions. One is the purchase of securities (collateral) by an investor from a bank or dealer. The other is the commitment by the bank or dealer to repurchase the securities at the same price at some mutually agreed future date. The collateral used is most frequently Treasury, mortgage-backed or other agency securities, but may also include money market instruments or corporate securities.

166

This dual transaction, which the market has dubbed a "repo" or simply an "RP" has developed into a meaningful money market instrument in its own right. It provides banks and dealers with an attractive alternative for financing positions, and it provides investors who want a short-term investment with a money market instrument that can be tailored to their exact maturity needs.

Early in their development, RPs were written mainly overnight or for very short terms. However, the market has now expanded so that RPs can be executed for maturities of between one day and one year (occasionally longer under special circumstances). The vast majority of RPs mature in three months or less. One-day transactions are called overnight RPs; longer transactions are called term RPs.

Participants in the long-term RP market include all major classes of private and government institutions who may have lendable collateral or excess investable funds. The long-term RP is frequently employed to increase interest return. For example, when the yield curve was favorable, customers were able to "reverse" Treasury or GNMA securities to a dealer and reinvest the proceeds in higher yielding CDs.

The RP rate is the rate of interest that the dealer pays the investor (lender) for the use of his funds. The RP typically trades· at high yields relative to other money market instruments. Rates depend on the type of collateral. In general, the higher the credit quality and the easier the security is to deliver and hold (wireable versus physical, semiannual coupon versus monthly pay), the lower the RP rate. Rates also depend on whether the collateral is generic or special. Collateral becomes special when it is in high demand by government securities dealers to make deliveries to customers. The interest rate dealers are willing to accept when bidding on these issues can be several hundred basis points less than the rate for generic collateral.

The principal upon which interest is paid is based on the price assigned to the collateral at the time of the transaction. The purchaser does not care what the market price of the security is, whether it goes up or down, or what coupon or maturity the security carries. The market risk of the collateral is completely borne by the seller. If market prices go down during the life of the RP so that the collateral is worth less than the principal amount of the trade, the purchaser is exposed should the seller default, file for bankruptcy, or be placed in receivership by the applicable regulatory authority. The purchaser would require that the transaction be marked to market, either through a repricing (return of cash in excess of the now lower market value of the collateral) or through the delivery of additional collateral. The seller would have similar remedies, should market prices rise.

Customarily, collateral is priced at some discount from current market value in order to provide a margin of protection against price declines which might occur over the term of the RP. A typical margin would be between 1% and 3% of the trade principal, although "haircuts" required on reverse RP transactions may be substantially higher. If CDs are the collateral, they are usually priced at par.

There are several delivery alternatives for the RP collateral:

- Delivery: The seller delivers the securities to the purchaser versus the principal of the trade. At the maturity of the RP, the purchaser delivers the securities back versus the trade principal and financing interest.

- Safekeeping: The seller holds the securities for the purchaser. The purchaser receives confirmations for the transaction, but the collateral is held in a segregated customer account by the seller.

- Third Party: Collateral is delivered to the purchaser's account at the seller's clearing bank. Since collateral moves within the bank, this arrangement has the operational advantages of safekeeping while still accomplishing delivery.

Securities dealers also often borrow the securities they need to make deliveries. These loans are collateralized by other securities of equal value or cash. If the loan is collateralized by securities, the borrower pays the lender a fee. If collateralized by cash, the borrower receives a below market interest rate on the money. The fee or rate differential is determined by how special the security is (its relative availability), but is currently at least 30 basis points. Securities loans are generally done on an open basis (terminable at the option of the lender), but may have specific maturities.

The smallest customary amount of an RP is $1 million, and round lots are $25 million. As with other money market instruments, interest is calculated on a 360-day year, and transactions are settled in federal funds.

Reverse repurchase agreements, technically called matched sales/purchase agreements, are essentially the mirror image of RPs. In this instance, the investor is the owner of the collateral, and the bank or dealer is the lender of money. All other aspects remain similar to the RP.

Short-Term Tax-Exempt Notes and "Commercial Paper"

Short-term tax-exempt notes are money market instruments that generally have maturities of less than one year. The bulk of these notes are obligations issued by states, municipalities, or other public agencies in anticipation of tax revenues or federal grants, or as interim financing prior to a bond sale. Interest paid on these securities is exempt from federal income tax. The notes are backed by the credit of the issuing body pursuant to borrowing authority granted by the voters. The credit of the issuer is generally the sole guarantee. Increasingly, issuers are employing "credit enhancements" such as third party insurance and bank letters of credit. Tax-exempt notes sell at yields that depend on current money market and municipal market rates and the credit ratings of the issuer as assessed by the various rating agencies (Moody's, Standard & Poor's, or Fitch). The yield may be further affected by whether the securities are tax or revenue anticipation notes or bond anticipation notes (TANs, RANs, or BANs, respectively).

In the primary new-issues market, notes vary in maturity from one month to the more common six-month and one-year maturities. Occasionally, longer maturities of up to several years are issued and may or may not be coupon bearing. During 1989, according to *The Bond Buyer*, a total of $27.7 billion of short-term obligations was sold.

The general obligation short-term notes of state and local governments are legal investments for commercial banks and most other classes of investors. Since state laws vary, they should be consulted for applicability in particular cases.

Tax-exempt "commercial paper" is becoming an increasingly important component of the short-term market. Like taxable paper, it provides both issuer and buyer with a highly flexible instrument that typically has maturities ranging from one to 60 days and may be "rolled" or renegotiated at maturity for a new period.

The proceeds from the sale of tax-exempt "commercial paper" are typically used for interim financing or to provide working capital during seasonal shortfalls in taxes or revenues. Tax-exempt paper is rated like other commercial paper and prices are competitive with other short-term notes.

Two other recently developed techniques for providing issuers with access to the short-term tax-exempt market are variable-rate demand notes and adjustable rate "put" bonds. These securities have been particularly attractive to tax-exempt money market mutual funds because of their frequent rate adjustments that guarantee current market rates of return, put options with notice of as little as one week or less, and superior credit quality resulting from various credit enhancements. Issuers have used the proceeds from the sale of such securities in place of conventional sources of short-term credit for bridging seasonal cash flow shortfalls, as well as for providing alternative permanent financing (at short-term rates) for public construction projects.

In most instances, short-term notes and "commercial paper" of states, municipalities or local agencies are also exempt from state and local income tax in the state of issuance, thus providing a multiple exemption to residents of those states. An exemption from all state income taxes also applies to notes of issuers in Puerto Rico, the Virgin Islands, Guam, and the various American Indian nations.

Short-term tax-exempt notes and "commercial paper" are both issued in fully negotiable bearer form. (The registration requirement that applies to tax-exempt obligations generally does not apply to obligations that have a maturity at issue of not more than one year.) Denominations for notes usually range from $5,000 to $1,000,000 at the option of the underwriter or the issuer, while for paper the usual minimum denomination is $100,000. Principal and interest are paid at maturity (with the exception of maturities longer than one year, which may be coupon bearing) at the paying agency designated on the note – a bank or trust company selected by the initial underwriter or designated by the issuer. Transactions are usually in federal funds. Interest is generally computed on the basis of a 30-day month or 360-day year, but occasionally on the actual number of days in relation to 365 days. Initial delivery is normally on the date of issue for newly auctioned notes. In the secondary market, regular delivery is normally five days, but trading for same- or next-day delivery is quite common.

Eurocurrency Deposits

A Eurocurrency deposit is created when a banking office in one country accepts a deposit denominated in the currency of another. The Eurocurrency deposit is then typically loaned or redeposited by the receiving bank (which may be a foreign branch of an American bank) through the mechanism of the Eurocurrency market. This market had its beginnings in the late 1950s. By December 1989, total Eurocurrency liabilities were approximately $3.7 trillion. The part of the Eurocurrency market denominated in dollars is referred to as the Eurodollar market.

The principal instrument of the Eurocurrency market is the nonnegotiable time deposit ("Depo"). Other instruments include certificates of deposit, bankers' acceptances, letters of credit, commercial paper, and bank loans of various maturities. In a majority of cases, of course, the borrower is a bank receiving a time deposit rather than borrowing in the conventional sense.

A bank, corporation, political entity, etc., owning foreign currency in excess of working balances may seek to deposit these funds on a fixed-term basis, at the best rate available from those depositaries whose standing is acceptable to the lender. When mutually satisfactory terms are arranged, the borrower and the lender simply exchange written confirmations detailing the terms of the deposit and acknowledging the transfer of funds. The commonly accepted minimum deposit amount is one million currency units. No negotiable instrument is created, mainly because of legal obstacles to the issuance and clearance of negotiable instruments. Should the lender need short-term funds prior to the maturity of the deposit, he simply becomes a borrower for the required period by initiating another transaction in the Eurocurrency market. If the deposit is for a term of one year or less, interest is normally paid at maturity. Semiannual or annual, and occasionally quarterly, interest is paid on deposits of more than one year. The most frequently quoted rate at which these deposits are made among the leading international banks is the London interbank offered rate (LIBOR). The most common maturities available in the deposit market are one, two, three, six, and twelve months, plus the "short dates" used by banks to balance their positions. Short dates are deposits of fixed maturities such as two-, seven-, and occasionally 14-day "fix" and "over weekend," or on a quasi-demand basis such as 48-hour "notice." Deposit rates are usually fixed, but on longer term deposits they may be floating; that is, the rate may be reset periodically at a fixed spread to a certain quoted interbank short-term rate.

The Eurocurrency market in no way resembles a central marketplace. In recent years, the integration of diverse capital markets has led to the development of active Eurocurrency markets in major cities all over the world. Transactions are negotiated by telex, cable, and telephone. Trading is normally done for settlement on the second business day following the trade date. The "short dates" are frequently traded for settlement on the same day. Same-day contracts are usually arranged by 12:00 noon London time with funds transferred by 3:20 p.m., or earlier in the case of other European money centers. Funds are transferred either directly through correspondent banks in the home country of the relevant currency or, according to the broker's instructions, against delivery of the required instrument. All terms of the transaction (amount, maturity, rate, currency, provisions for the payment of interest and principal, commission, etc.) are agreed upon at the time the trade is executed and are confirmed in writing by the broker.

Foreign Currency Hedged Investments (Covered Interest Arbitrage)

Certain national and regional government securities, bank certificates of deposit, and other money market instruments can provide attractive fixed-rate short-term yields for multinational companies that choose to diversify investments outside their home currency. International currency "hedged paper" is readily available denominated in several foreign currencies, including the British pound, Canadian dollar, German mark, Japanese yen, and Swiss franc.

For investors in foreign securities to obtain a known fixed-rate, short-term yield in their own currency, they must protect against the possibility that exchange rates may change prior to maturity. Such protection, or "hedging," is arranged by simultaneously purchasing a foreign security and establishing a currency hedge position in the forward market or the futures market.

The forward market is an extension of the Eurocurrency market described in the previous section. Forwards are traded through a worldwide interbank market where investors can reduce foreign exchange exposure by committing to convert a specified amount of currency at a set exchange rate on an agreed upon date in the future. Since all the terms of a forward market transaction are negotiated when the trade is executed, investors may establish a hedge which exactly matches the amount and maturity date of the foreign security.

The futures markets are confined to recognized exchanges that list standardized contracts through which investors agree to exchange a specific amount of currency on a set date in the future. Final settlement dates are limited to certain maturities, typically following a March, June, September, December schedule. Due to the standardized contract specifications established by the exchanges, the futures market provides somewhat less hedging flexibility than the forward market. Currency futures are traded in several major urban centers including Amsterdam, Chicago, London, Montreal, Singapore, and Sydney.

Example: In the following example of a foreign currency hedged investment, a forward contract—the oldest, most liquid, and flexible currency hedging vehicle—is used to cover the foreign exchange risk.

On day one, a U.S. investor purchases a French 90-day security denominated in French francs (FF) at a yield (in French francs) of 10%. Assuming the investor buys FF 5,000,000 face value of securities, he must purchase a like amount of French francs to deliver against the bonds. To protect himself against adverse currency movements that could reduce the yield, the investor simultaneously contracts to sell French francs in the forward market.

Assume that the spot (two-day settlement) rate for French francs is 5.6920 per U.S. dollar. On the same day, the quoted three-month forward (90-day settlement) rate is 5.7145 French francs per U.S. dollar. The difference between the two rates (5.6920 less 5.7145) is a discount of 0.0225, called the "three-month forward swap."

The following example outlines the steps followed by a U.S. investor to hedge a 10% French security with a maturity of three months through the forward market.

Day 1: Investor buys FF 5,000,000 spot

U.S. \$ cost = FF face value ÷ spot

$$= 5,000,000 \div 5.6920$$

$$= \text{U.S. } \$878,425.86$$

Day 1: Investor contracts to sell total FF proceeds forward

FF proceeds = FF face value + interest

$$= 5,000,000 + (\text{face value} \times \text{rate} \times \tfrac{\text{days}}{365})$$

$$= 5,000,000 + (5,000,000 \times 0.10 \times \tfrac{90}{365})$$

$$= \text{FF } 5,123,287.67$$

U.S. \$ proceeds = FF proceeds ÷ forward rate

$$= 5,123,287.67 \div 5.7145$$

$$= \$896,541.72$$

Day 90: Investor receives U.S. \$896,541.72

In U.S. dollar terms, the hedged investment yields:

$$\frac{\$896,541.72 - \$878,425.86}{\$878,425.86} \times \frac{365}{90} = 8.36\%$$

Using the 360-day year U.S. money market convention, the hedged investment yield is:

$$8.36\% \times \frac{360}{365} = 8.25\%$$

On rare occasions, a discrepancy might emerge between foreign and domestic interest rates that provides the U.S. investor with a hedged investment yield that exceeds comparable returns from equivalent credits denominated in U.S. dollars. In these circumstances, the forward hedging strategy is called a "covered interest arbitrage." When international money markets function normally, such discrepancies are quickly bid away.

Interest Rate Futures

Interest rate futures on money market instruments were introduced in January 1976 when three-month U.S. Treasury bills futures contracts began trading at the International Monetary Market (IMM) of the Chicago Mercantile Exchange (CME). The Treasury bill futures contracts offered for trade are based on a quarterly cycle. The contract months are March, June, September, and December. The Treasury bill contract is quoted in terms of the "IMM Index," which is 100 minus the discount rate; thus, a Treasury bill discount rate of 8.00% would be quoted in terms of the IMM price index as 92.00. Price fluctuations occur in increments of 0.01, or one basis point, with each 0.01 valued at $25.

The Treasury bill futures contract calls for physical delivery of U.S. Treasury bills. Positions that are still open after expiration of the contract are settled by delivering a U.S. Treasury bill with a face amount of $1 million that matures three months from the date of delivery. (The date of delivery is the day following the day the contract expires.) For example, the June 1990 T-bill futures contract expires (stops trading) on Wednesday, June 27. Positions that are still open after expiration are settled by delivering a U.S. Treasury bill that matures three months from Thursday, June 28, 1990, the first day of delivery. (The face amount, or the amount due from the U.S. government at maturity, must be exactly $1 million for each contract still open). Thus, the time period reflected in the June 1990 T-bill futures contract is June 28 to September 27, 1990. In other words, trading the June contract is the same as trading the rate to be charged to the U.S. government for borrowing for three months, from June 28, 1990 to September 27, 1990. Average daily volume in 1989 was 5,962 contracts, and open interest at year end was 34,392 contracts.

Three-Month Eurodollar Time Deposit Futures

Since January 1976, the CME has introduced other interest rate products based upon money market instruments. In December of 1981, three-month Eurodollar Time Deposit futures contracts began trading. The Eurodollar contract is traded in the same quarterly cycle contract months as the T-bill futures contract (i.e., March, June, September, and December).

Each Eurodollar futures contract is settled to the three-month LIBOR rate (i.e., the London Interbank Offered Rate for U.S. dollars) for funds that would be deposited the third Wednesday of the contract month, though the contract stops trading two business days earlier. For example, the June 1990 Eurodollar futures contract stops trading on Monday, June 18, 1990. On that date a 3-month LIBOR rate for a $1 million deposit to be made on Wednesday, June 20 is determined, which in turn determines the final settlement price for the contract. Thus the time period reflected in the June Eurodollar futures contract is June 20, 1990 to September 19, 1990. Trading the June 1990 Eurodollar futures contract is the same as trading the rate to be charged to the largest, most creditworthy commercial banks for borrowing Eurodollars for three months, from June 20, 1990 to September 19, 1990.

The Eurodollar time deposit futures contract, which (in contrast to Treasury bill futures) is a cash-settled contract, has become the most liquid money market futures contract. During 1989 the average daily volume in the Eurodollar futures contract amounted to 161,977 contracts. With each contract calling for a million dollar deposit, the average daily dollar value of trading in Eurodollar futures was almost $162 billion. As testament to the growing importance of the Eurodollar market, in 1989 the futures contract posted an 88% volume gain over the previous year. Year-end open interest on Eurodollar futures was 610,473. (See the accompanying chart displaying the historical growth rate of CME interest rate futures and options products.)

Among a myriad of applications, interest rate futures and options are utilized by:

- Investors with long positions in money market assets, to hedge against rising interest rates during the holding period.

- Future borrowers of short-term funds, to hedge the issuance of their liabilities.

- Investors, to hedge against having to roll over short-term investments at lower rates.

- Speculators, to try to profit from anticipated changes in interest rates.

Interest Rate Futures and Options Volume
(CHICAGO MERCANTILE EXCHANGE)
(In millions of dollars)

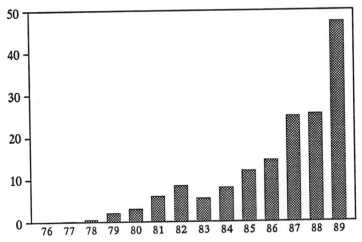

Options On Money Market Futures Contracts

The CME offers trading in options on both its Treasury bill and three-month Eurodollar time deposit futures contracts, with Eurodollar options commanding the greater portion of volume. The average daily volume during 1989 for Eurodollar options was 23,816. Total volume in Eurodollar options topped 6 million contracts in 1989, with year-end open interest reaching 241,684 (representing roughly $242 billion). One option represents the right to buy or sell one Eurodollar time deposit futures contract at the specified strike price. Call buyers have the right to *buy* (go long) the futures position, and put buyers have the right to *sell* (go short) the futures position.

178

The Government Securities Market

The Market Mechanism

Practically all trading in U.S. Government securities takes place in the over-the-counter market. Bond issues are listed on the New York Stock Exchange, but volume there is small. The over-the-counter market consists of a group of dealer firms, including First Boston, and several large banks that operate government bond departments. They deal directly with banks, insurance companies, corporations, brokers, and other large investors interested in the government securities market. Small investors have ready access to this market through their local banks, securities dealers, and brokers. A small group of government bond brokers serves to facilitate interdealer trading. Unlike the dealers, these brokers do not take positions themselves, but rather match the bids and offers placed with them by the dealer community. The best of these bids/offers are disseminated by the brokers to all dealers by means of a modern telecommunications network. As a result, the prevailing quotations from any dealer on a particular issue at a given time will be identical, or nearly so. The major government securities dealers are represented by the Primary Dealers Committee, Government and Federal Agency Securities Division of the Public Securities Association, which currently has a regular membership of 42 firms.

At present, normal domestic trading hours in the over-the-counter market are from 9 a.m. to 4 p.m., New York time. Trading often extends beyond these hours, however, when markets are active. In addition, active markets in London and Tokyo create a virtually around-the-clock market. Prices of government securities other than Treasury bills normally are quoted in terms of 32nds. Thus, a price quotation of 96–16, or 96.16, means 96 16/32. Occasionally, quotations are made in terms of 64ths, denoted " + ". Thus, 96.16 + means 96 33/64. Treasury bills are quoted in terms of rate of bank discount (see page 67). Dealers customarily buy and sell government securities at net prices; that is, no commission is added. A dealer's quotation, such as 93–5 bid, 93–7 asked, usually indicates that on full lots (usually 100 bonds — $100,000 face value — or more) the dealer will pay the bid price and will sell at the asked price. Service charges or price adjustments are made on small odd-lot transactions or transactions involving registered securities.

The difference between bid and asked price is called the "spread." Variations in the spread between issues with different characteristics and/or maturity reflect the relative activity and market risk of holding the issues. The spread in the quotations on Treasury bills may be only $50 per million par value or even less.

On other short-term issues the spread may be 1/32 to 4/32s of a point ($312.50 to $1,250 per million), while on longer-term or inactive issues it may be somewhat greater. The volume of market activity in the issue is a dominant factor in determining the width of the spreads.

Payment for and delivery of government securities normally take place on the next full business day following the day of the transaction, except in instances where the dealer and the investor agree on settlement the same day — termed a "cash" transaction — or on some later day — termed a "delayed delivery" transaction. Accrued interest to the delivery date is added to the price of coupon obligations. Payment is normally made in federal funds. Odd-lot transactions are normally on a five-business-day settlement basis.

The Federal Reserve Bank of New York publishes daily composite closing quotations for government securities. It also reports consolidated statistics each week on the market activity of the primary dealers, showing volume, type of customer, positions, and financing. (Some of these data are shown in the table on page 149.)

Telegraphic Transfer of Government and Agency Securities
Telegraphic transfer facilities for all unmatured marketable securities of the U.S. Treasury are available through the Federal Reserve Banks. The Federal Reserve Banks will transfer such securities for any purpose, including securities

borrowed by primary dealers and collateral thereto. In addition to Treasury issues, agency securities that are eligible for custody in book-entry form are also eligible for telegraphic transfer (see below) through this nationwide communications network.

Telegraphic transfers are subject to certain limitations: in general, transfers of securities are not authorized on or after the date of maturity of an issue or on or after the date on which securities are called for redemption and on which they will cease to bear interest.

The fee for interdistrict transfer of securities of any one issue or series to be delivered to a single recipient is $2.25 and is payable at the time securities are presented for transfer.

Book-Entry and the Telecommunications Transfer System
All the large New York City banks, including those that handle the bulk of the transactions of the major government securities dealers, now clear most of their transactions with each other and with the Federal Reserve through the use of automated telecommunications and the "book-entry" custody system maintained by the Federal Reserve Bank of New York. These banks have deposited with the Federal Reserve Bank a major portion of their government and agency securities holdings, including securities held for the accounts of their customers or in a fiduciary capacity. Virtually all transfers for the account of the banks, as well as for the government securities dealers who are their clients, are now effected solely by bookkeeping entries. The system reduces the costs and risks of physical handling and speeds the completion of transactions.

Treasury bills are offered in book-entry form only. New issues of marketable Treasury bonds and notes have been entirely in book-entry form since 1986. Older issues remain available in definitive form as well.

Most of the major federal agencies have issued regulations requiring use of the book-entry procedure for issuance of their securities. To further assist the smooth functioning of the market, the Federal Reserve will lend securities from its own portfolio to primary dealers when needed to complete transactions on which there has been a "fail" — that is, when a security has not been delivered because it has been delayed in transit to the dealer. The usual charge for such loans of securities is at a rate of 1½%. The Federal Reserve requires the securities it lends to be fully collateralized by the borrowing dealer and, in addition, sets limits on the amount of an individual issue, $50 million on any one bill and $10 million on any one note or bond, that a dealer may borrow. In addition, a dealer may not borrow more than $150 million per day. The Federal Reserve may charge an additional penalty if the securities are not returned to it within five business days.

Zero Coupon Treasury Securities

Beginning in the 1970s, aggressive interpretations of federal tax law encouraged some dealers and investors to separate the component pieces of U.S. Treasury bonds and notes. The separation allowed the holder to sell the corpus, or principal payment, at a deep discount price of $0.05 to $0.10 on the dollar and claim a capital loss on the difference between the selling price of the corpus and the price paid for the whole bond. The income stream was still realized as regular income, but no tax was paid on the accretion until the securities were sold or had matured. Through this process, therefore, an investor could delay his tax liability and also be allowed a significant capital loss. Because of the significant loss of tax revenue, the Treasury by 1979 had asked the primary dealers to discourage this process. The practice was eliminated among the primary dealers, although it persisted among some smaller dealers and investors.

In 1982, the Congress, through the Tax Equity and Fiscal Responsibility Act (TEFRA), required the holders of zero coupon and original-issue discount securities to accrue a portion of the discount toward par each year, and to report this unrealized accrual as taxable income. The tax status of coupon "stripping" was thus legally defined. Dealers consequently began again to separate coupon and principal payments, and an active secondary market developed for the component pieces.

TEFRA also mandated that as of January 1, 1986, all new U.S. Treasury issues would be available only in book-entry form. The process of stripping had depended on the availability of bearer bonds from which to physically separate the coupons; dealers now had to find a way to create separate principal and interest payments from registered bonds. They did so by introducing proprietary zero coupon certificates. These were certificates of ownership of Treasury cash flows. Proprietary certificates differed from physical zeros in that a Treasury note or bond could be deposited with a custodian, who could then issue certificates against the coupon and principal cash flows. In practice, all Treasury issues could be stripped in this indirect manner.

While this system apparently solved the immediate problem of the diminishing supply of raw materials for stripping, it created a segmented market as dealers rushed to create proprietary certificates attributable to their own firm. These various brands of Treasury-based zero-coupon products were not interchangeable and therefore lacked the secondary market liquidity investors had come to expect in physical zeros. Furthermore, creation of the product slowed as dealers began to realize that a tremendous capital and trading commitment was required to maintain an active secondary market in a proprietary item.

In early 1984, First Boston and a group of other dealers who had been actively creating and trading physical strip securities developed a generic security. Treasury Receipts (TRs), the result of this effort, were first issued in January 1984 and were readily accepted by both the dealer and investor communities. By the end of 1984, over $50 billion face value of TRs had been created, and the average trading volume climbed to several hundred million dollars per day.

The rapid development of this market and the large investor response once again drew the attention of the Treasury. This time, however, it approved of zeros because of indications that the demand for these securities was producing savings on government interest cost. After extensive study and consultation with the investment community, the Treasury announced that as of January 1985 all future note and bond issues with

Treasury Related Zero Coupon Products

Product Name	STRIPS	TRs	Physicals	Proprietary Receipts
	Separate Trading of Registered Interest and Principal of Securities.	Treasury Receipts		CATs, Cougars, ETRs, LIONs, STARs, TIGRs, ZEBRAs, etc.
Description	Generic, multiple market maker zero-coupon securities consisting of interest or principal on U.S. Treasury securities.	Generic, multiple market maker zero-coupon securities representing interest or principal payments on U.S. Treasury securities.	Generic, multiple market maker zero-coupon securities consisting of interest or principal payments on U.S. Treasury securities.	Proprietary, usually single market maker zero-coupon securities representing interest or principal payments on U.S. Treasury securities.
Unit Size	Interest and principal in $1,000 increments.	Interest payments denominated in multiples of the coupon on all issues where underlying Treasury is dated prior to August 1, 1984. On issues with underlying Treasury dated after this date, coupon certificates issued in $1,000 multiples. All principal certificates denominated in $1,000 units.	Interest payments denominated in multiples of the coupon on all issues. Principal payments always denominated in $1,000 units.	Principal and interest certificates usually denominated in $1,000 units.
Round Lot Size	$5,000,000	$5,000,000	$1,000,000 to $5,000,000	$1,000,000 to $5,000,000
Trading Spread	2–3 basis points.	10 basis points.	10 basis points.	10 basis points.
Yield Spread to Strips	--	25 basis points.	25 basis points.	35 basis points
Delivery	Wire transfer versus federal funds through Federal Reserve book-entry system.	Physical delivery of certificates versus federal funds.	Physical delivery of coupon or corpus versus federal funds.	Physical delivery of certificates versus federal funds.

maturities of at least 10 years would be transferable in their component pieces on the Federal Reserve wire system, thereby creating a generic, book-entry Treasury zero. This product was named STRIPS (Separate Trading of Registered Interest and Principal of Securities).

The process of stripping bonds involves wiring Treasury bonds to the Federal Reserve Bank of New York and receiving generic coupon strips and a principal strip in return.

As of May 1987, the Treasury has allowed the reconstitution of stripped bonds. Generic coupon strips, in the proper face amount and maturities, are combined with the corresponding principal strip to reconstitute Treasury bonds. Since the program's inception, an average of two billion notes and bonds have been either stripped or reconstituted each month. With the enhanced ability of market participants to strip and reconstitute bonds, the liquidity and efficiency of the strip market has been vastly improved. Generic coupon strips generally trade on a two to three basis point market. The liquidity of principal strips is dependent on the liquidity of the underlying bond. For very liquid bonds, the principal strip will trade in large size on a two basis point market.

Since the accretion of zeros is taxed annually as ordinary income, the principal investors in Treasury zeros are tax advantaged accounts such as domestic pension funds, insurance companies, and individual retirement accounts. Applications range from the matching of specific maturities to future liabilities to the use of long maturity zeros for adjusting portfolio volatility and convexity. Because of the elimination of reinvestment risk (a zero pays no interest until maturity and the rate of return is "locked in" at the time of purchase), zeros are frequently used to defease (in effect, guarantee the payment of) future liabilities. This can be either a simple cash flow match such as with a lottery payment or a guaranteed income contract, or a more complicated transaction such as a municipal bond defeasance or pension fund dedication. In contrast with this more passive role, longer maturity zeros with their low dollar price and high duration are often used to add volatility (potential of capital appreciation) to actively managed portfolios. Intermediate zeros, with duration similar

Government Agencies Related Zero Coupon Products

Product Name	FICO STRIPS	REFCORP STRIPS	GTCs
	The Financing Corporation	The Resolution Funding Corporation	Government Trust Certificates
Description	Authorized by the Competitive Equality Banking Act of 1987 and chartered by the Federal Home Loan Bank Board (FHLBB) on August 28, 1987. Its purpose is to advance funds for part of the costs associated with liquidating insolvent thrifts.	Established by the Financial Institutions Reform, Recovery and Enforcement Act of 1989 to provide financing for the Resolution Trust Corporation (RTC) to fund thrift resolutions.	GTCs have been issued since 1988, under a program that allows refinancing of Defense Security Assistance Agency (DSAA) loans made to various countries.
Guarantee	FICO bonds are not guaranteed by the U.S. government; however, the principal is to be fully repaid from the proceeds of noninterest bearing securities held in a segregated account. The primary source of interest payments is to be proceeds from pre-enactment and special assessments on member thrifts.	REFCORP bonds are not guaranteed as to principal by the U.S. government. However, the principal is to be fully repaid from the proceeds of interest bearing obligations of the U.S. government. Treasury is to pay all interest to the extent not paid from specified sources which include FHLB assessments on member thrifts and proceeds from thrift asset sales.	Although GTCs are not agency securities, the loan notes held by the trusts are backed by the full faith and credit guaranty of the U.S. government for 90% of all principal and interest payments. The remaining 10% of loan payments are collateralized by U.S. government or government guaranteed securities.
Market Size	Authorized to issue up to $10.825 billion in obligations. As of May 31, 1990, $8.04 billion of 30-year bonds were issued; a majority has been stripped.	Authorized to offer up to $30 billion in securities. As of May 31, 1990, $13 billion REFCORP bonds had been auctioned, and 56% converted to strip form.	Turkey, Pakistan, Morocco, Jordan, Israel and Tunisia have completed transactions under the refinancing program, totalling about $15.6 billion. Of this amount, $11.7 billion (face amount) are zero coupon certificates.
Special Features	The Federal Reserve has provided for the conversion of FICO bonds into book-entry zeros.	May be stripped into their separate interest and principal components in book-entry form and may be reconstituted into whole bonds.	GTCs are rated triple-A by Moody's and Standard and Poor.
Taxation	Subject to federal, but exempt from state and local taxation.	Subject to federal, but exempt from state and local taxation.	The Trusts are classified as grantor trusts for income tax purposes; certificates are subject to federal, state and local taxes where applicable.

Government Agencies Related Zero Coupon Products (continued)

FNMA and FHLB STRIPS

Portions of the following securities have been stripped by several dealers, including First Boston:

FNMA 8.95s of 2/12/18 Senior
    Capital Debentures

FNMA 9s of 2/1/19 Subordinated
    Capital Debentures

FHLB 9.50s of 2/25/04
    Consolidated Bonds

FNMA strips are subject to Federal, state and local taxes where applicable. The FHLB strips are Federally taxable, but exempt from state and local taxes.

Zero Coupon Agency Debentures

Several zero coupon agency debentures are actively traded, particularly the large, longer maturity issues. The more popular ones are listed below. Arbitrage opportunities frequently occur against Treasury STRIPS as well as among themselves.

Amount Outstanding	Issue		Maturity	Issue Date
$ 600 MM	FHLMC	Sub. Cap. Deb.	6/23/92	6/14/82
300	SLMA	Notes	11/1/94	9/27/84
250	FHLMC	Sub. Cap. Deb.	11/30/94	11/14/84
$2000 MM	SLMA	Notes	5/14/14 -09C	8/1/84
6000	FNMA	Debentures	7/5/14	7/5/84
6750	FNMA	Sub. Cap. Deb.	10/9/19	10/9/84
7000	FHLMC	Sub. Cap. Deb.	11/29/19	11/14/84
5059.05	SLMA	Bonds	10/3/22	9/12/84

The FHLMC and FNMA securities are subject to Federal, state and local taxation. SLMA issues are subject to Federal, but exempt from state and local taxes.

Holdings of Treasury Securities in Stripped Form

(As of May 31, 1990; in millions of dollars)

Maturity date	Coupon	Total outstandiang	Held in stripped form	% of total	Reconstitutions[1] in May 1990
Nov. 1994	11 5/8	6,659	1,394	20.9	0
Feb. 1995	11 1/4	6,934	520	7.5	0
May 1995	11 1/4	7,127	1,432	20.1	52
Aug. 1995	10 1/2	7,956	635	8.0	0
Nov. 1995	9 1/2	7,319	837	11.4	0
Feb. 1996	8 7/8	8,575	253	3.0	0
May 1996	7 3/8	20,086	221	1.1	0
Nov. 1996	7 1/4	20,259	300	1.5	0
May 1997	8 1/2	9,921	62	0.6	8
Aug. 1997	8 5/8	9,363	0	0	0
Nov. 1997	8 7/8	9,808	16	0.2	0
Feb. 1998	8 1/8	9,159	1	0	0
May 1998	9	9,165	30	0.3	0
Aug. 1998	9 1/4	11,343	128	1.1	0
Nov. 1998	8 7/8	9,903	6	0.1	0
Feb. 1999	8 7/8	9,720	3	0	0
May 1999	9 1/8	10,047	869	8.6	0
Aug. 1999	8	10,164	82	0.8	0
Nov. 1999	7 7/8	10,774	5	0	0
Feb. 2000	8 1/2	10,673	0	0	0
May 2000	8 7/8	10,496	0	0	0
Nov. 2004	11 5/8	8,302	4,669	56.2	0
May 2005	12	4,261	2,426	56.9	0
Aug. 2005	10 3/4	9,270	974	10.5	0
Feb. 2006	9 3/8	4,756	0	0	0
Nov. 2014	11 3/4	6,006	4,291	71.4	50
Feb. 2015	11 1/4	12,668	10,247	80.9	24
Aug. 2015	10 5/8	7,150	5,389	75.4	25
Nov. 2015	9 7/8	6,900	4,702	68.1	0
Feb. 2016	9 1/4	7,267	865	11.9	148
May 2016	7 1/4	18,824	1,995	10.6	111
Nov. 2016	7 1/2	18,864	7,732	41.0	321
May 2017	8 3/4	18,194	11,012	60.5	130
Aug. 2017	8 7/8	14,017	4,814	34.3	138
May 2018	9 1/8	8,709	5,237	60.1	0
Nov. 2018	9	9,033	7,415	82.1	0
Feb. 2019	8 7/8	19,251	12,408	64.5	627
Aug. 2019	8 1/8	20,214	7,959	39.4	350
Feb. 2020	8 1/2	10,229	2,341	22.9	0
May 2020	8 3/4	10,159	0	0	0

Source: Monthly Statement of the Public Debt of the United States.

[1]Effective May 1, 1987, securities held in stripped form were eligible for reconstitution to unstripped form.

to Treasury notes and bonds, can be used as a substitute, generally at a higher yield, for coupon Treasury securities. Zeros of all maturities can be combined with high coupon Treasuries or other securities to create "synthetic" securities. These hybrids theoretically perform much like a current coupon Treasury, but can often be created at significantly higher yield and lower dollar price.

For income tax purposes, Treasury zeros are considered to be an original issue discount debt obligation. (See chapter on Taxation beginning on page 215.) In general, the difference between the acquisition price and the maturing value is taxed as original issue discount. Treasury zeros are exempt from most forms of state and local taxation.

Financial Futures Market

A futures contract is a standardized agreement to make or take delivery of a specified security or commodity at a specified price on a future date. Delivery and payment specifications are established by the exchange where the contract is traded. Financial futures are contracts to deliver or receive securities such as Treasury bonds, notes or bills, or foreign currencies. Some contracts, such as Eurodollar time deposit, municipal index, and stock index futures, are different in that they refer to an underlying index rather than a specific security. In the case of index futures, settlement is made by a cash payment based on the movement in the underlying index. The vast majority of financial futures commitments are never delivered; they are usually "closed" through offsetting transactions prior to the specified delivery date.

Interest rate futures began trading in October 1975 when a GNMA futures contract was introduced on the Chicago Board of Trade (CBOT). The success of this contract prompted the CBOT to add contracts based on Treasury bonds; ten-year, five-year, and two-year Treasury notes; and Municipal Bond Index futures. The International Monetary Market of the Chicago Mercantile Exchange (IMM) introduced contracts on U.S. Treasury bills and Eurodollar time deposits. The Financial Instrument Exchange (FINEX) introduced Treasury note futures contracts with maturities of one and two years. Currency futures, which predate interest rate futures, are also traded on the IMM, while various stock index futures are traded on the Kansas City Board of Trade, the New York Futures Exchange, the Chicago Mercantile Exchange, and the Chicago Board of Trade.

For the majority of futures contracts, there are up to eight deferred contract months. The nearby contracts exhibit more liquidity than the deferred months. When the yield curve is positively sloped, outright holdings of actual cash securities can be financed with positive carry. To compensate investors for foregoing this income and holding futures instead, prices for future delivery must be lower in the deferred months. By the same token, with a negatively sloped yield curve, the deferred prices will be higher.

The financial futures market enables investors in fixed income assets to transfer market risk inherent in long or short security positions to others who are willing to assume these risks. The act of reducing risk by taking a position in the futures market is referred to as hedging. Hedging through financial futures can be employed by:

- Those intending to borrow in the future, to lock in a particular rate of interest and protect themselves from rising interest costs.

- Holders of fixed-income securities, to offset declines in the value of their assets during periods when they expect interest rates to rise.

- Those intending to lend in the future, to lock in currently low interest rates if they expect rates to rise.

In contrast to hedgers, who use futures to reduce their risk, speculators and arbitrageurs are willing to assume risk with the expectation of profiting from perceived price anomalies.

The most common arbitrage technique is "spreading," which may be "intramarket" (purchasing a futures contract of one delivery month and selling another delivery month of the same contract) or "intermarket" (buying a contract on one commodity and selling a contract on a different commodity).

Dealer Volume and Positions in Treasury and Agency Futures

(Daily averages; dollar value of contracts in millions of dollars)

	Dealer transactions			Dealer positions		
	Treasury securities		Agency	Treasury securities		Agency
	Bills	Coupons	securities	Bills	Coupons	securities
1988						
Jan.	2,790	9,401	1	-2,128	7,826	0
Feb.	2,660	9,526	2	-4,556	5,066	0
Mar.	2,768	9,413	6	-4,192	5,406	0
Apr.	2,995	8,772	0	-3,681	5,101	0
May	3,193	9,080	0	-2,027	4,460	0
June	2,205	11,565	0	-2,695	4,137	0
July	1,886	8,524	0	904	7,454	0
Aug.	2,592	9,485	0	1,157	8,476	0
Sept.	2,555	9,393	0	-4,049	7,745	0
Oct.	2,776	10,678	0	-4,388	6,534	0
Nov.	2,466	11,015	0	-1,878	5,875	0
Dec.	2,643	9,490	0	1,014	6,613	0
1989						
Jan.	2,924	9,832	0	-1,609	3,319	0
Feb.	3,947	10,658	0	4,512	2,895	0
Mar.	3,139	9,087	0	1,829	2,925	0
Apr.	2,782	8,676	0	-5,134	877	0
May	2,497	10,300	0	-5,721	-322	0
June	1,852	12,837	3	-4,741	-2,311	14
July	1,602	9,026	21	-5,792	-3,261	57
Aug.	1,696	10,547	8	-5,376	-2,664	7
Sept.	2,648	8,797	38	-6,106	-4,798	-26
Oct.	2,797	10,332	20	-7,459	-9,304	68
Nov.	1,898	9,313	7	-9,455	-11,364	25
Dec.	2,523	5,836	3	-10,135	-11,022	30

Source: Federal Reserve Bulletin.

The need of large institutions and securities dealers to protect or hedge their investments in stocks, bonds and other financial instruments has spurred extraordinary growth in financial futures trading volume. Daily dollar turnover in stock index futures exceeds that of cash trading on the New York Stock Exchange.

Average Daily Trading Volume in Treasury Bond Futures and Underlying Cash Bonds[*]

(In billions of dollars)

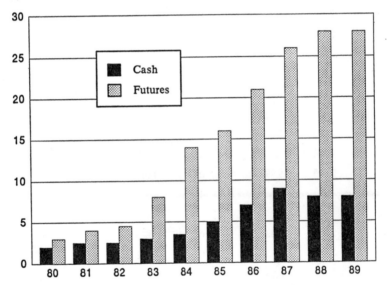

* Average daily cash trading volume, as reported by the Federal Reserve, divided by two (so as to count a purchase and sale only once).

The importance of stock index and bond futures for asset allocation strategies continues to grow. Spread trades like the TED (Treasury bill versus Eurodollar), the MOB (municipal futures versus Treasury bond futures), and curve trades such as note versus bond futures, continue to attract investors.

To trade in the futures market, an investor is required to deposit an initial margin in the form of cash or Treasury bills

192

which evidences the contract holder's ability to bear price risk. The initial margin is typically less than 5% of the face value of the position being held. Every day, the futures exchanges require that all price changes in every contract be settled in cash. A futures holder can make or lose more than the original investment and therefore should be cognizant of the face amount traded and not merely the amount of initial margin that is required.

Major strides were taken during 1987 toward creation of a truly global futures market. The London International Financial Futures Exchange (LIFFE) decided to make the delivery procedure of its U.S. Treasury bond futures contract conform to the CBOT procedure. For its part, the CBOT initiated night trading sessions to coincide in timing with the Tokyo bond market and so facilitate futures trading for Pacific Rim participants. The CBOT's night trading has been very successful, and now includes all of its Treasury note and bond futures and options.

Five-year Treasury futures were introduced by the Financial Instrument Exchange (FINEX), a division of the New York Cotton Exchange, to fill the gap on the yield curve between Eurodollar futures (based on three-month LIBOR) and Treasury note futures (based on seven-year to ten-year Treasuries). When five-year Treasury note futures were also introduced on the CBOT they quickly became the more liquid and actively traded of the five-year Treasury note contracts.

The number of Eurodollar futures contracts traded on the Chicago Mercantile Exchange (CME) was expanded from 12 to 16. The four additional contracts provide market participants the opportunity to create synthetic instruments with a strip of Eurodollar futures as long as four years. It also enhances pricing efficiency in the interest rate swap markets and offers short-term investors hedging flexibility.

Dealer Volume and Positions in
Treasury and Agency Forward Transactions

(Daily averages; in millions of dollars)

	Dealer transactions		Dealer positions	
	U.S. Govt. securities	Agency securities	U.S. Govt. securities	Agency securities
1988				
Jan.	1,707	6,549	-1,175	-14,396
Feb.	3,555	6,914	735	−15,610
Mar.	1,453	8,426	734	-16,442
Apr.	1,502	7,421	1,090	-16,528
May	2,516	8,597	2,191	-14,976
June	2,329	9,369	1,114	-17,834
July	1,670	7,087	1,353	-18,780
Aug.	2,283	8,701	641	-17,258
Sept.	1,478	7,601	-347	-16,988
Oct.	1,787	8,026	-968	-17,557
Nov.	3,112	8,188	-768	-16,963
Dec.	1,748	9,217	-451	-12,847
1989				
Jan.	1,679	8,211	114	-12,787
Feb.	3,054	7,656	872	-14,873
Mar.	1,819	8,322	-641	-15,662
Apr.	2,021	7,875	-1,328	-15,334
May	2,752	9,976	-1,380	-16,748
June	1,529	9,829	-1,885	-20,199
July	1,629	10,265	-1,353	-19,556
Aug.	2,923	12,087	-1,466	-20,639
Sept.	2,119	8,616	-607	-17,478
Oct.	2,163	10,560	1,380	-15,367
Nov.	2,009	10,894	-109	-17,372
Dec.	1,821	9,520	-145	-16,522

Source: Federal Reserve Bulletin.

Options on fixed income securities began trading in the fourth quarter of 1982 when options on Treasury bond futures were introduced. By any standard, this product has been enormously successful. At present, options on Treasury bills and notes are traded on the American Stock Exchange, options on Treasury bonds on the Chicago Board Options Exchange (CBOE), and options on Treasury bond and 10-year and 5-year Treasury note futures on the Chicago Board of Trade (CBOT). Options on Eurodollar futures are traded on the International Monetary Market of the Chicago Mercantile Exchange (IMM). Of the exchange-traded interest rate options, options on bond futures and Eurodollar futures are by far the most active and liquid.

Unlike the stock options market in which initially only call options were traded, debt options have been available from the start as both puts and calls. A call option gives the buyer the right to purchase (exercise) from the seller a security or commodity for a fixed price (known as the exercise or strike price) at any time within a certain time period. This is known as an American-style option, whereas in a European-style option, exercise is allowed only at expiration. The buyer of a put option purchases the right to sell an underlying security to the seller of the option at a set price within a given time period. Call option buyers profit when prices on the underlying security rise, whereas the buyer of a put option profits when the price of the underlying security declines.

The sum of money that the purchaser of the option pays for the rights granted by the option is the option premium. The buyer of an option is known as the holder, while the seller is often referred to as the writer. The option's expiration date is the last day on which the option can be exercised. If the option is not exercised by that date, then it ceases to exist. The buyer of an option can lose no more than the option premium. Purchasing a call option allows the investor to achieve gains as the market rises, but limits the loss to the option premium no matter how far the market declines. Analogously, the holder of a put option gains when prices fall (interest rates rise), but stands to lose only the option premium should prices advance. Thus, the investor may be able to increase the return on his portfolio and to hedge against interest rate risk. Furthermore, an investor can use fixed income options in a variety of complex combinations to manage and improve the risk, return, and volatility characteristics of a bond portfolio.

Fixed income options are employed by:

- Investors, to diminish portfolio risk, by purchasing options while investing their funds in relatively riskless short-term investments.

- Those intending to borrow in the future, to lock in a ceiling on their financing costs, thereby protecting themselves from increases in interest rates.

- Holders of fixed-income securities, to hedge against adverse price moves or to lock in minimum returns without forfeiting the ability to benefit from a market rally.

Options on bond futures began trading on October 1, 1982. Each options contract calls for delivery of a single, $100,000 face value Treasury bond futures contract of a specified delivery month. The option expiration date is in the month preceding the futures delivery month. Premiums are quoted in 64ths of a point, and strike prices are set at two-point intervals. Presently, there are three contract months that are traded, with the nearby contract exhibiting more liquidity than the deferred months.

The valuation of options requires at least five parameters: the term of the option, the exercise price, the value of the underlying security or commodity, the short-term rate of interest, and the volatility of the underlying commodity or security. The first two, the term of the option and the exercise price, are contractual features of the option, while the value of the underlying security and the short-term rate are easily observable from the market. It is the fifth parameter, the price volatility of the underlying security, that is difficult to measure accurately. Volatility refers to the tendency of the security to change in value over a given time frame. It is usually measured as the standard deviation in the expected annual rate of return from holding the security. Higher volatility is always associated with higher option premiums, whether the option is a put or call. The reason for this is that when the underlying security is more volatile, it is more probable that its value will fluctuate by large amounts, which will render option exercise profitable. An estimate of the volatility is often obtained by using past data. Using historical prices, the table on page 198 traces the actual volatility in the Treasury bond futures market, based on day-to-day price changes over the most recent thirty days, from January 3, 1978 through June 1, 1990. Another method for estimating volatility is to use the market's opinion. By taking the known market prices of options and their underlying securities and working backwards through an option-pricing formula, one can obtain the expected volatility that is implied by existing option premiums. Patterns in this "implied volatility," particularly in comparison to historical or actual volatility, are a commonly used indicator of market sentiment.

In an options transaction the buyer pays the premium in advance in cash, while the seller of an option is obligated to post margin in the form of cash or securities. The initial margin evidences the writer's ability to bear price risk. At the end of each trading session, each seller's position is marked to market to reflect gains or losses in the position. When the margin requirement exceeds the funds on deposit, the option writer is required to deposit additional funds or securities.

Futures and options users are continuing to find new applications for risk management. First Boston has developed sophisticated pricing models for variable-maturity securities, including adjustable rate mortgages (ARMs) and floating-rate collateralized mortgage obligations (FRCMOs). Cap structures and prepayment risk make ARMs and FRCMOs subject to price risks that had previously been difficult to quantify. The latest models enable accurate hedging since they describe the price sensitivity of these securities to changes in yield levels. ARMs now represent over 50% of all new mortgage originations. The cap structure of ARM-backed securities is best hedged with options, which should increase their use as a risk management tool. Furthermore, development of option-adjusted pricing models for all mortgage and corporate

Price Volatility of Treasury Bond Futures*

(Daily, percent annualized)

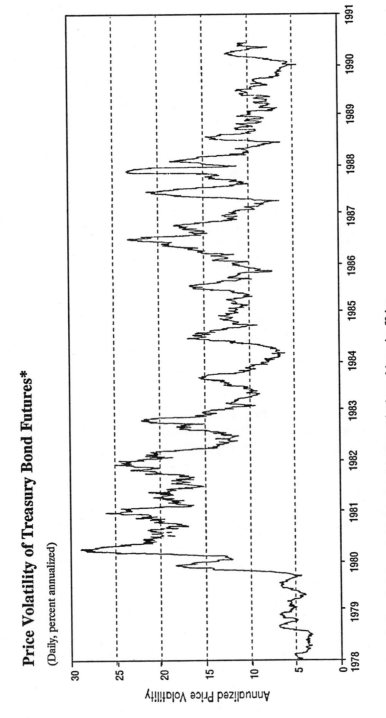

*Each daily observation is the standard deviation around the average price change of the previous 30 days.

securities enables construction of effective hedging strategies for entire portfolios of all corporate and mortgage-backed securities.

First Boston has been involved in the financial futures and options markets since their inception. First Boston professionals worldwide support hedging and arbitrage activities for customers. An extensive price database and wide array of fundamental and technical analyses are available to help in designing and executing specific strategies.

Interest Rate Swaps

An interest rate swap is an agreement between two parties to exchange payments that are based on specified interest rates and a notional amount. The exchange takes place over a specified period of time. Although swaps can take a variety of forms, typically one party pays fixed-rate and receives floating-rate payments, and the other party receives fixed and pays floating-rate payments.

Interest rate swaps were created to take advantage of arbitrage opportunities in the various fixed- and floating-rate capital markets. Arbitrage opportunities exist because some markets react to change more rapidly than others, because credit perceptions differ from market to market, and because receptivity to specific debt structures differs from market to market. If, for instance, a corporation wants term floating-rate funds but finds that the market for its fixed-rate debt is comparatively cheaper than that for its floating-rate debt, then it can issue a fixed-rate bond and swap it into floating, for an all-in cost lower than that for a floating-rate bond or loan.

Financial engineering and structured transactions play an important role as investors and issuers use the swap market to transform existing cash flows on capital markets issues into more desirable cash flows. The most frequent example of such transformation is the generation of callable interest rate swaps (swaptions) using callable bond deals. Issuers find that they can sell the call provision in their bond deals by receiving fixed rates and paying floating rates to hedgers seeking to create fixed rate liabilities, but requiring flexibility regarding maturity. Deep discount and zero coupon swap structures also are commonplace, driven primarily by the significant supply of Japanese equity warrants, Eurobonds and associated asset swaps.

Federal Government Loan Asset Sales

Sales of loan assets of federal agencies, mandated by the Omnibus Budget Reconciliation Act of 1986 (OBRA), have been undertaken as a means of reducing the current federal deficit and enhancing the management of federal credit programs. The sales are designed to provide an incentive for federal agencies to improve loan origination and documentation so as to clarify the level of subsidy provided by the federal government in the related loan programs. The original guidelines for loan asset sales, prepared by the Federal Credit Policy Working Group and issued by the Office of Management and Budget, called for loan asset sales to be structured without future recourse or the right to make a claim against the federal government or its agencies in the event of borrower default. From 1987 through May 1990, loans with a face value of approximately $10 billion were sold or prepaid by borrowers and yielded $7.1 billion in net receipts. The schedule for the 1990 fiscal year included loan asset sales by the Department of Education, Farmers Home Community Program, Veterans Administration, and the Departments of the Interior and Housing and Urban Development.

Nondollar Government Bonds

Financial market globalization has encouraged increased U.S. investor involvement in the nondollar bond markets. This represents the beginning of a trend, as the U.S. bond market now comprises less than half of the world bond market. The foreign bond markets have become sophisticated, liquid, and accessible in recent years as financial market liberalizations have advanced market-making capabilities and spurred innovations in all the major markets. Moreover, the global infrastructure developed by financial institutions facilitates foreign bond investing. Because of the impact of these factors

200

Comparison of Federal Loan Asset Sales

	Farmers Home Administration		Department of Education	Department of Housing and Urban Development	Department of Veterans Affairs
Offering	Rural housing Sept. 23, 1987	Community Program Sept. 2, 1987	Series I: Sept. 21, 1987 (Subordinate Certificates) Series II: Dec. 5, 1989	Public Facility Loan Trust Sequential Pay Bonds Aug. 22, 1988	AHT–AHT VI
Par Amount of Security Sold	$2.3 billion	$1.8 billion	Series I: $127 million Series II: $28 million	$235.9 million	$1.4 billion
Security	Mortgage pass-through	Bonds	Bonds	Bonds	Mortgage pass-through
Type of Loan	Mortgage loans for low- and moderate-income rural residents	Loans to small local governments to finance water and sewer systems and other essential community facilities.	Loans to post-secondary educational institutions to build college and other academic facilities.	Loans to municipalities, special districts, and not-for-profit organizations to refinance public work loans for construction of water, sewer, hospital and other public facilities.	Loans to finance the sale of residential properties acquired by VA through foreclosure on defaulted GI loans
Principal Amount of Collateral	$3.0 billion	$2.3 billion	$237 million	$271.9 million	$1.9 billion
Rating	Aaa/AAA	Senior Bonds Aaa/AAA	Series I: Aaa/AAA	Aaa/AAA	Aaa/AAA

Long-Term Market Rates

(Quarterly averages)

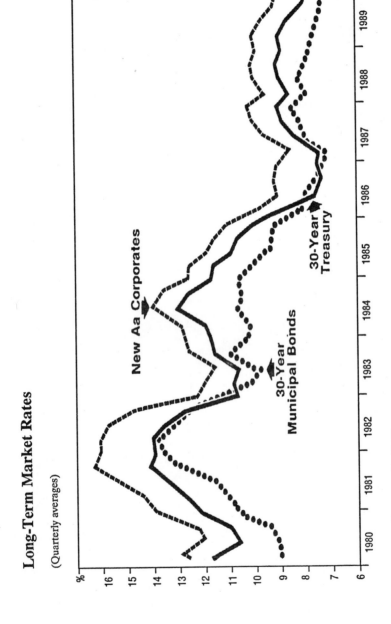

*Reproduced by courtesy of the U.S. Treasury.

on the U.S. fixed income market, U.S. investors now have an enhanced awareness of international developments.

Diverse investor groups account for the U.S. institutional participation in the foreign bond markets. The proliferation of global bond funds and unit trusts reflects the increased retail investor demand for international bonds. Public and private pension funds have diversified into nondollar investments, while total return money managers have sought enhanced performance. High yield buyers also have been attracted to several sectors.

Investors have a wide choice of instruments within the various government bond markets. In Europe, Dutch and French securities provide an alternative to German bonds, while U.K. gilts represent another option. The Japanese bond market is the world's second largest. Many investors view the Canadian sector as a high-yielding alternative to the U.S. market, given the high correlation of these sectors and the relatively stable Canadian-U.S. currency relationship. The Australian sector also has received new prominence in global portfolios.

Holders of the Public Debt

The distribution of ownership of the public debt has undergone large changes over the years (see table on page 72). Investors are always adjusting their portfolios, reflecting not only variations in the funds they have available and the types of securities the Treasury is offering, but also each buyer's particular investment preferences, the attractiveness of alternative investments, and the legal or other constraints under which the buyer may be operating.

In general, financial institutions are sellers of government securities when business is strengthening and higher yielding loans and investments are readily available. They are buyers at times of slack business activity and interest rates when, partly reflecting expansionary Federal Reserve policies, their inflows of funds exceed normal investment outlets. Similarly, non-financial corporations tend to accumulate government securities when capital spending is low, and to "spend" these liquid assets when outlays on fixed capital and inventories expand. In recent years, individuals have become major buyers, both directly and through mutual funds. Foreign official and private financial institutions have greatly increased their purchases as well, investing funds derived primarily from balance-of-payments surpluses. The Federal Reserve itself is a sizable owner of marketable issues, largely as a result of its open market operations in its conduct of monetary policy. These operations are discussed in the next section. It should be noted that considerations of profit or loss to the Federal Reserve do not enter into its decisions to buy or sell securities.

Government investment accounts comprise trust funds that by law are under the control of the Secretary of the Treasury or of the Treasurer of the United States and accounts under the control of certain U.S. Government agencies whose investments are handled through the facilities of the Treasury Department. These accounts also hold some marketable public debt, most of which was bought in the past when purchases would improve yield or help to cushion a market declining in price. Recently, however, they have not been actively acquiring marketable issues.

Federal Reserve Open Market Operations

The execution of monetary policy through open market operations frequently, and during certain periods almost daily, brings the Federal Reserve into the government securities market. Purchases of securities by the Federal Reserve create bank reserves and provide the underpinning for monetary and credit expansion. Sales of securities by the central bank absorb bank reserves and reduce the potential for monetary expansion. The Federal Reserve may purchase or sell securities outright or it may enter into repurchase agreements and so-called "reverse repurchase" agreements (formally designated as "matched sale-purchase agreements"). In repurchase or reverse repurchase transactions, the Federal Reserve buys or sells securities under agreements that call for automatic reversal of the operation within a specified number of days (at most 15 for repurchase agreements, but more generally only two or three). These agreements are in effect loans between the Federal Reserve and the dealers. The effective interest rate is set by an auction technique whereby dealers bid for or offer funds in competition with one another.

Over the long term, the Federal Reserve normally is a large buyer of securities. This is to create the bank reserves needed to offset the loss of reserves resulting from increases in the public's holdings of currency, as well as to provide the reserve base to support growth in the quantity of deposits.

The Federal Reserve added $15.1 billion of government securities to its outright holdings in 1988 but withdrew $10.0 billion in 1989 because a large buildup in its holdings of foreign currencies added reserves. Net purchases of coupon issues were $9.7 billion in 1988 and $1.3 billion in 1989. Treasury bill holdings increased by $5.4 billion in 1988 but decreased by $11.3 billion in 1989.

Since September 1971, the Federal Reserve has also engaged in open market operations in the securities of federal agencies and government-sponsored enterprises. Authorization for such transactions was given by law in 1966, but until September 1971 was used only for repurchase agreements. Under guidelines established by the Federal Reserve, its market purchases or sales of issues maturing in five years or less are limited to those of which at least $300 million is outstanding, while for longer-term issues the cutoff is $200 million. Holdings of agency securities were reduced by $0.6 billion in 1988 and a further $0.4 billion in 1989. The gross volume of Federal Reserve transactions is much larger than the net acquisitions because, for seasonal or other reasons, the Federal Reserve may be both a seller and buyer of Treasury bills.

Total transactions in bills and other Treasury securities through the market for the Federal Reserve's own account was $20.4 billion in 1988 and $30.0 billion in 1989. These figures do not include enormous additional transactions on behalf of foreign monetary authorities, the Treasury, and others, nor redemptions of Treasury bills and repurchase or reverse repurchase agreements.

Reserve Balances of Depository Institutions at Federal Reserve Banks and Related Items

(As of December 31; in millions of dollars)

	1985	1986	1987	1988	1989
Factors providing reserves:					
U.S. Gov't securities [1]	191,248	221,459	231,420	247,489	235,417
Loans to Depository Institutions	3,060	1,565	3,815	2,170	481
Float	988	1,261	811	1,286	1,093
Other assets [2]	20,020	22,493	20,855	23,821	48,149
Gold stock	11,090	11,064	11,078	11,060	11,059
Treasury currency outstanding	17,052	17,567	18,177	18,799	19,615
Factors absorbing reserves:					
Currency in circulation	197,465	211,995	230,213	247,649	260,443
Treasury cash holdings	550	427	446	395	455
Treasury deposits with Federal Reserve Banks	9,351	7,588	5,313	8,656	6,217
Service-related balances	1,490	1,812	1,687	1,605	1,618
Foreign and other deposits	1,521	1,204	1,271	895	1,887
Other Federal Reserve accounts	6,622	6,088	7,129	7,683	8,486
Reserve balances of depository institutions: [3]					
Federal Reserve Banks	27,928	38,659	37,055	37,106	35,131
Currency and coin	23,612	24,729	26,960	27,927	29,415
Total reserves [4]	48,950	61,417	62,160	63,631	63,033
Required reserves	47,644	59,369	61,354	62,550	62,015
Excess reserves	1,307	2,048	806	1,081	1,018
Federal Reserve Bank security holdings					
Totals:	191,248	221,459	231,420	247,489	235,418
Held outright:Treasury bills	85,425	103,775	107,691	112,782	104,581
Treasury notes	67,647	68,126	82,973	90,950	91,381
Treasury bonds	24,726	25,724	28,242	29,930	30,814
Agency securities	8,227	7,829	7,553	6,966	6,525
Held under repurchase agreement	5,223	16,005	4,961	6,861	2,117

Source: Federal Reserve Bulletin.

[1] Also includes federal agency obligations, eligible acceptances, and securities held under repurchase agreements.
[2] Includes Federal Reserve assets not elsewhere classsified and SDR certificates.
[3] Daily averages; last reserve period of the year.
[4] Includes reserve balances and vault cash used to satisfy reserve requirements.

Federal Reserve Discount Rates

(Percent)

Date effective			Discount rate (New York)	Surcharge[1]	Date effective			Discount rate (New York)
1979	July	20	10		1982	July	20	11 ½
	Aug.	17	10 ½			Aug.	2	11
	Sept.	19	11			Aug.	16	10 ½
	Oct.	8	12			Aug.	27	10
						Oct.	12	9 ½
1980	Feb.	15	13			Nov.	22	9
	Mar.	17		3		Dec.	15	8 ½
	May	7		0	1984	Apr.	9	9
	May	30	12			Nov.	21	8 ½
	June	13	11			Dec.	24	8
	July	28	10					
	Sept.	26	11		1985	May	20	7 ½
					1986	Mar.	7	7
1980	Nov.	17	12	2		Apr.	21	6 ½
	Dec.	5	13	3		July	11	6
1981	May	5	14	4		Aug.	12	5 ½
	Sept.	22		3				
	Oct.	12		2	1987	Sept.	4	6
	Nov.	2	13		1988	Aug.	9	6 ½
	Nov.	17		0	1989	Feb.	24	7
	Dec.	4	12		In effect March 31, 1990			7

Source: Federal Reserve Bulletin.

[1] As of March 17, 1980, a surcharge was applied to institutions with deposits of $500 million or more that had short-term adjustment credit borrowings in successive weeks or in more than four weeks in a calendar quarter. As of October 1, 1981, the basis for application of a surcharge was changed from a calendar quarter to a moving 13-week period. The surcharge was eliminated on November 17, 1981.

Specifications from Directives of the Federal Open Market Committee and Related Information

Date of meeting	Specified short-term growth rates [1] M2	M3	Borrowing assumptions for deriving nonborrowed reserves path (millions of dollars)	Discount rate (percent)	Committee preference	Guidelines for modifying reserve pressure	Prospective reserve restraint modifications — Factors to consider for modifications (in order listed) 1	2	3	4	5
12/15 to 12/16/87	November to March 5	6	300 250 on 1/28	6.00	Sought to maintain the existing degree of pressure on reserve positions[2]	A somewhat lesser or somewhat greater degree would be acceptable	Conditions in financial markets	Strength of the business expansion	Indications of inflationary pressure	Developments in foreign exchange markets	Behavior of the monetary aggregates
2/9 to 2/10/88	November to March 6 to 7	6 to 7	250 200 on 2/11	6.00	Sought to maintain the slightly reduced degree of pressure on reserve positions adopted in recent days[2]	A somewhat lesser or somewhat greater degree would be acceptable	Conditions in financial markets	Strength of the business expansion	Indications of inflationary pressure	Developments in foreign exchange markets	Behavior of the monetary aggregates
3/29/88	March to June 6 to 7	6 to 7	200 300 on 3/30 400 on 5/9	6.00	Sought to increase slightly the degree of pressure on reserve positions[2]	A somewhat greater or somewhat lesser degree would be acceptable	Conditions in financial markets	Strength of the business expansion	Indications of inflationary pressure	Developments in foreign exchange markets	Behavior of the monetary aggregates

Date	Period / range	Amounts	Rate	Policy on reserve pressure	Later in inter-meeting period	Factors cited
5/17/88	March to June 6 to 7	400 500 on 5/25 550 on 6/22	6.00	Sought initially to maintain the existing degree of reserve pressure but anticipated that a slight increase would be appropriate in weeks ahead, depending on factors cited	Later in inter-meeting period, a somewhat greater degree would be acceptable; a slightly lesser degree might be acceptable	Conditions in financial markets Strength of the business expansion Indications of inflationary pressure Developments in foreign exchange markets Behavior of the monetary aggregates
6/29 to 6/30/88	June to September 5½ 7	550 600 on 7/1 ³	6.00 6.50 on Aug. 9	Sought to increase slightly the existing degree of pressure on reserve positions	A somewhat greater degree would be acceptable; a slightly lesser degree might be acceptable	Indications of inflationary pressure Strength of the business expansion Developments in foreign exchange and domestic financial markets Behavior of the monetary aggregates
8/16/88	June to September 3½ 5½	600	6.50	Sought to maintain the existing degree of pressure on reserve positions	A somewhat greater degree would be acceptable; a slightly lesser degree might be acceptable	Indications of inflationary pressure Strength of the business expansion Behavior of the monetary aggregates Developments in foreign exchange and domestic financial markets

209

Specifications from Directives of the Federal Open Market Committee and Related Information (continued)

Date of meeting	Specified short-term growth rates [1] M2 (percent)	M3	Borrowing assumptions for deriving nonborrowed reserves path (millions of dollars)	Discount rate (percent)	Committee preference	Guidelines for modifying reserve pressure	Prospective reserve restraint modifications — Factors to consider for modifications (in order listed) 1	2	3	4	5
9/20/88	August to December 3	5	600	6.50	Sought to maintain the existing degree of pressure on reserve positions	A somewhat greater degree would be acceptable; a slightly lesser degree might be acceptable	Indications of inflationary pressure	Strength of the business expansion	Behavior of the monetary aggregates	Developments in foreign exchange and domestic financial markets	
11/1/88	September to December 2½	6	600 400 on 11/22	6.50	Sought to maintain the existing degree of pressure on reserve positions	A somewhat greater degree would be acceptable; a slightly lesser degree might be acceptable	Indications of inflationary pressure	Strength of the business expansion	Behavior of the monetary aggregates	Developments in foreign exchange and domestic financial markets	
12/13 to 12/14/88	November to March 3	6½	400 500 on 12/15 600 on 1/5	6.50	Sought to increase somewhat the degree of pressure on reserve positions	A somewhat greater degree would be acceptable; slightly lesser degree might be acceptable	Indications of inflationary pressure	Strength of the business expansion	Behavior of the monetary aggregates	Developments in foreign exchange and domestic financial markets	

Date	Period					Indications of inflationary pressure	Strength of the business expansion	Behavior of the monetary aggregates	Developments in foreign exchange and domestic financial markets
2/7 to 2/8/89	December to March 3½	2	600 700 on 2/14 [4] 500 on 3/9 [5]	6.50 7.00 on 2/24	Sought to maintain the existing degree of pressure on reserve positions	A somewhat greater degree would be acceptable; slightly lesser degree might be acceptable	Indications of inflationary pressure	Strength of the business expansion	Behavior of the monetary aggregates	Developments in foreign exchange and domestic financial markets
3/28/89	March to June 3	5	500	7.00	Sought to maintain the existing degree of pressure on reserve positions	A somewhat greater degree would be acceptable; slightly lesser degree might be acceptable	Indications of inflationary pressure	Strength of the business expansion	Behavior of the monetary aggregates	Developments in foreign exchange and domestic financial markets
5/16/89	March to June 1½	4	500 600 on 5/17 [5] 500 on 6/6	7.00	Sought to maintain the existing degree of pressure on reserve positions	A somewhat greater or somewhat lesser degree would be acceptable	Indications of inflationary pressure	Strength of the business expansion	Behavior of the monetary aggregates	Developments in foreign exchange and domestic financial markets

Specifications from Directives of the Federal Open Market Committee and Related Information (continued)

Date of meeting	Specified short-term growth rates [1] M2	M3	Borrowing assumptions for deriving nonborrowed reserves path (millions of dollars)	Discount rate (percent)	Committee preference	Guidelines for modifying reserve pressure	Prospective reserve restraint modifications — Factors to consider for modifications (in order listed) 1	2	3	4	5
7/5 to 7/6/89	June to September 7	7	500; 600 on 7/7 [e]; 550 on 7/27	7.00	Sought to decrease slightly the degree of pressure on reserve positions	A somewhat greater or somewhat lesser degree would be acceptable	Indications of inflationary pressure	Strength of the business expansion	Behavior of the monetary aggregates	Developments in foreign exchange and domestic financial markets	
8/22/89	June to September 9	7	550	7.00	Sought to maintain the existing degree of pressure on reserve positions	A slightly greater degree might be acceptable; a slightly lesser degree would be acceptable	Progress toward price stability	Strength of the business expansion	Behavior of the monetary aggregates	Developments in foreign exchange and domestic financial markets	
10/3/89	September to December 6½	4½	550 [5]; 500 on 10/5 [5]; 400 on 10/19 [5]; 350 on 11/2 [5]; 300 on 11/6 [5]; 250 on 11/9 [5]	7.00	Sought to maintain the existing degree of pressure on reserve positions	A slightly greater degree might be acceptable; a slightly lesser degree would be acceptable	Progress toward price stability	Strength of the business expansion	Behavior of the monetary aggregates	Developments in foreign exchange and domestic financial markets	

Date							Progress toward price stability	Strength of the business expansion	Behavior of the monetary aggregates	Developments in foreign exchange and domestic financial markets
11/14/89	September to December	7½	4½	250 [5] / 200 on 11/15 [6] / 150 on 12/11 [6]	7.00	Sought to maintain existing degree of pressure on reserve positions	A slightly greater degree might be acceptable; a slightly lesser degree would be acceptable	Progress toward price stability	Strength of the business expansion	Behavior of the monetary aggregates	Developments in foreign exchange and domestic financial markets
12/18 to 12/19/89	November to March	8½	5½	150 / 125 on 12/20	7.00	Sought to decrease slightly the existing degree of pressure on reserve positions	A slightly greater or slightly lesser degree would be acceptable	Progress toward price stability	Strength of the business expansion	Behavior of the monetary aggregates	Developments in foreign exchange and domestic financial markets

Source: Federal Reserve Bank of New York.

[1] No specific targets were established for M1 in 1988.

[2] Factors calling for special flexibility:
 — Sensitive conditions in financial markets.
 — Uncertainties in the economic outlook.

[3] On August 8, the borrowing assumption was increased to $700 million, but it was returned to $600 million the next day when the discount rate was raised.

[4] On February 23, the borrowing assumption was increased to $800 million, but it was returned to $700 million on the next day when the discount rate was raised.

[5] Borrowing assumption changed for technical reasons.

[6] Change in borrowing assumption reflected a technical adjustment and a change in reserve pressures.

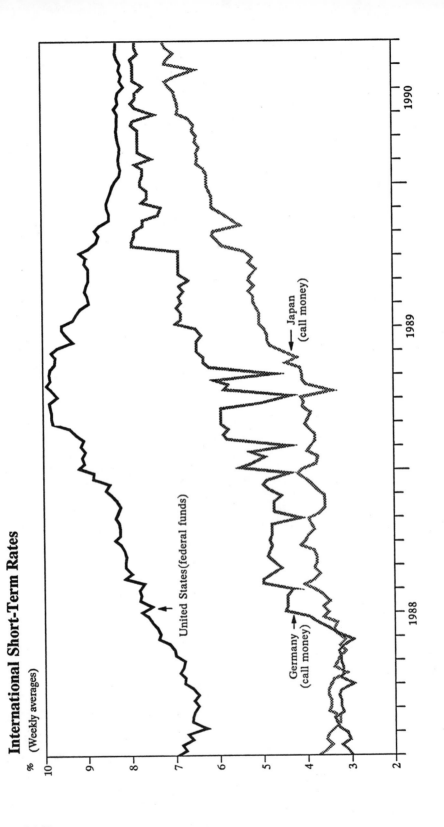

International Short-Term Rates

% (Weekly averages)

United States (federal funds)

Germany (call money)

Japan (call money)

1988 1989 1990

Federal Taxation of Income from Government Securities

The purpose of this section is to provide a general summary of tax considerations, as we understand them, and not to provide tax advice. Within this limitation, we attempt to outline certain of the more important provisions of the Internal Revenue Code as amended through May 31, 1990, as they relate to the taxation of income from government securities. Provisions relating to money market instruments are not discussed because of wide variations in the characteristics of those instruments. No attempt is made to discuss changes in the tax law that were being considered by the Congress at the time this outline was written, such as capital gains tax proposals.

Tax Status of U.S. Government Issues

Generally, the interest on obligations of the U.S. Government is subject to federal income tax unless there is legislation exempting specific obligations or classes thereof. Taxable securities, that is, those on which the income is subject to federal income tax, include all Treasury bills, certificates of indebtedness, notes and bonds, depository bonds, U.S. savings bonds, Federal Housing Administration debentures, Government National Mortgage Association (GNMA) securities, and most other agency obligations. They also include the obligations of government-sponsored enterprises—The Federal Land Banks, Federal Intermediate Credit Banks, Banks for Cooperatives, Federal Home Loan Banks, Federal Home Loan Mortgage Corporation, Federal National Mortgage Corporation, Resolution Funding Corporation, Student Loan Marketing Association, and United States Postal Service. Such obligations are also subject to federal capital gains, estate and gift taxes.

Subject to certain exceptions, interest payments on all such obligation are subject to a 20% backup withholding tax if the payee fails to furnish to the payor a correct taxpayer identification number, or if the payee fails to include the proper amount of interest income on the payee's tax return.

Obligations of the United States are exempt both as to principal and interest from all taxes imposed by any state, or any local taxing authority, except estate or inheritance taxes. Interest on and the principal or market value of such obligations, however, may be included in the base for state or municipal franchise taxes imposed on the privilege of doing business in the state or municipality.[1]

The exemption from state and local taxes applies only to "obligations of the United States Government," and this requirement is construed in a highly technical manner. As a general rule, obligations that are insured or guaranteed by the United States are not considered "obligations of the United States" for this purpose where the primary obligor is an individual or a private corporation. On the other hand, obligations of federal agencies and government-sponsored enterprises may qualify for the exemption. The reader should refer to the chapter on government-sponsored enterprises and federal agencies for the status of particular securities.

Certain outstanding issues of United States Treasury bonds, if held by an individual at the time of death, may be tendered and redeemed at par in payment of federal estate taxes imposed on the estate (see page 75). Such bonds are no longer issued.

The federal income tax provisions applicable to financial futures and put and call contracts covering government securities are too complex to be summarized here. In addition, other complex provisions apply if a "position" in government securities is held as part of a "straddle." Anyone considering

---

[1] "Stocks and obligations of the United States Government are exempt from taxation by a State or political subdivision of a State. The exemption applies to each form of taxation that would require the obligation, the interest on the obligation, or both, to be considered in computing a tax, except (1) a nondiscriminatory franchise tax or another nonproperty tax instead of a franchise tax, imposed on a corporation and (2) an estate or inheritance tax." Title 31, United States Code, § 3124.

Not all states have taken advantage of their power to include interest on and principal of U.S. securities in the base for their franchise taxes (as distinguished from corporation income taxes). New York, Pennsylvania, California, New Jersey, and Connecticut are some of the states that include such interest or principal in the measure of their franchise taxes.

entering into any such transactions should become familiar with the applicable provisions.

Amortization of Bond Premium

Corporations and individuals (other than dealers in securities) may elect to amortize any premium paid on the acquisition of government interest-bearing securities.

The election applies to all bonds of the same class held as of the beginning of the year in which the election is made or later acquired, and is effective for subsequent years unless permission to revoke the election is granted by the Commissioner of Internal Revenue.

In the case of bonds acquired after December 31, 1957, the amount amortizable is the difference between the cost and the amount payable at maturity (or an earlier call date, if it results in a smaller amount). The period of amortization is from the date of acquisition to the maturity date (or earlier call date, if applicable).

In the case of bonds issued after September 27, 1985, the constant yield method of amortization must be employed by the taxpayer. In the case of bonds issued prior to September 28, 1985, the method of amortization may be any method customarily used by the taxpayer, if it is deemed reasonable. In the latter case, amortization must conform to methods prescribed by the Internal Revenue Service, the two most common of which are the so-called "straight line" method and the constant yield method. Without considering the problem of changes in tax rates, the "straight line" method is generally better for investors because it produces a larger amortization deduction and, thus, a smaller net income subject to taxation, in the early years of the investment.

Generally, in the case of bonds acquired after December 31, 1987 (or at the taxpayer's election, October 22, 1986), the amount of bond premium will be treated only as an offset to any interest payment made on the bonds. In the case of bonds acquired after October 22, 1986 and before January 1, 1988 and which are not subject to the election referred to in the preceding sentence, the amount of bond premium is treated as a separate interest deduction item for all purposes, regardless of whether the taxpayer has any interest income from the bonds. In the case of bonds acquired prior to October 23, 1986, the amount of bond premium is treated as an itemized deduction.

If a bond is called before maturity, any unamortized premium (other than premium attributable to the period before the election to amortize was made) is amortized in the year the bond is called.

The basis of a security is reduced each year, beginning with the year in which it is acquired or in which election is made to amortize, by the amortizable bond premium for the year. At call or maturity, any unamortized premium attributable to the period prior to the election to amortize will constitute a capital loss to the investor. In the event of sale, the difference between sale price and the adjusted basis (cost less amortization) will represent a capital gain or loss.

Securities Issued or Purchased at a Discount

Government securities are not ordinarily issued at a discount except for short-term Treasury bills and savings bonds. A purchaser of government securities such as a dealer may "strip" some or all of the coupons (or rights to receive interest not evidenced by coupons) from the principal and resell the coupons (or rights to receive the interest) and principal to separate purchasers at discounts based on the present value of those amounts. A taxpayer who purchases stripped principal or a stripped coupon or right to receive interest must treat as original issue discount the excess of the amount of the principal or interest over the amount of the purchase price and must include in income annually a portion of the discount, determined on the basis of the implicit constant interest rate compounded semiannually (annually for stripped principal or stripped coupons or rights to interest purchased after July 1, 1982 and before January 1, 1985).

For government securities originally issued at a discount, initial holders and subsequent purchasers of the securities are required to include in income annually a portion of the discount at original issue, determined on the basis of the implicit constant interest rate compounded semiannually, adjusted in the case of a subsequent purchaser for the excess of the purchaser's cost over the issue price plus the original issue discount accrued to the date of purchase.

No original issue discount would be deemed to exist for this purpose if the amount of the discount at original issue was less than one-fourth of one percent of the principal amount multiplied by the number of complete years to maturity, but this rule apparently does not apply to stripped principal, coupons, or rights to interest.

Any increment in the value of savings bonds represented by the difference between the price paid and the redemption value receivable, whether at or before maturity, is considered interest. Taxpayers reporting income on the cash basis method of accounting may, under certain conditions, elect to treat the annual increase in redemption value as income for the taxable year, even though it is not realized in cash.

On the disposition of an obligation with an original maturity of over one year, issued after July 18, 1984, taxpayers are required to report as ordinary income any part of the gain, up to the amount of any market discount on the obligation (generally, the excess of the sum of the issue price and any original issue discount accrued to the date of purchase over the taxpayer's purchase price) that accrued while the taxpayer held the obligation. The accrued market discount is generally determined by multiplying the market discount by a fraction, the numerator of which is the number of days the taxpayer held the obligation and the denominator of which is the number of days after the taxpayer acquired the obligation through the date of maturity. Taxpayers are permitted to calculate the accrued market discount on a compound interest basis instead of this straight line method.

No deduction is allowed for interest paid or accrued during the taxable year on indebtedness incurred to purchase or carry an obligation with market discount acquired after July 18, 1984, (in excess of interest on the obligation included in income) to the extent the interest does not exceed the market discount accrued (calculated on either the straight line or the compound interest basis) during the taxable year while the taxpayer held the obligation. The disallowed interest is allowed as a deduction in the year the taxpayer disposes of the obligation (or, at the taxpayer's election, in a year subsequent to the year of disallowance and prior to the year of disposition to the extent of the excess of interest income over interest expense for that year). This limitation on interest deductions does not apply if the taxpayer elects to include in income annually the market discount accrued (on either a linear or an economic accrual basis) on all obligations held by the taxpayer.

Different rules apply to obligations that have a fixed maturity date not more than one year from the date of issue ("short-term obligations"). Certain taxpayers, including those using an accrual method of accounting, dealers, hedgers, banks, regulated investment companies, common trust funds, and certain other pass-through entities, are required to include in gross income the daily portions of the acquisition discount (whether original issue discount, market discount, or both) for each day on which a short-term government obligation (such as a Treasury bill) is held. A taxpayer not subject to this rule treats a ratable share of acquisition discount as ordinary income on the sale, exchange or retirement of a short-term government obligation, and such a taxpayer can deduct net direct interest expense with respect to short-term government obligations only to the extent the expense exceeds the acquisition discount for the year, unless the taxpayer makes an election to include in gross income the acquisition discount on a daily basis. In the case of nongovernment short-term obligations, the inclusion and deduction rules apply only with respect to original issue discount. A taxpayer may elect to compute the annual inclusion of original issue discount on the basis of the taxpayer's yield to maturity and daily compounding.

Foreign holders having close economic connections with the United States are, in the absence of an applicable tax treaty, taxed in the same manner as U.S. persons. For this purpose a foreign holder is considered to have close economic connections with the United States if (a) the holder is a resident individual or (b) in the case of a nonresident individual or corporation, the holder is engaged in a trade or business in the United States and the income earned is effectively connected with the conduct of that trade or business. An applicable tax treaty would be a treaty between the United States and the foreign holder's country of residence or, in the case of a corporation, the country in which the corporation is organized.

In general, foreign holders not having a close economic connection with the United States, in the absence of an applicable tax treaty, are taxed on gross interest income from United States sources at a 30% rate, and the 20% backup withholding tax imposed on interest generally does not apply. The tax is collected by means of a withholding tax at the U.S. source of payment. Exemption from withholding is available to foreign governments, their political subdivisions, organizations created by foreign governments which meet certain requirements, certain international organizations, foreign central banks of issue, and certain foreign organizations which would qualify as charitable organizations under U.S. law.[2]

With respect to obligations issued after July 18, 1984, the 30% withholding tax on interest (including original issue discount as described below) does not apply, subject to certain exemptions, to (1) obligations with respect to which the withholding agent has received a statement from the beneficial owners that they are not U.S. persons, or (2) targeted obligations (designed for sale outside the U.S.) with respect to which the withholding agent has received a statement from a qualifying financial

[2] Interest paid to nonresident aliens and foreign corporations on obligations of the International Bank for Reconstruction and Development (World Bank), the Asian Development Bank, and the Inter-American Development Bank generally is not subject to federal tax in the case of a foreign holder not having a close economic connection with the United States, because such interest is treated as derived from sources outside the United States.

institution, which is the registered owner of the obligations, that the beneficial owners are not U.S. persons. The Secretary of the Treasury may exclude from this exemption interest paid to persons within or with addresses in any foreign country on obligations issued after the Secretary determines that the exchange of information between the United States and the foreign country is inadequate to prevent the evasion of U.S. income tax by U.S. persons.

With the exceptions noted below, the 30% withholding tax, when applicable, applies only to payments of stated interest. It does not apply to gains on instruments due to market fluctuations.

In the case of obligations with original issue discount but without stated interest, issued after March 31, 1972, and payable more than 183 days from the date of original issue, and not exempt from the 30% withholding tax, the portion of the gain realized by a foreign holder on sale, exchange or redemption that is attributable to the original issue discount earned by the holder is taxable as interest income. Similar obligations with an original maturity of 183 days or less are exempt from such taxation. In the case of obligations with both original issue discount and stated interest and with a stated maturity of more than 183 days, the original issue discount earned by the holder between payments of stated interest is taxed, by means of withholding, to the extent of the stated interest payment that is available after the withholding tax applicable to the stated interest is paid.

When a discount obligation with an original maturity of over 183 days is sold by a foreign holder, a withholding tax is payable with respect to original issue discount to the extent not theretofore collected, except that under current rulings the only person obligated to collect such withholding is the original issuer of the obligation if it is the purchaser.

If the foreign holder's country of residence is a party to a tax treaty with the United States and the holder or the obligation is not exempt from the 30% withholding tax, the rate of taxation on interest income including original issue discount may be

222

reduced below the 30% rate or eliminated entirely, provided that the foreign holder's interest income is not attributable to a permanent establishment in the United States through which the foreign holder conducts a trade or business.[3]

Capital Gains and Losses

Capital gains and losses from securities acquired after December 31, 1987 or before June 23, 1984, and held one year or less, are classified as short term, and if held more than one year are classified as long term. In the case of securities acquired after June 22, 1984, but before January 1, 1988, the holding period for long-term capital gains and losses is six months.

For tax years beginning after December 31, 1986, the distinction between long-term and short-term capital gains and losses has limited application because there is no tax rate differential.[4]

Individuals

Individuals are required to include in income the excess, if any, of net capital gains (long-term and short-term) over net capital losses (long-term and short-term).

In any case where combining capital gains and losses results in an overall net capital loss for the year, the loss up to $3,000[5] may be taken as a deduction against ordinary income. To the

---

[3] Tax conventions that grant full exemptions to interest received by certain nonresident aliens and foreign corporations when not effectively connected with the conduct of a trade or business through a permanent establishment within the United States were in effect as of December 1989 with Austria, Denmark, Finland, France, Germany, Greece, Hungary, Iceland, Ireland, Luxembourg, the Netherlands, Norway, Sweden, the United Kingdom, certain colonies and former colonies of the United Kingdom, Poland, and the Union of Soviet Socialist Republics. Tax conventions that grant reduced withholding rates were in effect as of December 1989 with Australia, Barbados, Belgium, Canada, China (People's Republic), Cyprus, Egypt, Italy, Jamaica, Japan, Korea, Malta, Morocco, New Zealand, the Philippines, Romania, and Switzerland.

[4] For example, a charitable deduction is allowable for unrealized appreciation on donated securities only if the appreciation would constitute long-term gain if it had been realized.

[5] $1,500 in the case of a married individual filing a separate return.

extent not thus used as a current deduction, any net capital losses may be carried forward and used against capital gain and up to $3,000 of other income in any number of subsequent years.

Corporations

Corporations are subject to tax on net capital gains at the regular rates applicable to ordinary income.

A net capital loss is not deductible from ordinary corporate income, but may be carried back for three years and utilized to offset net capital gains arising in those years. In addition, a corporation may carry forward a net capital loss for five years to the extent that the loss is not exhausted by the carryback.[6]

Banks

If any taxable year in which a bank, including a mutual savings bank or a domestic building and loan association, sustains a net gain or loss from sales or exchanges of debt obligations, the gain or loss is includable in, or deductible from, ordinary income without limitation. Net operating losses of banks for any taxable year beginning after December 31, 1986 may be carried back for 3 years, and to the extent not exhausted, carried forward for 15 years. Losses from bad debt writeoffs are subject to different carryback and carryforward rules than losses from sales or exchanges.

Wash Sales

If any security held for investment is sold at a loss, and the taxpayer purchases, or enters into a contract or option to acquire, "substantially identical" securities within 30 days before or after the sale, no deduction for the loss is allowed for tax purposes.

---

[6] Carrybacks may not increase or produce a net operating loss in the year to which a capital loss is being carried. Special rules on carrybacks and carryovers apply to foreign personal holding companies, regulated investment companies, real estate investment trusts, S corporations, and foreign investment companies.

Whether one security is to be considered "substantially identical" to another depends upon the particular facts. The "wash sale" rule does not apply to a dealer in securities. With respect to short sales after July 18, 1984, the wash sale rule applies to losses realized on the closing of the short sale where the taxpayer sold "substantially identical" securities or entered into another short sale of "substantially identical" securities within 30 days before or after the closing.

Tax-Free Exchanges of U.S. Obligations

The Secretary of the Treasury is authorized to provide for nonrecognition of gain or loss on the surrender to the United States of obligations of the United States, including savings bonds, issued under the Second Liberty Bond Act (31 U.S.C. 774(2)) when the obligations are exchanged solely for other obligations issued under that Act. This is an exception to the general rule that an exchange of government debt securities is a taxable event. The special treatment is available only if the offering circular of the Treasury Department with respect to a particular exchange contains a declaration that no gain or loss shall be recognized for federal income tax purposes on the exchange or, in the case of bonds issued at a discount, grants the privilege of continuing to defer the reporting of the income on the bonds exchanged until such time as the bonds received from the exchange are redeemed, disposed of, or have reached final maturity, whichever is earlier.

Coupon Rate Equivalents [1]

Coupon rate %	Interest per million per day	No. days to equal 1/32nd	Coupon rate %	Interest per million per day	No. days to equal 1/32nd
			4	$109.58904	2.9
⅛	$ 3.42466	91.2	4⅛	113.01369	2.8
¼	6.84932	45.6	4¼	116.43836	2.7
⅜	10.27397	30.4	4⅜	119.86301	2.6
½	13.69863	22.8	4½	123.28767	2.5
⅝	17.12329	18.2	4⅝	126.71233	2.5
¾	20.54795	15.2	4¾	130.13699	2.4
⅞	23.97260	13.0	4⅞	133.56164	2.4
1	27.39726	11.4	5	136.98630	2.3
1⅛	30.82192	10.1	5⅛	140.41096	2.2
1¼	34.24658	9.1	5¼	143.83562	2.2
1⅜	37.67123	8.3	5⅜	147.26027	2.1
1½	41.19910	7.6	5½	150.68493	2.1
1⅝	44.52055	7.0	5⅝	154.10959	2.1
1¾	47.94521	6.5	5¾	157.53425	2.0
1⅞	51.36986	6.1	5⅞	160.95390	1.9
2	54.79452	5.7	6	164.38356	1.9
2⅛	58.21918	5.4	6⅛	167.80322	1.9
2¼	61.64384	5.1	6¼	171.23288	1.8
2⅜	65.06849	4.8	6⅜	174.65753	1.8
2½	68.49315	4.6	6½	178.08219	1.8
2⅝	71.91781	4.3	6⅝	181.50685	1.7
2¾	75.34247	4.1	6¾	184.93151	1.7
2⅞	78.76712	4.0	6⅞	188.35616	1.7
3	82.19178	3.8	7	191.78082	1.6
3⅛	85.61644	3.6	7⅛	195.20548	1.6
3¼	89.04110	3.5	7¼	198.63014	1.6
3⅜	92.46575	3.4	7⅜	202.05479	1.6
3½	95.89041	3.3	7½	205.47945	1.5
3⅝	99.31507	3.1	7⅝	208.90411	1.5
3¾	102.73973	3.0	7¾	212.32877	1.5
3⅞	106.16438	2.9	7⅞	215.75342	1.4

Coupon Rate Equivalents[1] (continued)

Copupon rate %	Interest per million per day	No. days to equal 1/32nd	Copupon rate %	Interest per million per day	No. days to equal 1/32nd
8	$219.17808	1.4	12	$328.76713	.9
8⅛	222.60274	1.4	12⅛	332.19178	.9
8¼	226.02740	1.4	12¼	335.61644	.9
8⅜	229.45206	1.4	12⅜	339.04110	.9
8½	232.87671	1.3	12½	342.46576	.9
8⅝	236.30137	1.3	12⅝	345.89041	.9
8¾	239.72603	1.3	12¾	349.31507	.9
8⅞	243.15069	1.3	12⅞	352.73973	.9
9	246.57534	1.3	13	356.16438	.9
9⅛	250.00000	1.2	13⅛	359.58904	.9
9¼	253.42466	1.2	13¼	363.01370	.9
9⅜	256.84932	1.2	13⅜	366.43835	.9
9½	260.27397	1.2	13½	369.86301	.8
9⅝	263.69863	1.2	13⅝	373.28767	.8
9¾	267.12329	1.2	13¾	376.71233	.8
9⅞	270.54795	1.2	53⅞	380.13698	.8
10	273.97260	1.1	14	383.56164	.8
10⅛	277.39726	1.1	14⅛	386.98630	.8
10¼	280.82192	1.1	14¼	390.41096	.8
10⅜	284.24658	1.1	14⅜	393.83562	.8
10½	287.67123	1.1	14½	397.26027	.8
10⅝	291.09589	1.1	14⅝	400.68493	.8
10¾	294.52055	1.1	14¾	404.10959	.8
10⅞	297.94521	1.0	14⅞	407.53425	.8
11	301.36986	1.0	15	410.95890	.8
11⅛	304.79452	1.0	15⅛	414.38356	.8
11¼	308.21918	1.0	15¼	417.80822	.7
11⅜	311.64384	1.0	15⅜	421.23288	.7
11½	315.06849	1.0	15½	424.65753	.7
11⅝	318.49315	1.0	15⅝	428.08219	.7
11¾	321.91781	1.0	15¾	431.50685	.7
11⅞	325.34247	1.0	15⅞	434.93151	.7

[1] 365-day basis.

Discount Rates and Equivalent Bond Yields

Discount rate (percent)	Equivalent bond yields at varying maturities							
	1 mo.	2 mo.	3 mo.	4 mo.	5 mo.	6 mo.	9 mo.	1 yr.
5	5.09	5.11	5.13	5.16	5.18	5.20	5.22	5.27
5⅛	5.22	5.24	5.26	5.29	5.31	5.33	5.36	5.41
5¼	5.35	5.37	5.39	5.42	5.44	5.47	5.49	5.55
5⅜	5.47	5.50	5.52	5.55	5.57	5.61	5.63	5.69
5½	5.60	5.63	5.65	5.68	5.71	5.74	5.76	5.83
5⅝	5.73	5.76	5.79	5.81	5.84	5.87	5.90	5.97
5¾	5.86	5.89	5.92	5.94	5.97	6.00	6.03	6.10
5⅞	5.99	6.02	6.05	6.08	6.11	6.14	6.17	6.24
6	6.11	6.15	6.18	6.21	6.24	6.27	6.31	6.38
6⅛	6.24	6.27	6.31	6.34	6.37	6.41	6.45	6.52
6¼	6.37	6.40	6.44	6.47	6.51	6.54	6.58	6.66
6⅜	6.50	6.53	6.57	6.60	6.64	6.68	6.72	6.80
6½	6.63	6.66	6.70	6.74	6.77	6.81	6.85	6.94
6⅝	6.75	6.79	6.83	6.87	6.91	6.95	6.99	7.08
6¾	6.88	6.92	6.96	7.00	7.04	7.08	7.13	7.22
6⅞	7.01	7.05	7.09	7.13	7.18	7.22	7.27	7.36
7	7.14	7.18	7.22	7.27	7.31	7.36	7.40	7.50
7⅛	7.27	7.31	7.36	7.40	7.45	7.49	7.54	7.65
7¼	7.40	7.44	7.49	7.53	7.58	7.63	7.68	7.79
7⅜	7.52	7.57	7.62	7.67	7.71	7.76	7.82	7.93
7½	7.65	7.70	7.75	7.80	7.85	7.90	7.96	8.07
7⅝	7.78	7.83	7.88	7.93	7.98	8.04	8.10	8.21
7¾	7.91	7.96	8.01	8.07	8.12	8.17	8.24	8.35
7⅞	8.04	8.09	8.14	8.20	8.26	8.31	8.38	8.49
8	8.17	8.22	8.28	8.33	8.39	8.45	8.51	8.63
8⅛	8.29	8.35	8.41	8.47	8.53	8.59	8.65	8.77
8¼	8.42	8.48	8.54	8.60	8.66	8.72	8.79	8.92
8⅜	8.55	8.61	8.67	8.74	8.80	8.86	8.93	9.07
8½	8.68	8.74	8.81	8.87	8.93	9.00	9.07	9.21
8⅝	8.81	8.87	8.94	9.00	9.07	9.14	9.21	9.35
8¾	8.94	9.00	9.07	9.14	9.21	9.28	9.35	9.50
8⅞	9.07	9.13	9.20	9.27	9.34	9.42	9.49	9.65

228

Discount Rates and Equivalent Bond Yields (continued)

Discount rate (percent)	Equivalent bond yields at varying maturities							
	1 mo.	2 mo.	3 mo.	4 mo.	5 mo.	6 mo.	9 mo.	1 yr.
9	9.20	9.26	9.34	9.41	9.48	9.56	9.64	9.79
9⅛	9.33	9.39	9.47	9.54	9.62	9.69	9.78	9.94
9¼	9.45	9.52	9.60	9.67	9.75	9.83	9.92	10.08
9⅜	9.58	9.65	9.73	9.81	9.89	9.97	10.06	10.23
9½	9.71	9.79	9.87	9.95	10.03	10.11	10.20	10.38
9⅝	9.84	9.92	10.00	10.08	10.17	10.25	10.34	10.53
9¾	9.97	10.05	10.13	10.22	10.30	10.39	10.49	10.67
9⅞	10.10	10.18	10.27	10.35	10.44	10.53	10.63	10.82
10	10.22	10.31	10.40	10.49	10.58	10.67	10.77	10.97
10⅛	10.35	10.44	10.53	10.62	10.72	10.81	10.92	11.12
10¼	10.48	10.57	10.67	10.76	10.86	10.95	11.06	11.27
10⅜	10.61	10.70	10.80	10.89	10.99	11.09	11.20	11.42
10½	10.74	10.84	10.93	11.03	11.13	11.24	11.35	11.57
10⅝	10.87	10.97	11.07	11.17	11.27	11.38	11.49	11.72
10¾	11.00	11.10	11.20	11.30	11.41	11.52	11.64	11.87
10⅞	11.13	11.23	11.33	11.44	11.55	11.66	11.78	12.02
11	11.26	11.37	11.47	11.59	11.70	11.81	11.93	12.18
11⅛	11.39	11.50	11.61	11.72	11.84	11.95	12.08	12.33
11¼	11.51	11.63	11.74	11.86	11.98	12.10	12.23	12.49
11⅜	11.64	11.76	11.87	12.00	12.11	12.24	12.37	12.64
11½	11.77	11.89	12.01	12.13	12.26	12.38	12.52	12.79
11⅝	11.90	12.02	12.14	12.27	12.39	12.52	12.66	12.94
11¾	12.03	12.16	12.28	12.41	12.54	12.67	12.81	13.10
11⅞	12.16	12.29	12.41	12.54	12.68	12.81	12.95	13.25
12	12.29	12.42	12.55	12.68	12.82	12.96	13.10	13.40
12⅛	12.42	12.55	12.68	12.82	12.96	13.10	13.25	13.56
12¼	12.55	12.68	12.82	12.96	13.10	13.24	13.40	13.71
12⅜	12.68	12.82	12.95	13.10	13.24	13.39	13.55	13.87
12½	12.81	12.95	13.09	13.23	13.38	13.53	13.69	14.02
12⅝	12.94	13.08	13.22	13.37	13.52	13.68	13.84	14.18
12¾	13.07	13.21	13.36	13.51	13.66	13.82	13.99	14.33
12⅞	13.20	13.35	13.49	13.65	13.80	13.96	14.14	14.49

Decimal Equivalents of 32nds and 64ths per $100

32nds	64ths	Per $100	32nds	64ths	Per $100
+	1	$.015625	16 +	33	$.515625
1	2	.031250	17	34	.531250
1 +	3	.046875	17 +	35	.546875
2	4	.062500	18	36	.562500
2 +	5	.078125	18 +	37	.578125
3	6	.093750	19	38	.593750
3 +	7	.109375	19 +	39	.609375
4	8	.125000	20	40	.625000
4 +	9	.140625	20 +	41	.640625
5	10	.156250	21	42	.656250
5 +	11	.171875	21 +	43	.671875
6	12	.187500	22	44	.687500
6 +	13	.203125	22 +	45	.703125
7	14	.218750	23	46	.718750
7 +	15	.234375	23 +	47	.734375
8	16	.250000	24	48	.750000
8 +	17	.265625	24 +	49	.765625
9	18	.281250	25	50	.781250
9 +	19	.296875	25 +	51	.796875
10	20	.312500	26	52	.812500
10 +	21	.328125	26 +	53	.828125
11	22	.343750	27	54	.843750
11 +	23	.359375	27 +	55	.859375
12	24	.375000	28	56	.875000
12 +	25	.390625	28 +	57	.890625
13	26	.406250	29	58	.906250
13 +	27	.421875	29 +	59	.921875
14	28	.437500	30	60	.937500
14 +	29	.453125	30 +	61	.953125
15	30	.468750	31	62	.968750
15 +	31	.484375	31 +	63	.984375
16	32	.500000	32	64	1.000000

Value of One Day's Discount per $1,000 at Various Discount Rates

(360-day basis)

Discount rate percent	Amount	Discount rate percent	Amount	Discount rate percent	Amount
4	$0.11111111	8	$0.22222222	12	$0.33333333
4⅛	0.11458333	8⅛	0.22569444	12⅛	0.33680555
4¼	0.11805556	8¼	0.22916667	12¼	0.34027778
4⅜	0.12152778	8⅜	0.23263889	12⅜	0.34375000
4½	0.12500000	8½	0.23611111	12½	0.34722222
4⅝	0.12847222	8⅝	0.23958333	12⅝	0.35069444
4¾	0.13194444	8¾	0.24305556	12¾	0.35416667
4⅞	0.13541667	8⅞	0.24652778	12⅞	0.35763889
5	0.13888889	9	0.25000000	13	0.36111111
5⅛	0.14236111	9⅛	0.25347222	13⅛	0.36458334
5¼	0.14583333	9¼	0.25694444	13¼	0.36805556
5⅜	0.14930556	9⅜	0.26041667	13⅜	0.37152778
5½	0.15277778	9½	0.26388889	13½	0.37500001
5⅝	0.15625000	9⅝	0.26736111	13⅝	0.37847223
5¾	0.15972222	9¾	0.27083333	13¾	0.38194445
5⅞	0.16319444	9⅞	0.27430556	53⅞	0.38541667
6	0.16666667	10	0.27777778	14	0.38888890
6⅛	0.17013889	10⅛	0.28125000	14⅛	0.39236112
6¼	0.17361111	10¼	0.28472222	14¼	0.39583334
6⅜	0.17708333	10⅜	0.28819444	14⅜	0.39930557
6½	0.18055556	10½	0.29166667	14½	0.40277779
6⅝	0.18402778	10⅝	0.29513889	14⅝	0.40625001
6¾	0.18750000	10¾	0.29861111	14¾	0.40972224
6⅞	0.19097222	10⅞	0.30208833	14⅞	0.41319446
7	0.19444444	11	0.30555556	15	0.41666669
7⅛	0.19791667	11⅛	0.30902778	15⅛	0.42013890
7¼	0.20138889	11¼	0.31250000	15¼	0.42361113
7⅜	0.20486111	11⅜	0.31597222	15⅜	0.42708335
7½	0.20833333	11½	0.31944444	15½	0.43055557
7⅝	0.21180556	11⅝	0.32291667	15⅝	0.43402780
7¾	0.21527778	11¾	0.32638889	15¾	0.43750002
7⅞	0.21875000	11⅞	0.32986111	15⅞	0.44097224

Dollar Equivalents

(.01% discount per $1 million)

Days to mat.	.01% equiv.	Days to mat.	.01% equiv.	Days to mat.	.01% equiv.	Days to mat.	.01% equiv.	Days to mat.	.01% equiv.	Days to mat.	.01% equiv.
1	$ .28	36	$ 10.00	71	$ 19.72	106	$ 29.44	141	$ 39.17	176	$ 48.89
2	.56	37	10.28	72	20.00	107	29.72	142	39.44	177	49.17
3	.83	38	10.56	73	20.28	108	30.00	143	39.72	178	49.44
4	1.11	39	10.83	74	20.56	109	30.28	144	40.00	179	49.72
5	1.39	40	11.11	75	20.83	110	30.56	145	40.28	180	50.00
6	1.67	41	11.39	76	21.11	111	30.83	146	40.56	181	50.28
7	1.94	42	11.67	77	21.39	112	31.11	147	40.83	182	50.56
8	2.22	43	11.94	78	21.67	113	31.39	148	41.11	183	50.83
9	2.50	44	12.22	79	21.94	114	31.67	149	41.39	184	51.11
10	2.78	45	12.50	80	22.22	115	31.94	150	41.67	185	51.39
11	3.06	46	12.78	81	22.50	116	32.22	151	41.94	186	51.67
12	3.33	47	13.06	82	22.78	117	32.50	152	42.22	187	51.94
13	3.61	48	13.33	83	23.06	118	32.78	153	42.50	188	52.22
14	3.89	49	13.61	84	23.33	119	33.06	154	42.78	189	52.50
15	4.17	50	13.89	85	23.61	120	33.33	155	43.06	190	52.78
16	4.44	51	14.17	86	23.89	121	33.61	156	43.33	191	53.06
17	4.72	52	14.44	87	24.17	122	33.89	157	43.61	192	53.33
18	5.00	53	14.72	88	24.44	123	34.17	158	43.89	193	53.61
19	5.28	54	15.00	89	24.72	124	34.44	159	44.17	194	53.89
20	5.56	55	15.28	90	25.00	125	34.72	160	44.44	195	54.17
21	5.83	56	15.56	91	25.28	126	35.00	161	44.72	196	54.44
22	6.11	57	15.83	92	25.56	127	35.28	162	45.00	197	54.72
23	6.39	58	16.11	93	25.83	128	35.56	163	45.28	198	55.00
24	6.67	59	16.39	94	26.11	129	35.83	164	45.56	199	55.28
25	6.94	60	16.67	95	26.39	130	36.11	165	45.83	200	55.56
26	7.22	61	16.94	96	26.67	131	36.39	166	46.11	201	55.83
27	7.50	62	17.22	97	26.94	132	36.67	167	46.39	202	56.11
28	7.78	63	17.50	98	27.22	133	36.94	168	46.67	203	56.39
29	8.06	64	17.78	99	27.50	134	37.22	169	46.94	204	56.67
30	8.33	65	18.06	100	27.78	135	37.50	170	47.22	205	56.94
31	8.61	66	18.33	101	28.06	136	37.78	171	47.50	206	57.22
32	8.89	67	18.61	102	28.33	137	38.06	172	47.78	207	57.50
33	9.17	68	18.89	103	28.61	138	38.33	173	48.06	208	57.78
34	9.44	69	19.17	104	28.89	139	38.61	174	48.33	209	58.06
35	9.72	70	19.44	105	29.17	140	38.89	175	48.61	210	58.33

Dollar Equivalents (continued)

(.01% discount per $1 million)

Days to mat.	.01% equiv.	Days to mat.	.01% equiv.	Days to mat.	.01% equiv.	Days to mat.	.01% equiv.	Days to mat.	.01% equiv.	Days to mat.	.01% equiv.
211	$ 58.61	237	$ 65.83	263	$ 73.06	289	$ 80.28	315	$ 87.50	341	$ 94.72
212	58.89	238	66.11	264	73.33	290	80.56	316	87.78	342	95.00
213	59.17	239	66.39	265	73.61	291	80.83	317	88.06	343	95.28
214	59.44	240	66.67	266	73:89	292	81.11	318	88.33	344	95.56
215	59.72	241	66.94	267	74.17	293	81.39	319	88.61	345	95.83
216	60.00	242	67.22	268	74.44	294	81.67	320	88.89	346	96.11
217	60.23	243	67.50	269	74.72	295	81.94	321	89.17	347	96.39
218	60.56	244	67.78	270	75.00	296	82.22	322	89.44	348	96.67
219	60.83	245	68.06	271	75.28	297	82.50	323	89.72	349	96.94
220	61.11	246	68.33	272	75.56	298	82.78	324	90.00	350	97.22
221	61.39	247	68.61	273	75.83	299	83.06	325	90.28	351	97.50
222	61.67	248	68.89	274	76.11	300	83.33	326	90.56	352	97.78
223	61.94	249	69.17	275	76.39	301	83.61	327	90.83	353	98.06
224	62.22	250	69.44	276	76.67	302	83.89	328	91.11	354	98.33
225	62.50	251	69.72	277	76.94	303	84.17	329	91.39	355	98.61
226	62.78	252	70.00	278	77.22	304	84.44	330	91.67	356	98.89
227	63.06	253	70.28	279	77.50	305	84.72	331	91.94	357	99.17
228	63.33	254	70.56	280	77.78	306	85.00	332	92.22	358	99.44
229	63.61	255	70.83	281	78.06	307	85.28	333	92.50	359	99.72
230	63.89	256	71.11	282	78.33	308	85.56	334	92.78	360	100.00
231	64.17	257	71.39	283	78.61	309	85.83	335	93.06	361	100.28
232	64.44	258	71.67	284	78.89	310	86.11	336	93.33	362	100.56
233	64.72	259	71.94	285	79.17	311	86.39	337	93.61	363	100.83
234	65.00	260	72.22	286	79.44	312	86.67	338	93.89	364	101.11
235	65.28	261	72.50	287	79.72	313	86.94	339	94.17	365	101.39
236	65.56	262	72.78	288	80.00	314	87.22	340	94.44	366	101.67

Index

A

Adjustable rate mortgages, 197
Agreement Establishing the Asian Development Bank, 138
Agricultural Credit Act, 94, 95, 97, 98
Agricultural Credit Association, 94
American-style option, 195
Amortization of bond premium, 217-18
Arbitrage techniques, 190
Asian Development Bank, 85, 138-41, 221n
Asian Finance and Investment Corporation, Ltd., 141

B

Balanced Budget and Emergency Deficit Control Act, 89
Bank discount, 67-68
Bankers' acceptances, 151-55
Bank Insurance Fund, 102
Banks for Cooperatives, 93, 94, 95
Bearer bonds, 45
Bond-equivalent yield, 68-70
Bond futures, options on, 196
Bonds, Treasury, 60-61, 75
"Book-entry" form, 45, 181
Book-entry and telecommunications transfer, 181-82
Budget receipts, expenditures, and debt, 42, 44

C

Call option, 195
Capital gains and losses, taxation of, 223-25
Cash Management Bills, 57-58
Cash transaction, 180
CDs. *See* Certificates of deposit
Certificate of deposit notes, 157
Certificates of beneficial ownership, 128
Certificates of deposit, 155-64
    computation of proceeds, 160-63
    deposit notes, 157-58
    Eurodollar CDs, 158-59
    Yankee CDs, 159-60
Certified Development Company Program, 134-35
Chicago Board of Trade, 189, 193
Chicago Mercantile Exchange, 176, 178, 189, 193
Chronology. *See* Economic climate
CoBank, 94

H

I